See You Tomorrow…
Reclaiming the Beacon of Hope

Gary Matloff

See You Tomorrow . . . Reclaiming the Beacon of Hope
High Street Publishing
All rights reserved

Copyright © 2013 by Gary Matloff, Ph.D.

No part of this book may be reproduced or transmitted in any form or by any means, electronic or mechanical, including photocopying, recording, or by any information storage and retrieval system without the written permission of the author, except when permitted by law.

ISBN: 978-0-9899218-0-0

Cover design by SPDesign and under creative continuous copyright.

To my father . . . and all fathers who do all they can to be there for their children and provide the tools so that they might become better than him.

It goes without saying that most of my gratitude for having written this book goes to my beloved family, especially those key players in our story--my mother, Miriam; nephew, Michael; cousins Gayle and Jake; and our family's "big brother," Sean. Without their abiding love and support there would be no book to write. As I also believe that it takes a village to raise a child, I am eternally grateful for our neighbors, Miss Mary, Mr. Sean, Jacob, and Jared, who have opened their hearts and have generously given of themselves so that we may further thrive as a family. A special thank-you also goes to close family friend, Ellen Brazer, who lovingly encouraged me to write, and that what I had to say and how I wanted to tell it was worthwhile. As for the writing, much appreciation goes to my editor, Tiffany Yates Martin, whose candid guidance was an inspiration toward the book's final composition. Thank you to the folks at LIMIAR, One World Adoption Services, and JAFCO for their frank endorsement of the single father, and the robust role he can play in the life and maturity of a child in need. Also close to my heart are brothers Bobby and Brandon; even as married young men with lives of their own now, they are forever my two "little brothers," and perhaps the catalyst for even my inclination to adopt a pair of brothers of my own. And, as the best is usually saved for last, my two sons, Matheus and Davi, are my inspiration every day. Not a day goes by that I am not reminded of the shared need for humility, patience, and unconditional love and regard.

Table of Contents

Part 1 | Here I Come, Here I Go, and There I Was   1

Chapter 1 | With the Closing of One Door   3

Chapter 2 | So Opens Another Door   13

Chapter 3 | Crisscrossing Paths in the Dark   20

Chapter 4 | Why Not Buy American?   29

Chapter 5 | Brazil or Bust   42

Part 2 | Crossing Over   55

Chapter 6 | Breaking the Language Barrier   57

Chapter 7 | War and Peace—Overcoming the Love of Power with the Power of Love   67

Chapter 8 | The Simple Pleasures in Life   76

Chapter 9 | You Can't Go Home Again   84

Chapter 10 | How Do You Say Goodbye in Portuguese?   90

Chapter 11 | Father's Day   98

Part 3 | Settling In   107

Chapter 12 | Putting It Together ... Bit by Bit   109

Chapter 13 | All Roads Lead to Home   117

Chapter 14 | Dear Teacher ...   125

Chapter 15 | The Arrival of the Great Pumpkin   133

Chapter 16 | Sibling Rivalry: The Tangled Twisting of Brotherly Ties   145

Chapter 17 | 'Tis the Season   152

Chapter 18 | Passage to Manhood   160

Chapter 19 | The Circle of Life   169

Chapter 20 | *Feliz Aniversário* ... Happy Anniversary   178

Chapter 21 | Jumpin' June   186

Part 4 | Looking Toward the Future ... One Day at a Time   195

Chapter 22 | Macho, Macho, Man ...   197

Chapter 23 | Checks and Balances   205

Chapter 24 | That's the Way the Cookie Crumbles   218

Chapter 25 | The Truth of the Matter Is ...   228

Chapter 26 | A House Divided ...   238

Chapter 27 | Educated Guesses   250

Chapter 28	What Comes Around Goes Around	262
Chapter 29	Walking the Emotional Tightrope	275
Chapter 30	See You Tomorrow . . .	289
Epilogue		296

Enquanto há vida, há esperança
"While there's life, there's hope."

Part 1

Here I Come, Here I Go, and There I Was

Chapter 1

With the Closing of One Door

On the eve before my departure for Brazil to meet my two sons for the first time, I found myself quietly standing in the small entryway separating the boys' waiting bedrooms, taking a peek into each of their rooms. The comforters were neatly folded, pillows fluffed, pictures hung straight, and a few toys, games, and books smartly arranged. If these walls could talk, there was not yet much to be said. The picture-perfect arrangement of the boys' bedrooms was anything but a metaphor for the chaos that had prevailed over my own life for the past few years.

Two months shy of my 45th birthday, I was about to give up my life of independence to become a single father of two. As a young teen, I adored being with children and fantasized about becoming a father. It seemed natural for me to gravitate toward a career as a child psychologist, assisting those who were troubled, and in need of an extra guiding hand to overcome their struggles. No matter how successful I was in my work, however, I never gained the kind of personal contentment I believed was achievable only in parenting a child. Never one who felt pressured to be married as the means to have a family, even as a teen I was attracted to the prospect of saving a child through adoption. Through the years, I also gradually found myself becoming more passionate about working with older children and adolescents. It seemed easier, more natural for me to relate with their more sophisticated mental development. I never tired of taking on their youthful angst, influenced by the frenzy of their often larger-than-life emotional expressions and social relations. I believed it was my destiny to take in an older child in need of a family, and to nurture him in a way that countered his compromised beginnings in life; unlike the objectivity I maintained in my role and practice as a psychologist.

As my parents adopted my sister as an infant, my only sibling when I was three years old, adoption was an integral part of my life early on. I never regarded my sister any differently than if she were born into our family. She, however, distinguished herself as different from us and had unresolved issues about her adoptive circumstances that played out in angry outbursts, in full force during her teen years that wreaked havoc on her self-worth. Not until many years later were my parents and I able to reconcile with the extent of her problems that became resistant to our attempts to nurture and support her. I knew there were risks involved in any adoption, but so were there risks with having children naturally.

As I surveyed the stillness of my son's new bedrooms five years since having officially started my adoption pursuits, I was prepared in the superficial, materialistic sense, yet I really did not know what to expect. I was excited, yet fearful of the unknown, and what it meant to be taking on fatherhood amidst my life's challenges. I had waited so long to adopt, and it was not enough to have to contain the minefield of my family's struggles on my back. I also had to withstand the pain of too much rejection any one person should have to bear as I had throughout my adoption pursuits. When all was said and done, the information about the boys I chose to adopt seemed enough for me to have made an informed decision; I really knew so little about them, yet it was what I had to go on for me to feel that it was meant to be. I thought I knew, but how much did I really know about myself and how ready I was, as I stood at the threshold of the journey of my life? I barely managed to keep from sliding off the edge of the reality of impending fatherhood and into the abyss of uncertainty.

* * *

After accepting the referral to adopt a pair of brothers from Brazil, I pushed forward and navigated the seemingly endless stream of paperwork to satisfy both the American and Brazilian bureaucracies. Although approved to adopt as a single father by the Brazilian courts, I still felt as though the rug could be snatched from under me at any moment. There was no guarantee that I would get these two boys. First having to wait out the courts' closure during the customary five-week holiday break over Christmas was too much to bear. Were there others who put in to adopt them? I did not know that I was the only one who had come forward on their behalf. Would the courts approve of my suitability to adopt these boys? I was constantly reassured that the ruling in favor of proposed matches between waiting children and identified families was usually approved. Did I accept the boys' referral in haste? Should I wait to see what other children were available? I was told most tended to accept their first referral. As I originally focused on adopting just one, would adopting two be too much to undertake? Should I wait to see whether a single child became available? All my instincts told me to adopt eleven-year-old Matheus and eight-year-old Davi. I was already emotionally attached, and invested in being their father.

The four months following my commitment to adopt the boys had seemed a one-sided affair. I did all the planning, hoping, and envisioning of what might be for the three of us as a new family, knowing that Matheus and Davi had no idea they were slated to be adopted. They were unaware that I or anyone else was interested in them. They were being prepared for adoption in therapy, yet they would not be told of their adoption plans or their impending move to America until just two weeks before my arrival to meet them. I went about wrestling with my unrelenting fear of the unknown alone. As is customary in the Brazilian courts, the boys were protected from potential disappointment. They would not be told of their adoption until everything was finalized and the date for their new father's arrival was set. Who would protect me from the threat of disappointment?

I found myself challenged by so many setbacks, in ways I never expected in this precarious journey to adopt; yet fear especially pervaded my senses on the drive into work one mid-April morning. It was the day the court social worker would tell Matheus and Davi of their impending adoption. What would their reactions be? What kinds of questions would they have? Would they accept the prospect of being adopted by a single father? Or would my greatest fear be realized – that they would not want me as their father? It was a struggle to keep from unraveling the exposed threads of my resolve.

That evening, chained to my computer, I finally received word from the Brazilian caseworker guiding me through the coming weeks that the boys had been told. They found out all about me and were shown pictures of me, of my immediate family, and the house they would live in. The wrapped presents I had sent ahead also were given to them. They wore their new Florida State University Seminole shirts and caps in the photos that were e-mailed to me. I had hoped for them to establish a connection to their new family straight away with the paraphernalia of my alma mater. Their photographed faces wore somewhat dazed expressions fronted by wary smiles, yet the caseworker said it was highly unusual for adoptive children to be as inquisitive as Matheus and Davi were. They wanted to know all about their new father and his family and their impending move to Florida. Although still separated by continents, there was sense of a physical connection between us. There were shared expectations that we would soon be brought together as a unified family. Matheus and Davi had occupied all my thoughts for months. Now perhaps they were thinking of me, and also planning, hoping, and dreaming for what was soon to come.

* * *

The morning of my departure, just two weeks later was not like any one of my former trips abroad. This time, instead of tossing a compactly packed bag and knapsack into the car's backseat, I lugged two large, densely packed suitcases along with an overnight bag and my trusty knapsack into the trunk of the car. One of the suitcases contained a hodgepodge of clothes, games, and books earmarked for Matheus and Davi. The blank slate of my newly renewed passport was in stark contrast with my heavily stamped former passport that bore witness to the broad expanse of my travels throughout Europe and Asia. This would be my first venture into South America. I was used to being in charge of where I would be going and what I would be doing, but this time, I would be at the mercy of a caseworker's direction. Only until after thirty days of monitoring the bonding between us during our cohabitation would the court grant its official sanction of the adoption, clearing our way to finalize the paperwork.

My father was taking me to the airport that morning. It was one of his good days; at a passing glance, one could easily look past his ill health and carry on with business as usual. I was usually successful in doing so, yet the frailty of his appearance worried me, leaving me with a sense of regret in leaving.

For the moment, I pushed aside the pain of having had to deal with my father's terminal lung cancer the past six years.

In bidding me goodbye at the house before leaving for work, my mother kept her emotions in check. I knew better; she was only concealing her nervousness. Never mind that she always was uncomfortable with my predilection for roaming the globe. She tenderly looked me over as I stood on the threshold of a decision that was going to forever change all of our lives. As she always does before I leave to travel, she urged me to "kiss the mezuzah," firmly affixed to the doorframe of our Jewish household, before stepping out of the house. I regarded the bejeweled, protective case that stored the sacred parchment with its two portions of the Torah as our reminder of G-d's presence and of our duty to fulfill His commandments. "Honor thy mother, honor thy father," particularly came to mind, as I quietly considered my parents' cautious support of my decision to adopt these boys. Their dithering support, at times, was swayed by unanswered questions about not just what was going to happen to me in the days and weeks to come, but to all of us in the years ahead.

I also kept in mind my sister's death barely a year ago from an overdose, for which the pain of her troubled existence still plagued our lives. Details about the circumstances surrounding her adoption remained a mystery; she had refused adamantly any interest in seeking out information about her biological family. She began abusing drugs and alcohol early in her teenage years, which seemed to escalate in association with the development of a cluster of psychiatric diagnoses in early adulthood. It was a different time when we were growing up; understanding the issues and knowing to seek out counseling and other treatments for adopted children were not as ubiquitous as it is now. I was away at college by the time her difficulties began spiraling out of control; she later managed some semblance of control, keeping secret the extent of her substance abuse while successfully completing a master's degree and retaining high-profile job positions through the state government. Rotating personality disorders, panic attacks, and manic-depressive states of behavior frequently manifested themselves in fits of rage, despair, and withdrawal. Although having been out of our lives for the better part of eight years, the finality of her death destroyed even the smallest hope for her recovery, forever a reminder that she would remain estranged from us.

Her son, my nephew stood off to the side. For him, it was just another school day. Twelve-year-old Michael would go about his day as usual. He would return home in the afternoon and put off doing his homework, lie around and watch television, and make it his business to annoy his poppa with his physical pokes, noises, and aimless running around the house, trying to keep alive the waning spark that still flickered within my father. Six months after a failed marriage to an up-and-coming attorney that did not even last a year, my sister discovered she was pregnant with Michael, just as she was entering her second trimester. Who knows what she abused until she found out about the baby growing inside her. She remarkably maintained sobriety, cold turkey throughout the rest of her pregnancy, kept up with her prenatal care, and sustained a proper diet of vitamins and healthy eating. She was a different person during that short period of time. There were no panic attacks or mood swings, and relating with her was uncomplicated and agreeable; there was renewed closeness in our relationship as brother and sister as she thoughtfully planned for the caring of her newborn baby. Unfortunately, my parents and I did not fully understand at the time the significance of the bottle of wine we discovered tucked away in her overnight bag to "celebrate" Michael's birth at the hospital; she was barely holding on before she could re-engage her old, deeply entrenched substance abusing habits.

It only was a little over a month before my sister went through her first, unsuccessful stint in rehab and Michael began living with my parents. It only took another year and a half before my parents gained legal custody of Michael as my sister drifted in and out of jail, hospital emergency rooms, drug rehab centers, and group homes. My parents were successful in adopting Michael when he was 6 years old; by then, there was no contact with his mother and I had settled back to living in South Florida from Baltimore. Relief in being able to provide for Michael without the threat of interference from my sister would be extremely short lived; my father unexpectedly received his cancer diagnosis only a week after the adoption's finalization. By this time, Michael was settled with my parents as they were with him; I only lived a few miles away and was a constant presence in their household. It did not make sense to uproot him to live with me in my house. After another year and a half, I felt life for our family was finally as stable as it could be to start up my adoption plans.

Michael, too, kept his more personal thoughts and feelings about his new cousins to himself no matter how many times I tried to stoke more authentic discussions. He held the honored position as the *only* child in our immediate family. He was used to getting the sole attention, especially from me. After all, it was no secret that I gave up for him my fledgling life in Baltimore with its more readily available professional opportunities and my dreams of settling down in the northeast when he was not quite four-years-old. Throughout the years I made myself available for all things Michael; I attended his school functions, followed along with his revolving cycle of sporting pursuits, chauffeured and chaperoned outings with his friends, and vacationed with him. I wondered how he would handle having to share my attention, perhaps fearful that he would lose me to Matheus and Davi. It already was too much for him to fend off the denial of my father's impending mortality. Even so, there was innocence in his excitement to meet his new "brothers" who were sure to offset the then often too quiet solitude of his family life. I dutifully placed two fingers over my lips and walked out of the house after touching the mezuzah, which was covered over with the time-honored blotches of my mother's lipstick.

It was at the tail end of rush hour on my drive down to Miami. My father and I mostly made small talk about the random views of construction along the highway, the clear skies that made for good flying weather, the upcoming preparations for Michael's bar mitzvah, still eight months away, and negotiating the building up of the traffic the closer we made our way to the airport. There was little or no mention at all about the adoption, as if all the talking had been done; there was nothing left to say, nothing left to question, and nothing left to reason. After heaving the last of my luggage onto the curbside at the airport, I turned to face my father and hugged him goodbye. I tried not to notice the stooped posture, pastiness of his skin, advanced balding, and small stature of his head now precariously perched between oversized shoulders. Despite it all, my father was a picture of determination; he had living to do. Seeing me realize my long-held dream to become a father added some credence to all the suffering and sacrifice he was going through. Knowing this in my heart helped to alleviate some of my fear and guilt in leaving him behind. Although there was no immediate cause for concern about his health, there also was no guarantee as to its stability. As a turn toward the worse could happen at any time, we were forewarned about the often swiftness in the deterioration in a patient's health and subsequent death in such advanced cancer cases as his.

Perhaps in large part due to the "live for the moment" attitude he had adopted more passionately since he was diagnosed with his cancer, my father never flinched in his support of my moving forward in adopting Matheus and Davi. Though no less supportive of my dreams to adopt, my mother still could not help but express her doubts about the reality of the change these two boys would inevitably make in our family. She wanted to know how I would manage, where she would fit in, could she grow to love these two strangers, and, most important, what about Michael? My father's unconditional support balanced my mother's anxiety. I felt empowered by his building blocks of competence and commitment, character traits we shared in common; his subtle support further strengthened my resolve to adopt the boys.

Once I passed through security and check-in, I boarded the airplane and took my seat at the window. Waiting for others to board the plane, I glanced over at the two other empty seats in my row. Soon the seats would fill with strangers, who would likely stay as such; I rarely have luck finding agreeable companionship on long flights abroad. It was a bit surreal to think how Matheus and Davi would be occupying those two seats for the return flight home. As on most of my former trips abroad, I was traveling solo, and yet, unlike previous returns home, I would not be alone and sitting with random strangers.

Throughout the daylong flight to São Paulo, I focused on my readings and kept at bay the roiling doubts that threatened to dampen my spirits. This was the first time I had flown between the northern and southern hemispheres. The time change was only an hour, but I went from summer to winter. Although it was early May, I reached to pull on my coat upon landing. A slight chill in the air greeted me as I stepped out of the plane and onto the jetway. Passing through customs, I handed my passport with its specialized visa stamp issued for the purpose of adopting. With a customary air of indifference to the jumble of emotions churning in my insides, the agent then stamped my passport, officially clearing me to enter into Brazil.

Chapter 2

So Opens Another Door

I negotiated my way through the crowds at São Paulo's Guarulhos airport. Relying on the scant signage to guide me, and hauling around my luggage before checking it back in for the connecting flight to Curitiba, it was slow moving between terminals. Once relieved of my luggage, I sat down on the floor in the departure lounge for domestic travelers and watched the ticking of the clock as constant throngs of people filed into the terminal from all parts of Brazil, from places I had never heard of. It was a strain to hear the anonymous calls of the loud speaker as the next flights ready for boarding were announced. My little command of Portuguese from my few months' worth of Rosetta Stone tutorial exercises was of no help to me as I craned to hear the call for Curitiba. Minutes seemed like hours until the announcement was made to board.

It was late and I imagined the boys would be sleeping by now, having spent their last evening at the orphanage. I wondered how they were feeling about meeting me tomorrow. Were they as excited and nervous as I was? I wanted to think that I understood what was about to happen to my life. Even with my doctorate in psychology, I really had no idea. All the books I read, seminars I attended, and people in the know I had spoken to bore very little relevance at this point.

Having finally arrived in Curitiba, I deplaned with the others and wearily waited for my bags to come tumbling down the conveyer belt. In a flash, I had all of my bags stacked on the baggage cart. As I rolled toward the exit doors where the caseworker would be waiting for me, I stopped short at the corner, bowed my head and clasped my hands together, keeping myself steady against the jostling of others that rushed past me. As I wrestled with the mixture of feelings I had about going out to connect with my future, I shut my eyes and momentarily breathed deeply. I could not feel my beating heart as if time stood still. I was really going through with this, yet I trembled at the thought of having to round the corner where there would be no turning back.

Lino knew to look out for me, having seen the same pictures of me that were shown to the boys. I had no idea what he looked like, yet he seemed easy for me to spot in the waiting area. He looked to be roughly my age as he greeted me with a warm smile and a handshake. His demeanor was gentle, obviously influenced by his years of working with needy, troubled children. Lino readily put me at ease as he briefly laid out what I should expect over the next six weeks.

It was close to midnight and I was bleary eyed from both physical and emotional exhaustion. The streets were nearly empty as we drove into the night. The occasional street lamp illuminated isolated, anonymous pieces of the passing cityscape. Lino related the agenda for the next day, starting with a ride out to the orphanage to meet Matheus and Davi. He told me the boys were excited, and prepared to meet me. More small talk predominated until we reached our destination. I checked into Lar Rogate, a non-denominational Christian retreat and conference center. It was to be home throughout the cohabitation period for the boys and myself; my Jewish self was relieved as to the absence of any tangible overtones of Christianity on display. We had a two-room suite with my bed and the bathroom in the back room and two twin beds for the boys in the front room. I took another moment to regard the still emptiness of the boys' two beds, knowing they would be filled tomorrow night. Sleep did not come easy that night.

* * *

The following morning I woke with a start, followed by an adrenaline-fueled sprint out of bed. I was all too happy to set the day in motion and put an end to the night's fitful efforts to sleep. Lino was waiting for me as I finished what little breakfast I could manage. We set out for the orphanage, taking our place in the line of the morning's rush-hour traffic. We passed many a blighted area in our travels, highlighted by the congestion of poverty and overpopulation. We faced time constraints as it was Friday and the courts were due to shut down in the mid-afternoon. The traffic especially was stressful, because we had to be in court by two o'clock and that left me limited time to meet my sons.

We arrived at the office building for the orphanage, where the boys were waiting for us. The small building was nondescript, blending into the shabby neighborhood where the different group homes of the orphanage were scattered about. Standing outside, I asked Lino to take my picture for posterity's sake. It would be the last time I would pose as a lone person, as one who had to answer only to himself. For a second I looked backward, bidding my old self good-bye as Lino ushered me into the office. I was not nearly as nervous as I feared I would be. I was in a state of shock. My emotional system had shut down, a faint buzz of adrenaline still rushing through me. Brief introductions were made to the agency's social worker and a few of the people who cared for the children. Everyone was genuinely hospitable.

I kept my wits about me as I moved toward a closed door, behind which the boys were waiting. Lino simply said, "Well, are you ready?" I simply nodded as I heard their muffled voices from inside. They were real! Lino's counterpart back home in America, who had been guiding me through up until my departure, frequently encouraged me to attend to Brazilian culture. Luciana told me how Brazilian children are used to an unlimited, unconditional supply of physical affection from not only their parents, but most adults. "When you first meet them, hug them," she had urged.

I followed behind as Lino entered the room. I first spotted the boys in the back, contentedly playing on the floor. They turned to look in our direction, then got up and slowly, hesitantly approached me with shy smiles and open arms. We must have shared some of the same degree of disbelief, uncertain just what to make of this forced meeting of strangers. To this day, I do not remember whom I held in my arms first. I just remember how unbelievable it felt to actually be touching them. They seemed so small, so vastly unlike how big I had been building them up to be all this time. I could only imagine how I appeared to them a giant, all six feet, two inches of me. Towering over them, I got down on bended knee to meet and interact with them face-to-face.

Lino was right there to translate for us. My attempts to converse in Portuguese were futile. I struggled with missing vocabulary, mangled pronunciations, and mixed up grammar. The boys did not seem to care. Instead, they were eager to show me the random toys with which they were playing, encouraging me to engage with them through the universal language of play. At this point, Lino backed away, conversing with the social worker and taking pictures. It was a gentle first meeting.

Only about an hour had passed before it was time to go to court. The boys had their final packing and goodbyes to make before they would be ready. In the meantime, I had to meet with the court's social worker and judge. The boys were all smiles as we exchanged hugs and kisses. When asked in the car after leaving them behind, I did not know how to express what I was thinking, what I was feeling as I struggled to take everything in. The boys were very sweet, engaging, bright, and eager to please. I thought they liked me.

It was a short drive to the courthouse. The court social worker, Amelia, seemed pleased to hear the meeting with the children went well. Her fondness for the boys was apparent; she smiled broadly and was eager to talk about them. Thumbing through the weighty file folder on her desk, she offhandedly revealed intimate details of the boys' background; she told me what had led up to their mother's relinquishment of her parental rights. I was already privy to much of this information, yet I knew only cursory details of the boys' earlier history of poverty and neglect. It seemed that their mother loved and cared for them as best as she could and that she gave them up to better guarantee a future she could not give them. Amelia provided me with a letter their mother had written to them, for which they read at the time of her last meeting with them. It was on several sheets of lined notebook paper, and written in Portuguese; its words were interspersed with simplistic drawings of hearts and flowers. I was told that she wrote how much she loved them, hoped that they would find peace and forgiveness in their hearts, and how they were to be mindful of G-d's authority. I planned for its safekeeping until the time was right for it to be shown to them again.

Meeting the ruling judge was a rather informal affair. She wore jeans and a white turtle neck sweater. She smiled affably. As she spoke English, it was easy for me to engage her in idle conversation. There were no probing questions or expressed concerns. Her signing off on the temporary custody orders for our thirty-day cohabitation period seemed a mere formality.

We were on our way back to the orphanage when Lino mentioned his relief that she had been in a good mood that day. I had made a positive impression on her.

Back at the orphanage, Matheus and Davi were pining to leave. A few backpacks with their clothes and personal toys were waiting in the front office. While I was away, they'd had their lunch and said their good-byes. A few pictures with the social worker and other care workers were taken. Both boys were excited and the smiles remained plastered on their faces. Lino stayed and ate dinner with us at Lar Rogate, making sure we were settled in and that any immediate concerns were addressed. Afterward, it seemed all too soon for Lino to go, leaving us to fend for ourselves. He would be away for the weekend, but left me a cell phone to call for any questions or concerns that should happen to come up. He did his best to reassure me, yet nothing could have prepared me for the insecurity and vulnerability I felt once the door closed behind him.

The reality of suddenly having to move up from the back to the driver's seat was unnerving. I turned to look at the boys, as they stared back at me with hopeful, questioning smiles affixed to their innocent faces. By now, my limited command of Portuguese was finally registering with them, yet no words in any language came to mind. The humming sounds of some distant generator surrounding our awkward silence was deafening. Taking notice of the time, I turned to the venerable tradition of the day's closure for parents all over the world: sending their children to bed. Especially with children who came from a background dominated by uncertainty and chaos, I would discover again and again the boys' desire, their need for the structure of our bedtime routine.

Matheus and Davi readily laid claim to their beds, and that gave way to the beginnings of our bedtime routine; they showered, put on their "sleepy clothes," brushed their teeth, and took their places on one of the twin beds, one pressed against each side of me as we read along together *The Cat in the Hat,* one of the English language pictured story books I brought with me. Their eyes silently followed along with my finger trailing the printed words. I slowly read aloud. Taking care to read expressively and enunciate each word precisely, I sometimes stopped and pointed at the picture and said the word in English. It was my first attempt to teach them English. Reading aloud together would become a fixture in our bedtime routine. It was both calming and comforting for all of us, a chance to bond. Our forthcoming days would end with me wedged on one of the beds in between my sons, who held me upright like two bookends. It was everything I had hoped for ... and it was only the beginning.

Chapter 3

Crisscrossing Paths in the Dark

As I lay down on my bed that evening, with the boys asleep in the next room, the rapid shifting of my thoughts penetrated the stillness of the night. It was going to be another sleepless night for me. Perhaps to calm my restless spirits, my attention turned toward my "little brothers" from what seemed another lifetime ago, now young men, and off on lives of their own. I met them twelve years before, when I had taken a job as the sole school psychologist for a small, rural county in North Central Florida after finishing the coursework for my doctoral studies. The guidance counselor at one of the elementary schools recruited me a month after school started to talk to interested classes about what a school psychologist does. A group of fourth graders particularly were eager to engage; when I opened the floor for questions, hands shot up in the air, the students' teeming with eagerness to share their personal struggles: This one's parents were divorced; that one's grandmother had died; another's older brother was hitting her at home . . . I was overwhelmed by the candor with which each child wanted to share.

It was a sea of anonymous faces until my eyes rested on an Asian boy eagerly yet patiently raising his hand for a turn. Strikingly handsome, poised, articulate, and endearingly soft-spoken, he boldly began telling of his own difficult familial circumstances with his parents' impending divorce and his father's hostile relations toward him and his mother. I stopped him mid-sentence, protective of his privacy and the sensitivity of the details starting to unfold. He agreed to meet privately the next day.

We struck an affable rapport, yet his mother told me he was supposed to start outside counseling. I refrained from pursuing any further contact ... until his teacher approached me shortly after winter break and asked me to connect with him again. Bobby was displaying some aggressive behavior seemingly out of character for him. He hadn't followed through with the counseling, so we met weekly for about two months until he regained his composure. Coincidentally, my administrative cohorts were encouraging me to take on a particular fourth-grade boy earmarked for the county's grant funded mentoring program. My heart was already taken. I felt Bobby would thrive within the context of a consistent relationship with a "big brother," and I could not bear the thought of someone else taking on that role with him.

Also at the time, I was summoned by the school to evaluate his younger brother, who was a second-grader. I vividly remember walking into his classroom that first time to meet Brandon, spotting him seated off to the side at his own desk, away from the group. His teacher clearly had a dislike for him, judging by the way she spoke, casting him aside because she was unable to tolerate his fidgety, unfocused, impulsive mannerisms. His hulking size seemed a poor fit for his desk, his shy demeanor in stark contrast to his brother's forthcoming, outgoing personality. We clicked fast; an instant bond forged between us, with Brandon feeling at ease relating with someone who obviously found him delightfully funny and one who felt that he mattered. I found myself stretching the testing to numerous meetings, keeping him out for prolonged periods of time for game playing and more casual relations. It quickly became a given in my mind and heart that I would be taking Brandon on as a "little brother", as well.

Asian-American culture discourages seeking out mental health and/or social supportive services in favor of isolation behind a wall of privacy. Their mother seemed to belie this generalization in sharing with me her fear for her sons' welfare and her desire for assistance on their behalf. Without a moment's hesitation, she signed the permission forms, sending me on the task to introduce the idea to the boys. I spoke with Bobby first, who maintained a quiet sort of interest; he refrained from asking any particular questions or relating his thoughts. He cautiously agreed to try out this strange idea of a mentoring relationship. His mother reassured him that it would be good for him, and to give "Mr. Matloff" a try. Unlike his brother, Brandon was barely able to contain his excitement at home after I had approached him with the mentoring prospect. Though he, too, seemed rather quietly speculative when I first mentioned it to him. My eyes welled up with tears when he simply asked, "What did I do to deserve this?" Struggling to keep my composure, I whispered, "Nothing... just for being you." I knew Matheus and Davi had been "excited" to meet me, yet I wondered what kind of thoughts they had of me now that I had entered into their lives.

For the next year and a half, I met with Bobby and Brandon several times weekly, alternating between one-on-one time and fraternizing together as a trio; each month I plotted out a schedule of our meetings for them to keep track on their refrigerator at home. Most of our meetings were simple affairs, such as games of hide-and-seek at the nearby park, hanging out in my office after school, frolicking in my apartment complex's pool, or grabbing a pizza at Pizza Hut or burgers at Sonny's. As much as I cherished our one-on-one time together, I especially enjoyed our time together as a trio, and how Bobby and Brandon played off of each other that lent itself to a more familial type of atmosphere for me. Their younger brother, Sean, was in kindergarten and sometimes tagged along. I signed him up to receive his own mentor, yet he was never assigned one. Sean always was happy to be included and endeared himself to me as well; he never seemed to begrudge his brothers for the preferential attention they got from me.

It was easy for me to become caught up in the boys' lives as they indelibly embedded themselves within the far reaches of my heart. It was a time in my life that forever stands out for its blissfulness in how we carried on with one another in spite of the trials and tribulations we each struggled to toil through. I carried the strain of applying for internships and jetting around the country for interviews, getting my doctoral dissertation off the ground, and assisting my parents in taking over the care of my nephew from my sister during her first stint in rehab. The boys were adjusting to life with their mother trying to raise them properly under near-poverty-level conditions, her acculturation from her native Philippines to American culture and the English language, and their father's inconsistency, marked by their impression of his indifference toward them. Matheus and Davi did not carry with them the burden of having been rejected by their natural father; he had died shortly after Davi was born, and neither had remembered him.

Bobby and Brandon's mother never refused my requests to take them; the trust she instilled in me with her precious sons never ceased to move me. When I was successfully matched with my first choice for internship that would have me moving to Pennsylvania, it was not without heaviness and trepidation in my heart about leaving the boys behind. I waited three months before sitting down to tell them, trying to keep our carefree relations as long as possible. I hadn't even finished warming up to officially telling them when Bobby abruptly asked, "You're leaving, aren't you?" What they had become used to as a constant in their life was about to be disrupted, yet another reminder of the harshness of their reality; they had muted reactions, as if they expected all along that it would be only a matter of time for this also to eventually fade away. Matheus and Davi had also experienced so much loss already in their young lives. I wondered how they were looking at me on this first day. Were they expecting me to be their life's constant, or that I was just another who would be transient, and likely to abandon them at any moment?

We held onto our routine to the very end. It was the end of an era for us. I tried my best to reassure them *and* myself that we would maintain our ties to one another. As with any long-distance relationship, it was a challenge with our lives set to move ahead on different trajectories. Indeed, from the start, with the rawness of our separation still weighing heavily on my mind and heart, I could not reach them when their phone service was shut off; their mother had lost her job. I enlisted their school's guidance counselor to check in on them, for which they were able to call a few days later, after their phone service was restored and their mother resumed working.

Three months later, when I returned to meet with my dissertation committee, I could not get away fast enough to get to the boys. Entering their house, I found Bobby and Brandon with only the backs of their heads visible, sitting on the couch watching television. Both of them sprang up, flying over the couch and into my open arms. They knew I was coming, but it was as if they couldn't believe I would come back, readying themselves for disappointment . . . again. For the first few ensuing years, we again adopted a regular routine dictating our weekend visits, averaging three to four times a year. After a five-hour drive to pick them up around lunch time on Saturday, I took the boys to a park or the mall or some touristy site, or maybe the beach, dinner, and a night at a hotel; a movie with lunch the following Sunday followed before the drop-off and the five-hour drive south. Bobby was starting middle school and Brandon had advanced into the fourth grade that first year. They were roughly the same ages, then, as Matheus and Davi were now, asleep in their beds.

These visits kept us actively connected, allowing us a brief physical reminder of our ties to each other. By the time Bobby and Brandon moved onto high school, our weekends had dwindled to once or twice a year. Michael sometimes joined us, and Sean became a regular fixture. I was there for Bobby's and Brandon's high school graduations; Bobby's graduation from a two-year military college in Alabama, where he was on a wrestling scholarship; and Brandon's graduation from boot camp in the air force on base in Texas. Later that year, when I was visiting a friend in Minneapolis for a long weekend, just nine months before I received Matheus's and Davi's adoption referral, I boarded an overnight Amtrak train to Minot, North Dakota, where Brandon was newly stationed, to spend the day with him. Bobby was already in the air force, stationed in Alaska. Weekend visits were further reduced to meeting half way for a late lunch/early dinner whenever one of the boys came home for a rare visit, yet we continued to maintain our connection via the odd email, phone call, and Facebook contacts. The relationship we had cultivated together over the years inspired the type of bonding I was hopeful for when adopting a child of my own. And, even though I had set out looking to adopt one child, I dared to fantasize that a pair of brothers might be in my destiny.

* * *

I had gotten out of bed, and quietly opened the door separating my room from the boys' adjoining room. I let my eyes adjust to the room's prevailing darkness, gradually making out the boys' distinct shapes filling their beds. There was silence; neither made a sound as they slept. I stood in the doorway, gazing at the stillness of their slumber. My mind began to travel back even further, back to when I was living in New England doing direct-care work with children in a residential treatment center. I was remembering that first day when I walked into the main living quarters of the center's cottage, and became surrounded by the home's thirteen boys, ranging in age from six-to twelve-years-old. They were eager to get a look at their newest caretaker.

Eight-year-old Philip caught my eye. All the boys were keen on interacting with me, jockeying for a position that would get my attention, but Philip stood out to me; his angelic face supported a gentle, sweet smile, yet the sparkle in his hazel eyes seemed veiled by the shadows of a lifetime of sorrow. I enjoyed caring for all of the home's boys, yet I had formed a special bond with Philip over the two years I was there. There were times only I was able to coax him to rejoin the group, out from a state of despair and insolence when he had withdrawn to sulk. When he was the only one in the group who had not earned enough points to go on a day-long outing, I could not volunteer fast enough to stay back with him, where we spent the better part of the afternoon playing out back in the woods, steeped with imaginary tales of kings, castles, and battle conquests. When watching television at the house with the group, he often sat next to me on the couch, perhaps at times pressed up against me a little too closely. It took all I had to restrain myself from embracing him in return, in that most familiar of ways reminiscent of the physical bonding between a father and son.

I stood on the sidelines for two years watching Philip constantly disappointed by his family of origin, until parental rights were severed between him and his deadbeat father; his mother had passed away when he was much younger. I looked on as he transitioned into his new adoptive family, only to later hear of the disruption of his adoption and subsequent return to the group home. By then, I had moved to a neighboring state, having taken my first therapist job counseling children and teens at a mental health clinic.

Feeling that I could, that I *wanted* to love Philip in the way that he needed, I set out to adopt him myself. He was eleven-years-old, then. I drove through an ice storm after getting special permission to meet up with him at the group home; I needed to see whether that spark still existed, even if just a flicker. I recall how I entered the house, still feeling unnerved from the treacherous drive, having to flex my fingers for several minutes after uncurling them from their tight grip on the steering wheel. I was at a loss for words when we met face-to-face and he incredulously asked, "Why are you here?" My peripheral vision suddenly darkened; I only was able to see his face, as I felt the flicker in my heart ignite into a firestorm of affection.

I promptly put my bid in to adopt him, attending required prospective parent meetings, and meeting with caseworkers. I even interviewed for therapist jobs, with the intent to move back to the area if it would better my chances. I did not get very far. Because of his already failed adoption, the social workers were extra cautious in selecting his next placement. It soon became clear that Philip would not be allowed to leave the state, yet I could not just take any job, one that might not fit well professionally with me. I had not even completed attending all of the required prospective foster care meetings when Philip was swiftly matched with a married couple, who had other children. I was ignored as a serious contender as I was single, and still young in my late twenties, with not yet "enough" life experience to properly provide for a troubled child. I was crushed; I had not planned on pursuing adoption at this still new stage in my life, but I had felt that I was destined to adopt Philip. He never knew of my intentions, and

I never saw or heard of him again. Thinking about him that night, with him now being in his late twenties as I was when I tried adopting him, I wondered how he had fared in life, hoping that he had found peace and happiness.

Matheus and Davi remained in their peaceful slumber. Now that we were newly joined together, our life's journey had only just begun. They say that "getting there is half the fun," yet it was anything but "fun" in the years before that led me to this new beginning of my life's journey. It was another ten years before I officially launched the beginning of my adoption pursuits, a journey that would test my resolve across the bumpiest of roads, time and time again.

Chapter 4

Why Not Buy American?

As I was pursuing international adoption, and even after having adopted, friends and acquaintances unexpectedly would ask why I chose to adopt overseas when there are so many American children so badly in need of a loving family. Indeed, I knew the number of children in foster care in the Unites States is staggering. Numerous reports indicate that more than half a million children nationwide are at the mercy of the foster care system, yet most are not necessarily available for adoption. Too many adoptable children are older and typically escape the attention of those seeking to adopt younger children. Given my interests in adopting an older child, I did not expect the multiple roadblocks I experienced when first setting out to adopt a child domestically.

When I officially launched my plans to adopt an older child out of the foster care system, I thought my plan was a straightforward one. I did not expect three years to go by and still to come up empty handed. I learned quickly how much I vastly underestimated the complexities involved in the nation's foster care system. I started, innocently enough, with a short list of the potential issues I felt willing and able to parent in a child removed from his family of origin. I was looking for a boy ranging in age from about seven to twelve years old, who was of at least average intelligence, with related achievement potential, and lacking in severe acting-out, delinquent behaviors, or severe psychiatric problems. I also entertained the possibility of, or perhaps a preference toward adopting a pair of brothers. Little did I know how vastly different the many caseworkers searching for suitable families would interpret my professed interests.

I also was overconfident about what I had to offer for caseworkers to take notice of me over other prospective adoptive parents. After all, I was a psychologist with extensive experience in enhancing children's mental and behavioral health for a variety of issues and in multiple settings. Having been working in the schools since I returned to Florida from Baltimore, I also was well versed in how to access necessary supports as needed. I seemed extra qualified to parent a child with layers of emotional baggage in need of specialized nurturing guidance. I also was financially independent, with a solid support system of family and friends, for which I had their glowing testimonials as to my character and emotional stability.

Encouragement to adopt from the foster care system seemed omnipresent both locally and statewide. In Florida, television commercials, newspaper advertisements, and Heart Gallery announcements of traveling photographic and audio exhibits constantly were touted to find forever families for children *waiting* in foster care. Such publicity, glossy in its appearance and nobility, made the prospect look straightforward and relatively trouble-free. Although it was not necessarily widely publicized, I also found information about the many financial incentives designed to further support parents of foster children. There typically are no adoption fees, health care is covered by the state, college tuition at a state school is covered, and a small adoption subsidy is available in many special-needs cases. But idyllic smiles, photogenic faces, and carefully contrived statements all too often seemed a smokescreen for the incessant troubles plaguing the foster care system as I was soon to experience firsthand.

* * *

Already familiar with the positive reputation of a local adoption and foster care agency, I started with them. Straightaway I felt welcomed by the directors and social workers in response to my expressed interests in fostering a child with the potential for adoption. I felt valued for what I could offer as a prospective parent, respected for my professional background, and cared about regarding my particular interests in adoption. There was the required Model Approach to Partnerships in Parenting (MAPP) training to attend, and a home study to complete. In about three months I officially became a licensed foster parent with a home deemed suitable by the county to take in children in need of residence. I began to attend the agency's monthly foster parenting classes while I waited until a potential foster-to-adopt child came up.

On my own, I checked daily the numerous online adoption listings, including the national website www.adoptuskids.com and regional and individual state listings of children available for adoption. A photo usually accompanied a brief profile for each child listed. With a trained eye, I read between the lines and picked apart particular dynamics that seemed counter to my particular standards for adopting, helping me to narrow my focus. For those I felt had potential for my purposes, I enlisted the agency's foster care caseworker to send out my home study. Together, we made somewhere close to two hundred of these formal inquiries to caseworkers across the country.

Locally, there were limitations in the agency's referrals to child cases that came through their shelter, with the majority of cases being babies and toddlers and/or who had only short-term, transient placement needs. The needs of the children residing in their complex of group homes were considered too severe relative to my criteria. Soon after I'd started out with them, a rather curious occurrence began to unfold throughout the state, with mandates to halt the removal of children from their families unless the need for it was absolutely extreme. Shelters in the area, including the agency's own, quickly found their units nearly empty of children in need of at least short-term care for the better part of a year.

I continued to press forward, trying to network with caseworkers and supervisors, and follow-up on the inquiries that we'd made. Too many times, caseworkers would not even return my phone calls or e-mails. Those who did respond usually offered little encouragement, resisted sharing any further information about a particular child for confidentiality purposes, and were vague about time frames and the plans for moving forward on the child's behalf. With some of those children whose profiles strongly piqued my interest, I followed up initial inquiries with a "life book" I'd created, depicting my family life as told through photos and descriptive statements. I also wrote personal statements geared toward the particular child's needs and what I might be able to offer to meet those needs. I had hoped for my home study to stand out from the dozens of others collecting dust on some anonymous caseworker's desk. It often was hard to maintain a balance between appropriate boundaries in making contact with caseworkers and assertively promoting myself as a suitable prospective parent.

In hindsight, it was not that long before my efforts finally caught a caseworker's attention . . . and it was only the second child I'd formally inquired about. Like all the others, the profile for this preteen of eleven-years-old, offered only a brief glimpse of who he was and the problems with which he was struggling. I was one of three families selected to receive more detailed information about this boy in order to make an informed decision about whether to pursue further the prospect of his adoption. Contact was maintained through my agency's caseworker; I never had direct contact with the child's caseworker.

I could barely contain my excitement, despite my caseworker's benevolent tries to caution me about getting too hopeful for what was not yet known and most likely to be dispiriting as to the extent of this boy's needs. Weeks went by, and despite several calls to the caseworker and her supervisor, a month passed before the caseworker followed up on her promise for more information. The boy had already been in their state's custody for several years, after all; what difference would another month make? With a deafening thud, twenty-plus pages of information landed on my caseworker's desk for her review.

The report sharply contrasted with his public profile; it seemed as though we had gotten information about a different child. I was appalled by what his caseworker considered was a child *mildly* affected by emotional problems. The significance of his psychiatric difficulties, suggesting a history of psychotic-like symptoms and behavioral outbursts in need of heavy doses of medication, was too overwhelming for me to conceive of. His public profile also stated that he did not have learning problems, yet he was diagnosed with a developmental disability and had a neurological condition involving memory deficits. His was a very sad case that revealed tremendous upheaval throughout his young life, and the subsequent abandonment of an overwhelmingly large extended family many states away. I felt for this boy's innocence, so horrendously trampled upon, yet the damage inflicted on him was so extensive, I could not conceive of taking him on.

I had to let the boy go and wrestle with my disappointment. I also had to fend off some guilt, wondering what would happen to him, hoping he was receiving the treatment he needed. I separated my urge to think of him as though he were a prospective client from my own personal need to adopt. I stumbled across his profile again three years later, just before moving on to the international realm. I was taken aback upon seeing the exact same profile; nothing had been updated, with the exception of his photo. His profile made him seem even more juvenile than before now that he was fully in his adolescent years. How many others over the years were blindly attracted to his profile? Still, I remained true to what I realistically felt was feasible for me. I could not hold myself responsible for every child waiting to be adopted, even if it meant having to gently close one door and move on to another door waiting to be opened.

* * *

Months more went by until a full year slipped away, and more than halfway passed on into the next year. I grew tired of attending the agency's foster parent meetings month after month, only to declare myself still waiting for a placement and hearing how other families finalized adoptions of their young foster children, most of whom were toddlers. One couple who regularly attended the meetings had an older child in his later elementary school years they recently had adopted from foster care. I always was the only single man, and semi-regularly a single woman or two would be in attendance. The regulars politely received me, but that was all; I dreaded those meetings, and it probably showed. I refrained from speaking much during group discussions, as I did not have personal references like the others did about their own children at home. Occasionally I would speak up about my nephew, Michael, when it was relevant. I kept my professional knowledge and experience off the table, not wanting to come across as a supercilious know-it-all. Listening to what some of the parents spoke of, asked about, and worried over often made it difficult for me to keep quiet.

I also grew weary of sending out my information over and over again to no avail. Poring over the online adoption listings nightly became something of an obsession. Every night I took another spin of the same children's photos, only to come up without any new jackpot potential. Too many of these children's profiles began to ingrain themselves into my consciousness, threatening the weakening of my objectivity and my sending out an inquiry or two *just because*. Grabbing hold of my senses, I curbed my searches to a weekly endeavor.

In my contacts with caseworkers they often made it apparent that delays in responding, or perhaps not responding at all was not so much because there were concerns or doubts about my suitability. It seemed more about the indecisiveness in determining a particular child's best interests. Many of the children's biological parents had yet to have their rights legally terminated, stalling plans for any permanency planning. For those who were legally free to be adopted, there were many who had other members of their biological family stepping forward for consideration, a situation that needed to be played out before any other options could move ahead. Outside of the biological family's grip, there sometimes were the children's current foster parents, who still were considering whether to pursue adopting the child. So many other children simply had yet to have a specific adoption plan at all laid out, for which their being put out on public display to attract generic attention seemed senseless.

As frustrated as I was about not making any headway with the children I inquired about, I became even more exasperated by the phone calls I did receive from caseworkers. Encouraged by my professional background, they wanted to discuss a particular child on their caseload whom I might not have considered. These children typically presented with severe problematic behaviors and psychiatric diagnoses. The criteria I specified in my home study were completely disregarded by these caseworkers, as I, more than most, seemed ideally equipped to handle the severity of these children's problems. Too many of them appeared more appropriate for the round-the-clock care and supervision of residential treatment.

As I struggled to remain optimistic, the agency's caseworker and director unexpectedly approached me about a particular child in his early elementary school years who needed to be removed from another foster family. I occasionally heard the current foster mother speak about the boy and his two sisters at our monthly meetings. He was sweet, without any apparent malicious intent; he did not demonstrate any severe types of psychiatric problems. He was behind in school and struggled with inattention, maybe some impulsiveness as well that might or might not be diagnosable as an attention disorder. There were questions of an earlier history of unknown sexual abuse, for which he was starting to act-out mild degrees of sexualized behavior. There were concerns about whether he should continue living for the time being with his two sisters for their safety. There also were concerns about whether his current foster mother would be able to proactively and skillfully redirect his behavior. If I took him in, I would be provided with the agency's intensive financial, service, and counseling supports. It was the agency's hope to avoid placing him in one of their group homes, feeling that I was the one foster parent in their network they believed would be able to effectively handle his circumstances.

I struggled with taking him on. He seemed to fit well with many of my hopes for a child I wanted to adopt. I was saddened about having him separated from his sisters. The prospect of having to regularly relate with this particular foster mother, with whom I tended to zone out whenever she would endlessly interject her opinions in our meetings, also did not sit well with me. The director's faith in my ability to care for this boy was such that she did not hesitate to commit to the agency's funding him to join us on our planned family cruise in the Mediterranean later that summer. Even though permanency plans for him included a strong probability that he might be available for adoption, the agency's pressing concern was to proactively treat his behavior and further his emotional stability. As in any foster care situation, there were no guarantees.

I spoke at length with my parents and my trustworthy cousin, Gayle, and close friends. There was no doubt about my being able to provide for him and his needs; my loved ones' ready willingness to support the boy and me was touching. Yet most concerning was the potential impact on my nephew; Michael was about two years older than the boy at the time. Being told I would not even be able to have the two of them together in the backseat of the car echoed in the back of my mind. The intensive amount of care that would be required to monitor this boy's behavior was most disconcerting. I worried how difficult it would be to maintain the close, relaxed relationship between Michael and me, given the boy's intense supervisory needs.

After a year and a half, a possibly viable child for me had finally surfaced, yet the extent of his particular needs seemed too great given my familial commitments. I was afraid to turn this proposition down, fearful I might not get another chance. Perhaps this was the boy who was meant for me to take in. I also was concerned the agency would think less of my commitment to foster a child, that I was unrealistic about providing for a child with baggage of any significance. With a heavy heart, I decided taking in this boy would not have been realistic considering the needs of my family and myself. I still had to remain truthful to myself.

* * *

With nearly two years having passed, I came across another avenue to pursue from a random search on the Internet. There was an adoption agency in the Pacific Northwest corner of the country that had a program focusing on children in the foster care system. I was intrigued by the program's use of grants and other funding resources in its work to find families for legally available older foster care children across the country; only a nominal amount of fees were required. I completed the application process, which was expedited, since I already had a home study. Upon acceptance into their program and being connected with the program's caseworker, I had renewed hopes with having support and assistance on both sides of the country.

The caseworker seemed understanding of my criteria in our discussions over the phone. He was active in sending out my home study to draw the attention of other caseworkers, and promoted my candidacy in the many foster care review meetings he regularly attended. Even so, I still received some of those same phone calls from him about severely impaired children. He always prefaced these calls with his understanding what my answer would be; yet because it was another caseworker's request he needed to be sure I was made aware. Again, those children I was interested in still rarely went past our first inquiry, and still usually for reasons unknown.

Attempting to conserve my energy and overall sanity, I stopped bothering to make inquiries in certain less liberal areas of the country. We excluded the Southeast, including my home state of Florida and many states throughout the Midwest, in favor of those areas that were more liberal toward single prospective fathers. California, the Pacific Northwest and Idaho, New Mexico, and Texas were the more progressive areas where we seemed most successful in gaining interest in my candidacy.

A year and yet nearly another year passed before an eleven-year-old boy on the West Coast surfaced, seemingly earmarked for me. A conference call was scheduled between the boy's social worker in his home state and both of my caseworkers. Details of the boy's needs and the potential for a suitable match between this boy and me were to be discussed. Per the policy of the boy's home state, I would not be privy to any such information until after this briefing and discussion. Just as before, I did not know anything about the boy and his background other than what was shared in his public profile.

With excitement built to an all-time high for me in anticipation of the meeting, I was left dejected at the meeting's abrupt cancellation. My Florida caseworker received word of the boy's refusal to be adopted after having visited with his maternal grandmother. Seemingly out of desperation, he indicated to his social worker that he simply would go to work and earn money for his family to stay together, even though adoption rather than reunification with his family of origin was to remain the plan for him. He was placed on inactive status with intentions to provide him with adoption counseling. There was no time frame about a change in his status, and I was told I should just wait for news. I never did hear of him again.

I turned back to thinking about what it really was I wanted ... to be a father, to love and nurture a child into maturity. International adoption began to occupy my thoughts, with its appeal inspired by the potential for a more straightforward means to adopt. As I began to research further, with my West Coast caseworker's encouragement, I considered the possible advantage of going out to an upcoming adoption party in Seattle, sponsored by the state's adoption listing agency. I would get to meet personally some of the children available for adoption in the area, as well as some of the influential supervisors. It was early November and Seattle was experiencing an unusually vibrant autumn; when the plane dipped below the skies in its approach to land, I gazed dreamily at the trees' bounty of golden colors blanketing the landscape below, deflecting from the nervous energy I was feeling.

As I expected, attending the party was an awkward experience. I never was comfortable with the idea of openly meeting children as if shopping at the mall for clothes, trying them on for size and whether they were suited to my style and taste. It especially was disheartening to spy on some of the older teenagers I repeatedly had seen on their state's online listings for two or three years, seeing their fragile selves on display. Would they ever find a family? I felt self-conscious striking up conversations on my own with these children. Most interactions seemed to last no longer than a minute or two, until I became engrossed in chatting it up with a personable twelve-year-old, as if he were an irresistibly good book I could not put down. With dashed hopes, I learned he was not to be separated from his younger sister, who had significant psychiatric problems; they also were Native American and not permitted to be adopted outside of their tribe. Personal meetings with supervisors also did not change my prospects all that much. I was highly praised, yet they also expressed their difficulties convincing caseworkers of the viability of single fathers and a move to another state a considerable distance from the Pacific Northwest.

I returned to Florida further disillusioned, yet much stronger in my resolve to push on with international adoption. I felt as though I had drawn the final straw; there was nothing else to draw from. Domestic adoption no longer seemed a viable option for me. I did not have any more time to waste. The last of autumn's colors were fast fading away with winter soon to take charge. With the passing of autumn "one remembers one's reverence," as Yoko Ono said, yet with the soon passing of winter "one remembers one's perseverance." The child right for me was waiting and I needed to find him, wherever he might be. Little did I know that within days of my return from Seattle, on the other side of the equator, Matheus and Davi had returned to the orphanage for the last time, not yet understanding that adoption was in their future.

Chapter 5

Brazil or Bust

I did not know where to start. I aimlessly searched the Internet for inspiration, yet I only came up more confused. I took more time to structure my thoughts, considering the different countries and nationalities that most intrigued me in my travels. I quickly ruled out those countries in the U.K. and Western Europe, as well as Canada; adoption from these countries are not open to foreigners. Being a single adoptive parent, I also quickly ruled out many of those countries where only married couples are allowed to adopt. Even for some of those countries that considered allowing single-parent adoptions, only single females were permitted to adopt. The list of countries where single males were permitted to adopt was short, forcing me to narrow my search to those that seemed amenable.

I had a special affinity toward the Philippines early in my search as my "little brothers" are Filipino, and I found a record of single-male intercountry adoptions having occurred there in the past. Although verbiage about the current attitudes toward single adoptive fathers seemed vague, a few adoption agencies encouraged inquiries about their programs. I e-mailed one agency, asserting itself as a Christian organization, that was guided by Christian principles. After a few e-mails back and forth, I was taken aback when the director abruptly stopped responding to me when I questioned whether my Jewish religion would be a problem for them or for adopting in the Philippines. I found another agency that was more straightforward, informing me that single males were no longer being permitted to adopt in the Philippines. I shifted my thoughts in another direction.

Staying in Southeast Asia, I turned toward Vietnam. It seemed to be the only Asian country allowing single males to adopt. I contacted my West Coast agency's caseworker to discuss my interests in international adoption. With Vietnam being one of the countries the agency represented in their international adoption program, I felt comfortable exploring further my interests with those already familiar with and approving of me. The caseworker of the Vietnam program quickly introduced me to the prospect of a six-year-old boy available and eligible for special funding that would cover most of the costs involved. The boy did not seem to have a significant amount of needs on the surface; he was young and seemed likely to thrive upon being removed from the battering effects of isolation, poverty, and malnutrition. All the same, I was not yet ready, as I realized the many questions I posed about him seemed more in relation to my uncertainty about pursuing international adoption rather than regarding this particular child.

I still had not reconciled with making an actual commitment to pursue international adoption. On the surface, I was fearful of the expenses involved, having heard about the often-extraordinary cost of adopting a child from another country. I was protective over my savings, concerned about their depletion and what the ramifications would be for me if the adoption were not to work out in the end. Adopting domestically, I felt secure about the minimal costs involved, keeping my savings intact. I also was attracted to the available supports allowing me to financially provide for my child as needed. With an international adoption, I felt as though I would be on my own without any sense of a safety net if I should stumble.

While I waited for further information about the Vietnamese boy, it was not long before I received word that a family in Italy had snatched him up. Soon afterward, the agreement allowing Americans to adopt children from Vietnam also was terminated; there were no definite prospects any time soon for the reinstatement of amicable relations with Vietnam. None of the other countries the agency represented allowed single males to adopt. I had yet to fully commit to pursuing international adoption and already I was meeting with disappointment. Keeping the faith, I continued researching its viability for me.

Eastern Europe did not seem to offer much hope for me in spite of a sprinkling of countries seemingly open to adoptions by single males. Christian preferences still seemed to predominate. I was especially leery because of the well-documented troubles with the children from overpopulated, understaffed orphanages in such countries as Romania. The media had overexposed the plight of these adopted children with histories of their extreme neglect and abuse, perpetuated by detached caregivers in these orphanages. The children's subsequent struggles with severe forms of attachment disorders, and the negativity surrounding these stories, too often eclipsed those cases that were positive. When I'd traveled through Romania during the winter holidays a few years back, I was disheartened to see firsthand so many children and preteens on the streets, neglected, dirty, and desperate. Many of them were aggressively panhandling or inhaling glue or some other fumes from a plastic bag, seemingly to deaden the hunger pangs of their emaciated bodies. These scenes forever etched themselves in my consciousness.

With another spin of the globe, the countries of Central and South America began to prevail. Guatemala seemed heavily publicized for the country's openness to many different types of prospective parents, subsequent ease in gaining approval, and the ready availability of many children for adoption. Again, just as I was looking into the various programs, the significant corruption plaguing the adoption of babies in Guatemala abruptly caused its government to impose a two-year moratorium on intercountry adoptions. Still, I pushed aside concerns of the seemingly precarious state of international adoptions, subject to greed, inhumane interests, and ignorance.

I meandered around Columbia, Venezuela, Peru . . . but for no particular reason none of these countries seemed to hold much appeal to me. Covering nearly half of the South American continent, Brazil loomed large on the world map. I was instantly intrigued, given the many Brazilian children I had come across and worked with over the years in the two schools I was servicing as their psychologist. I had developed warm, close relations with many of them. In general, I typically found Brazilian children to be smart, personable, and endearingly affectionate, with giving hearts. They also seemed to come from nurturing, and fiercely loving parents and families. In my readings about Brazilian culture, children were portrayed as being held in high esteem, revered by all adults with whom they come into contact. Children coming out of orphanages frequently were described as having experienced a loving and nurturing environment that was in stark contrast to descriptions I came across for other countries.

I was encouraged by Brazil's policy of not imposing any fees for intercountry adoptions, highlighting the government's commitment to the children's welfare over the making of a profit. I did not come across any reports of corruption or parents being taken advantage of, as described in other countries. Both single female and male prospective parents also were permitted to adopt; there was a history of many single males who had been successful in adopting from Brazil. Adoptions seemed closely monitored by the courts to ensure a favorable match, yet my enthusiasm stalled when I noted the required thirty-day cohabitation period in Brazil, stretching into another ten days for the adoption's finalization. Could I be gone for that long . . . away from work, family, and other commitments? The more I researched, referring to stories told of completed adoptions, the more I was attracted to the benefits of the lengthy time Brazil required. Initial bonding experiences with the child in his familiar surroundings would be augmented by the lack of distractions of foreign surroundings and strangers in a new country.

There did not seem to be many adoption programs working with Brazil, yet multiple websites and referrals pointed to LIMIAR as a particular point of reference. On its website, LIMIAR clearly represented itself as an agency assisting with the international adoption of children in Brazil who would not ordinarily have a chance of being adopted by Brazilian families. I was charmed that LIMIAR's Portuguese translation referred to the threshold of a doorway; its symbolism of "the act of crossing over to a new beginning" resonated strongly with me. That proverbial doorway seemed wide-open, inviting as I began to peer more closely inside.

* * *

Another e-mail inquiry put me in touch with the U.S. representative for LIMIAR. She was the caseworker handling referrals for those children referred to the Brazilian courts that were available for adoption; she also assisted families in negotiating the paperwork leading to their departure for Brazil. She was a Brazilian native and previously worked as a caseworker directly assisting families during their stay in Brazil. I felt at ease speaking with her. She told me of the many single males who had successfully adopted from Brazil, and about the older children who typically became available for adoption. At my request she sent me a few sample referrals; both of the children were a bit older than what I had hoped for and did not pull any of my particular heartstrings. I kept my perspective; these were just samples of possible children available for adoption, and we had not yet specifically discussed what I was looking for.

The caseworker also put me in touch with two single fathers; each had adopted two older boys. The first father adopted quite a few years earlier, openly sharing his struggles with the pair of brothers he adopted. He described rather significant attachment-related problems, especially with his oldest son. He was frank about having known beforehand the potential significance of his son's problems, but was not deterred from adopting him. He remained upbeat about the positive direction both his sons were moving in, and the joys he experienced with his two boys as their father. The other father told how he adopted two boys who were unrelated, living in different cities before he came to Brazil to adopt them just a year earlier. He maintained a positive portrayal of his experiences thus far; the two boys were relating well with each other, as if they had known each other all their lives, and had adjusted to family life and to American society and schooling. Both fathers seemed to have made conscious choices about their decisions, seemingly pleased with the paths their lives had taken with their children. I was encouraged, ready to move forward.

The LIMIAR caseworker referred me to an adoption agency with a Brazil program that worked specifically with them. LIMIAR would take over after completion of the required U.S. paperwork and subsequent acceptance of a referral, ultimately leading to submission to the Brazilian courts for official approval. The agency was one of only two with whom

LIMIAR worked, and met the Hague international adoption convention requirements. The caseworker felt that this one agency was more liberal, welcoming of single males. It was a fairly straightforward beginning, with the explanation of procedures, getting answers to my questions, and generally relating with the agency's director, who would be my go-to person. Feeling as though my perspective was intact and my eyes were wide-open helped me to swallow the nervous tension I still felt about the prospect of international adoption. I wrote out that first big check and officially committed to this seemingly most auspicious phase of my adoption quest.

The next five or six months was a dizzying rush of finalizing my home study to meet the Hague Convention guidelines, completing a myriad of forms, getting fingerprinted here and gaining clearance checks there, and paying off more bills. Then all of a sudden, with the last batch of forms completed, the official U.S. government approval to bring home up to two children was issued. It was late August and I had just returned from a three-week sojourn through Southeast Asia. It was all done; there was nothing else to do but wait for a referral. Used to always having something to do, I was unprepared for how long the next few months of *waiting* would seem, not knowing what to expect.

* * *

One late evening in November, as I was on the computer researching for my winter break trip to Germany, I was caught off guard by the ding of an e-mail alert. Little did I know at the time, it was the catalyst for the realization of what I had been hoping for, for so long. The e-mail was brief, yet its emotional punch left me breathless. The agency's director simply requested, *Gary, I would like you to consider these boys...* All that was contained in the e-mail were their names and that they were brothers, ages eight and eleven, their grades in school, and brief statements from the court that they had "good hearts" and did well in school. Attached were a few grainy and not terribly attractive photos. She concluded, *Would you like for me to get further information about these boys?*

I started to shrug my shoulders, wondering what I was supposed to do next, until I took closer notice of their names. For as long as I can remember, always wanting a child of my own, I envisioned naming my son Matthew David. In turn, I was stunned by their names, Matheus e Davi, the Portuguese equivalent of *Matthew and David*. I never once imagined my wish possibly coming true in the form of a plural over the singular.

Looking more closely at the photos, I noticed Matheus's brilliant smile. One could almost see the twinkling of his perfect set of white teeth, yet his hair was unruly and his photographed demeanor may have suggested a hint of wildness in need of taming. Davi wore a long-sleeved Mickey Mouse sweatshirt; a somber look on his face predominated in most of the photos, and he seemed ill at ease being photographed. He was badly in need of a haircut, his hair dully plastered lopsidedly over his head as if he had just come in from the deluge of a rainstorm. I stopped short again, dumbfounded upon noticing in one of the photos next to where Davi was sitting a large sign with the word *Bavaria* boldly emblazoned on it. When the e-mail came, I was in the middle of making hotel reservations for my trip to Germany's Bavaria region. I felt another tingle travel down my spine. I struggled to maintain an impartial viewpoint, trying to pass off these odd coincidences as such and no more. I was not successful. Absolutely I wanted to know . . . *needed* to know more about these two boys.

It did not help that we left for a family cruise to the Caribbean the following week for the Thanksgiving holidays. My father was feeling well and he wanted to take advantage of his favorable health. I would have no access to the Internet for the week. I knew nothing more, yet my thoughts constantly revisited the photographic images I privately tucked away in the back of my mind. The mental reflections of their photos danced inside my head, making these two strangers seem alive in my consciousness. I agonized in private as I cruised the week away with my parents and Michael. I could not wait to get home to my computer.

Another week passed before the follow-up e-mail came, providing me with more professionally taken photos. I gasped at first notice of their fresh, shining faces. A ten-minute video also was attached. Their one-dimensional selves suddenly came alive, highlighting some of their endearing personal qualities I now cherish. With the LIMIAR caseworker, Lino's voice in the background, both boys were engaging as they answered his questions and played off of each other. This time, Davi appeared more comfortable in front of the camera; he did much of the talking, while Matheus often hesitated behind his shy, dazzling smile. I was captivated when they broke into song: "All you need is love, dah dah dah, all you need is love, dah dah dah, love is all you need. . . ." They concluded, "We wish you a merry Christmas, we wish you a merry Christmas, and a happy New Year. . . ." They were charming and sweet. I could not get enough of them.

The e-mail also included greater detail about the boys, with information about how they came to the orphanage and the reasons involved in their availability for adoption. Their presented issues seemed relative to the kinds of problems I felt able to parent, and were not indicative of any particularly serious psychiatric problems, and their personal qualities embodied resiliency potential. Davi was described as one who "expressed himself well, both his feelings and wishes. He adapted well with different people of different ages." He also was noted as having trouble with "agitation," as related with "excitability and his resistance to follow some rules that makes the adult in charge needing to be more assertive. He is an agitated child because of his need to know and do new things and be put to the challenge." Davi also was described as being "caring and respectful with those he is connected to." I did not know it at the time, but the court's description of Davi was flawless. Matheus's description was as accurate. He was noted as being "very social and has lots of friends. He is a leader for children of his age and smaller ones. The other side of this is that this leadership position can result in conflicts with adults. He challenges the power of the adults, testing them, but does not disrespect them. He is caring and likes to talk and make new friends."

I still took two days to think it through and talk it out with my cousin, Gayle and few close friends, even though my mind seemed made up from the start with the first e-mail. I refrained from getting my parents' input; I needed to decide for myself without the insecurities driving their influence. I do not really know what exactly propelled me off the diving board. I remembered the few times I'd become excited over the prospect of a certain child when attempting to negotiate my way through the foster care system, yet this was different. Whereas I had experienced excitement before, this time it felt more visceral. I found myself whispering in both mind and heart that these two boys were to be my sons. They were simply waiting for their father to come and bring them home.

* * *

After informing the agency's director to move forward, I entered a dreamlike daze. There were no guarantees, yet I felt oddly serene. We had to move quickly and get the preliminary forms in, formally requesting the Brazilian courts' approval of the adoption. The Christmas holidays were fast approaching, and the courts would be closed through January. We did not get the courts' attention in time, yet LIMIAR assured me not to be concerned; the boys were supposedly earmarked for me. I had no choice but to hunker down and surrender to a prolonged state of hibernation.

It was Chanukah, the festival of lights. With the darkness of so many years of floundering beginning to dissipate and the force of light growing stronger in my heart, I decided it was time to spread the news to the immediate family. Terrified of the reactions I might get from my parents, I recruited Gayle for moral support. It was the second night of Chanukah. After lighting the menorah and the opening their presents, Michael and Jake disappeared to play their video games. I gathered my parents, along with Gayle and her mother and mother-in law, around my laptop. I told my parents that this was my Chanukah present for all of us as I turned on the video with Matheus and Davi. The silence in the room betrayed the feelings of disbelief pervading the air. I was too choked up to say anything as the boys once again came alive on the screen.

My mother's face seemed to pale a bit as she stared at the video and exclaimed, "There are two?!" With the nod of my head, my mother bowed hers down onto the back of the chair she was leaning on. My father mostly kept quiet, determined to be supportive despite his own unexpressed doubts. My mother straddled the line of wanting to be supportive and expressing her lingering fears of my adopting even one child, let alone two from another country. After a few false starts, feeling her protests were in vain, she retreated in silence, forgoing any further objections in favor of her tacit support. Gayle's spirited enthusiasm in seeing the boys for the first time did little to deflect the staid emotions in the room, at times echoing off the strained silence that pervaded the room.

I had Michael and Jake come over soon afterwards from their playing so I could let them in on the news and show them the video. Despite having impatiently declared for months his excitement about the prospect of our expanding family, Michael's demeanor was rather subdued. With reality in the form of two faces now staring back at him, he also felt overwhelmed. He, as did the others, needed time to sort through conflicting thoughts and feelings that he was able to avoid dealing with, until now. With nothing more than a comment or two, their fleeting interest had them retreating back to their video games.

I breathed a sigh of relief. It was not the apocalypse I'd feared, although I could not help but feel disappointed with the restrained reactions among the family. It was no secret that I had been seeking to adopt all these years, and that the numerous hardships I encountered along the way often weighed heavily on my resolve. I was hopeful for a little more enthusiasm and excitement, but I also understood this overwhelming sting of reality after the many years of complacency and reduced expectations. Gayle and my friends repeatedly reassured me that they would come around; indeed, over the ensuing weeks and months they did.

Matheus and Davi became household names. The family began to band together and share in the preparations for the boys' arrival. I received hand-me-down clothes, forgotten-about toys and games, and suggestions, reminders, and opinions from anyone who felt that they had my ear. I put the boys' bedrooms together and organized the different spaces in the house for more efficiency in family functioning. I registered them for school in the fall, and reserved their spots for summer camp beginning the week before their arrival from Brazil. Sometimes it seemed forever for the final clearances to transpire; other times I felt as though there just was not enough time to prepare. Months turned into weeks; then weeks turned into days. The more time had passed and the shorter the to-do list became, the greater was the family's adjustment to the reality of "those two boys from Brazil."

My excitement had been steadily growing over the past four months. Once the courts handed down their official sanction in mid-February for the adoption, I branched outside my close circle of confidantes to spread the news. When I officially shared the news of my impending adoption of Matheus and Davi, among the well-wishes of many family and friends, my "little brother," Bobby surprised me with a poignant statement of gratitude for my having been in his life in those earlier years. Normally stoic in the overt expression of his emotions, he overwhelmed me with his heartfelt enthusiasm for my becoming a father.

Most of my family, friends, and colleagues at work knew of my efforts to adopt, yet many were unaware I had reached out internationally. I felt as though I walked on air, carting around my favored photo to show off to anyone who showed the slightest of interest. Some of them expressed surprise about my decision to adopt internationally, politely inquiring about my choice. I began to develop a standard response to counter innocent questions that tended to be veiled by uncertainty and ignorance. I referred to my long, embattled, and failed efforts as a single male against preconceived, narrow-minded views without specific regard for who I was and what I was about. I further pointed out the foibles of a broken, overwhelmed domestic foster care system that too often seemed to work against me and so many of its children in need, further aggravating their plight. In the end, my choice to reach out halfway around the world did not matter. All children are created equal, and deserve the love and care of a family so they may mature into connected, secure beings strong enough to withstand the threat of society's alienating forces. As I finally drifted off to sleep, I reminded myself that Matheus and Davi were no different.

Part 2

Crossing Over

Chapter 6

Breaking the Language Barrier

On our first morning together, I awoke to find the boys still in their beds asleep; I left them behind for the shower, but not before lingering over the sweetness of their innocent, restful faces. Upon emerging from the bathroom twenty minutes later, I found them standing at some sort of attention on opposing sides of my bed, which was now neatly made up. Each wore the same broad smile from the previous day, eager in their quest to please me. I wondered how much longer they were going to be able to keep this up. The frozen arcs of their smiles were bound to thaw at some point. I knew we were knee-deep into the honeymoon phase. It was only a matter of time before the limits would be tested. Still, I was going to enjoy their impeccable manners, unbridled affections, and prompt receptiveness to direction and guidance for however long that might last.

As we explored the walled grounds of Lar Rogate, checking out the grazing sheep and listening to the soft whistling of the wind among the pine trees, the focus of the day seemed to center around simply getting to know one another. Each boy's uniqueness steadily unfolded in the beginning hours of our togetherness. Davi readily displayed a rather fun-loving personality; he seemed eager to learn and experience the world around him, and loved to assert himself with perceptions that often had a humorous twist to them, readily showing off an apparently bright intellect. He was eager and quick to understand what was going on and articulate as such, often finding creative ways to communicate around our language differences, sometimes drawing or turning to pictures from the Internet or in some of the books he had brought with him. Matheus seemed more soulful with an interest in and flair for artistic endeavors; he readily gravitated toward a pack of colored pencils, and became absorbed in some of the drawings he had brought with him, highlighting their drawn features. He did not seem as forthright in asserting himself as Davi; rather, Matheus tended to gaze out over his surroundings in a pensive manner, his soft brown eyes staring intently at the smallest of details. He would finger the veins of a single leaf or pluck a gardenia perched on a tree branch to admire before tucking it behind his ear. I often wondered, in turn, what kind of impression I was making on them.

In preparing to leave for Brazil, I had used the Rosetta Stone language system to gain some familiarity with Portuguese. I hoped to communicate a little with Matheus and Davi within the context of their native language. From the start, Lino introduced us to the use of Google Translator, which became more affectionately referred as the *tradutor*. I was amazed with the near immediate gratification of being able to communicate in sync despite our language barrier. The boys appeared to be good readers in their native language, as well as eager typists. They readily were receptive to engaging the *tradutor's* help for communication and understanding of important points, directions/instructions, and explanations. It became routine for us each morning to first sit down in front of my laptop and attempt to exchange our thoughts and interests for the day. During our residency at Lar Rogate, the *tradutor* remained ready to assist.

With our language difficulties, conversation among us was fleeting, but it was not spoken language that was responsible for nurturing our bonding these first few days; it was about the emotional connections that were being made between us. I found it instinctively easy to meet the sweetness of their smiles with physical gestures of my affection in return. One armed hugs, tousling of their hair, strokes of their chin or cheek were often greeted by an arm occasionally winding its way around my waist, a hand slipping into mine, or a head leaning into my side. We already were beginning to relate with one another through genuine interaction and emotional expression, telltale signs we were belonging together. What stopped me dead in my tracks every time, however, were the many different ways they began using the *tradutor* to express, "*Eu te amo pai*" – *"I love you Daddy."*

After lunch on our first day, we turned back to the laptop, but this time to try out Skype and call home. Not yet forty-eight hours since I had left for Brazil, it already seemed a lifetime ago. I was relieved to see the familiar faces and hear the reassuring voices of my parents and Michael. Also, as part of our becoming a family, we reached out to my closest cousin, Gayle and her ten-year-old son, Jake. Gayle and I had grown up together, even graduating from college together. I regarded her more as a sister, even more so than my own sister was to me. Jake was our family's miracle child, born after years of struggle for Gayle and her husband to conceive.

I was excited to show off Matheus and Davi, who also were eager to meet their new family. Yet, trying to engage the boys beyond their inane hand waves and awkward smiles were not successful by those on the other side of our screen. I was able to communicate to the boys with my Portuguese and introduce them to their new relations, but reciprocal exchanges were lacking on this first call.

My parents smiled benevolently, perhaps regretting the lack of knowing any Portuguese words or phrases to throw out to the boys and being able to make an instant connection with them. Probably not noticeable to Matheus and Davi, my parents were anxious in their attempts to engage with us. Their smiles were perhaps a little too broad, their hand gestures a little too exaggerated, and their verbalizations overly affirmative. Our Skype communications progressed over the ensuing six weeks. My parents became more comfortable interacting with Matheus and Davi, won over by their enthusiasm in relating with "Grandma and Poppa."

Michael, seemingly forever the goofball at home, not one who liked to take things too seriously, would delight in being a source of entertainment for himself and the boys. He would make whooping and chortling noises, jump up and down and sway back and forth, and make silly faces. On camera, he kept the mood light, covering up any misgivings about the prospective changes Matheus and Davi would be bringing into his life; it would not take long for his fears and doubts to surface even before our homecoming from Brazil. There were times he declined from appearing on the screen altogether, staying away because of a "bad mood" for no explainable reason at the time.

Jake, who did not have as much at stake as Michael, made more concerted efforts to communicate directly with Matheus and Davi. He and his mother made use of the *tradutor* on an adjoining screen and read aloud in Portuguese what they wanted to say. The boys, in turn, sometimes tried matching Jake's Portuguese attempts with their own efforts to utter an English word or phrase. The broadening of their new worldview had begun. Almost daily we made use of Skype to bridge the gap across the two hemispheres. Michael and my parents and Gayle and Jake became more familiar faces for the boys;

they, in turn, became more familiar to the constants of their new family.

* * *

By the fourth day I adopted a routine to promote the direct adaptation of speaking English. It became a habit for me to commonly follow what I would say in Portuguese with its English translation. Almost immediately I found both of them making efforts to utter an English word here and there. Most mornings, with the *tradutor's* help, we engaged in a short, impromptu English lesson to encourage a functional grasp of basic conversation. Sometimes the drudgery of the writing and pronunciation of commonly used English vocabulary words and basic sentences would wear on their patience. Davi resisted the lessons the most, often whining and withholding real effort in spite of his reported self-motivated interests in academic endeavors. Seemingly more receptive and disciplined in writing out the different words in both English and Portuguese, Matheus seemed better able to appreciate the structure I was trying to impose on the lessons. I would tingle with excitement upon hearing the occasionally rehearsed phrase... "I want dinner," "I need the bathroom," "what time it is?" that fittingly popped up when least expected.

Having been born literally tongue tied, Matheus had surgery to release overgrown tissue underneath his tongue. A year and a half later he told me his family "had money" at the time for the operation, which did not correspond with the impoverished background they reportedly came from. Davi also apparently had the same condition, yet adapted to the tongue restriction. Matheus did not receive regular speech therapy until he and Davi came to the orphanage. Even in his native Portuguese, Matheus was described as having a severe articulation disorder that made his learning to speak English much more difficult than for Davi.

Aside from the forced inductions to English, the three of us found many ways to transcend the literal word in communicating with one another after only the first few days. We used gestures, pointed, drew pictures, and even made connections with antonyms of those words we knew in our respective languages. I had also brought with me a library of mostly Dr. Seuss books to read and Disney movies to watch. I chose those with stories the boys might be most familiar with, and through which they could make meaningful connections to spoken English. The Dr. Seuss books especially were a joy to read together; it was fun making our way through the stories' ubiquitous use of repetitions, rhymes, and clear images. We were beginning to communicate "here or there" what was on our minds and in our hearts just about "anywhere."

Six days into our first week together, the boys' true colors finally manifested themselves when they required some mediation for trouble playing together, simply because Matheus was better than Davi at *futebol*. Matheus's older age, greater experience, more refined skillfulness, passion for the sport, and not to mention his tendency to care only about himself when angered did little to even the playing field for his brother. Davi was three years younger and not as experienced, despite his good motivation and potential as a player. With Matheus deferring to his own bruised ego, Davi was left behind to wrestle with his fury. Reasons for the anger they began to unleash on one another were a mystery to me, and left me with fear in my heart over the potential escalation of their resentment without my being able to effectively problem-solve. Language differences aside, it was apparent early on, as we made our way back to our room from the playing field that bridging the emotional gap in their brotherly relations would be an ongoing challenge.

After returning to our room, their conflictual relations climaxed in the midst of a *tradutor* session, as I attempted to sort their differing perspectives following their flinging of Portuguese insults, fast and furious at one another with which I was not able to keep up. At a turning point in the *tradutor* discussion, Davi typed he did *not like playing with Matheus at all*. Upon reading Davi's proclamation, Matheus stormed outside to sulk. I typed back to Davi that his comment *made me sad* and *how great the two of you had been getting along up until now. You hurt Matheus's feelings.* I got up and told Davi *"Não tocar no computador"*—"Do not touch the computer" and *"Espera aqui"*—"Wait here."

I found Matheus by a tree just outside the entryway, looking down at the ground with a droopy, sad look on his normally radiant face. I felt helpless, unlike when counseling an anonymous child in distress; I was at a loss for words. For the first time, I actually felt responsible in a way I ordinarily did not feel for one of my child clients; his pain penetrated right through my objective mirror. Acting on emotional instinct, I silently approached him, spread out my arms and drew him into me. There he remained with his arms encircling my waist, his head resting against my chest, and tears rolling down the sides of his face. I stroked the curls of his hair and held him close amid the soft sounds of his cries. After waiting a few moments, I dared to speak, softly saying in my broken Portuguese, *"Eu preciso de você para ler o laptop."*—that I needed him to read what I wrote to Davi on the laptop. He nodded and let me usher him back inside, where we found a teary-eyed Davi waiting. After Matheus read my comment to Davi, I offered the laptop to Davi to respond; he simply typed, *"Eu, então, pedir desculpas a Matheus"*—"I will then apologize to Matheus." To my astonishment, they both turned and spontaneously hugged each other, putting an end to their differences for the moment. Capitalizing on their good will toward each other, I typed how proud I was of them, praising them for their expressed affection toward each other as *irmãos* – brothers, forever.

* * *

Also early into our first week, I was anxious to get out from feeling confined within the walls of Lar Rogate. We made like tourists and headed out into the city, where we toured the botanical gardens and went into a shopping mall to browse and get a snack. I was surprised by how aware Matheus and Davi were of the surrounding pop culture, despite their impoverished background and having spent the better part of the last three years in an orphanage. They had seen many of the current movies, watched the popular television shows, kept up with the local *futebol* teams, played the popular video games, and participated in the area's children's attractions and events. They had even participated in the annual Christmas performance of the children's choir at the Palácio Avenida. The children sang out to the public from the building's open windows; the darkness of the night was illuminated solely by the collective glow of the candle each child held. A year later we were even able to spot snippets of them preparing for the concert on various YouTube videos. The boys seemed well socialized in public, which belied my expectations that they would be more wide-eyed to the world as a function of having lived in the closed, confined spaces and experiences of an institution.

Having experienced the stripping of their birth family, Matheus and Davi also contended with the artificiality of group home living at the orphanage. The intimacy of family relations were lost on them; routine, structure, and detached caregiver affections became substitutes for maturing familial ties. With no sights on the future, life in an orphanage was just about living a day-to-day existence to survive. Even though they still had each other, brotherly relations were significantly strained. As I discovered after their first row, neither was a source of comfort to the other; both were mutely burdened by their own difficulty reconciling with the rawness of their feelings of loss, rejection, and abandonment.

I knew beforehand that they had been separated from each other into different residences for many months because of their relentless fighting. Reports of the fury of Matheus's rage against Davi, whether he was provoked or not, caused enough of a concern for the orphanage's caseworkers to separate them even though their behavior was dismissed as relatively normal brotherly relations. Before I stepped forward with my interest to adopt them, as there had been no expressed interest in them as a sibling set, the courts had considered adopting them separately. Because of Davi's still younger age of eight, he had much more of a chance of sparking a family's interest in adopting him on his own. All hope for the preteen Matheus would likely have been lost if he were sacrificed on behalf of his brother's welfare. They'd already lost their older brother, approximately two years older than Matheus. Lucas ran away from a different orphanage where he had been residing; where he went was unknown. He did not want to be adopted. Matheus and Davi were brought back together in the same home at the time the court sanctioned its approval of their adoption.

Even before that first row, it did not take long for the unrelenting friction between Matheus and Davi to present itself, starting with their competition for my affection. It seemed innocent at first. One would teasingly try to muscle in on the other to lay his claim, linking an arm into the crook of mine, saying *"Meu pai"*—"My father." The other would lean in and retort, *"Não, meu pai"* – "No, my father." Never one to appreciate being regarded as a piece of property, I struggled to resist shaking them both off, to free myself from the shackles of their neediness. Rather, I regarded the glimmers of their attachment to me as their father—leader, provider, supporter, nurturer. I looked to reassure them I had "room to love them both."

Upon completing the first ten days of our cohabitation period, the three of us had assumed a rather comfortable daily routine. We had our three meals a day, which dictated our movements at and around the compound, as well as our outings into the city for greater stimulation. We spread out across the day our time outside, playing video games, watching movies or television, playing games of Uno, reading, and conducting our English lessons. Visits with the court social worker were weekly and Lino stopped by every few days to check in with us. It was difficult to be away from my responsibilities at home for such a prolonged period of time—from my family, friends, work, and customary activities. Yet I valued our exclusive time alone together. We were able to relate with one another virtually uninterrupted, without distraction as I tackled fatherhood straight on. We could not possibly bond together as we had without this extended time away from what was to all too soon to become life's reality.

Chapter 7

War and Peace—Overcoming the Love of Power with the Power of Love

As we entered into our double digits in days together, the boys' patience began to wear thin. The emotional turmoil within started to emerge, sharply contrasting with their lighthearted ways and eagerness to please. As invaluable as the *tradutor* was, it often proved anything but a perfect communication tool. Thoughts, needs, and wants often would get lost in translation, requiring our patience, flexibility, and creativity to get the message across.

A series of miscommunications, misunderstandings, and misrepresentations finally broke Matheus, igniting a firestorm of rage. It came from nowhere, and so fast that I had no idea what really triggered him at the time, as I was not yet clued into the nuances of his emotions and behavior. In attempting to engage him about his apparent frustration as noted by his facial expressions and tense body language, I mistakenly took the *tradutor's* verbatim translation as a hurtful comment towards me. Unsure whether he was attempting to push me away, I tried to address his need for respect, regardless of his anger and frustration. Matheus became extremely angry and stormed out, slamming the door to our room. He promptly stomped back in, shoved papers onto the floor, threw a notebook out into the hall, and retreated to my room in the back to sulk. Davi and I carried on with our UNO game; I struggled to remain calm and collected, cognizant of my need to both reassure Davi of my levelheadedness and give Matheus time to cool off.

In between our game playing, still unnerved by the strained silence in the room, Davi wrote a quick note to Matheus, pleading with him to *not act like this tomorrow—Gary doesn't like us this way—PLEASE.* Although I knew he was worried about his brother, I also understood his concern was more about disrupting the adoption. Matheus promptly balled up the paper and threw it out from the back room, yet he came out not too long afterward. He calmly sat down on the bed with us and picked up the cards to deal for the next game. He wanted to leave it be for the rest of the night, agreeing to talk about it further in the morning. He put an end to the evening with his usual smiles, hugs, and kisses. He needed reassurance just as much as Davi.

During a lengthy *tradutor* session the next morning, Matheus and I were able to distinguish what was true versus what was misunderstood. Matheus denied having hostile thoughts toward me; his reactive behavior appeared driven by hurt feelings over my suspicions that he would even have such thoughts. I hoped I was able to reassure him that I then understood him. We discussed a little further his need for greater patience for talking through a problem to prevent future needless angry outbursts. We ended our discussion with a hug, a kiss, and a deep gaze into each other's eyes. Yet no sooner did I dare breathe a sigh of relief than another episode swiftly occurred.

With our morning movie interrupted due to minor bickering between brothers, Matheus became angry when I stopped him from moving onto playing a video game without having asked for permission to play. I had been following Lino's continued insistence that I needed to establish my authority and enforce limits on their behavior. Still feeling the sting from the previous night's events, he felt unfairly faulted for his behavior. His tantrum seemed slightly more heated this time. He stormed out again, yet I could still see the shadows of his feet under the door. He came in and went back out several times, keeping to himself whenever he came back in, after parading around ranting and raving to no one in particular. At one point, he plopped himself down at my laptop. I refrained from my instincts to stop him in favor of seeing how he pulled out a particular *foto* to stare at from his *favoritas* file of my nephew Michael, flanked on both sides by my parents when he recently had been inducted into the National Honor Society.

Throughout Matheus's antics, Davi also kicked it up a notch. Attempting to lessen the tension in the room, he scurried about, busying himself cleaning and putting away the clutter of the papers and books hurled to the floor. I thought to stop him, yet it seemed important for him to contribute to renewing the peace. Feeling unsure about how to proceed further, I called Lino for assistance; Matheus readily took the phone when I motioned for him to come over. Shortly after speaking with Lino, Matheus got up from his sulking position on the bed, approached me, and quietly laid his head on my shoulder. I asked how I could help him; he simply stated he did not know. "Then I will just love you," I responded. He began to cry, holding on to my waist and responding to my embrace with an even tighter one. It was over, again—just in time for us to meet with the court social worker that afternoon for our weekly progress update.

Lino had come over an hour earlier to help further sort out any lingering differences and work through Matheus's difficulties over the last two outbursts. He confirmed Matheus's behaviors for what they were: his testing of the limits, which still seemed to me to be par for the course rather than indicative of something more concerning. I felt vindicated when

Lino simply stated that he wished we might just go home, so that we may get our lives started. With the expected decrease in language difficulties and life feeling more normal, he felt such potentially explosive situations would be more swiftly handled. Amelia later agreed. She continued to express her approval of my parenting and how well the boys were committing to relating and adjusting with me. I had been carrying around so much self-doubt about my parenting that it was a relief to get Amelia and Lino's endorsement. I was able to ease up on the tension I held inside and regard myself as being soundly competent, emotionally responsive, and . . . well, human. I was going to get the hang of this parenting thing in spite of my fears and insecurities about being the father I should be—the kind of father I wanted to be.

* * *

I took a chance on a change in scenery and planned a weekend getaway for the three of us to Ilha do Mel, a tiny dot of an island off the coast of Parana. I was hopeful for the prospect of a break from the city's hustle and bustle, on an island where there were no cars, no large hotels, or any big business. We would be staying in a small pousada, a bed-and-breakfast that promised to be rustic in charm and with ready access to the island's idyllic lighthouse and long, isolated stretches of white sandy beaches. It was the perfect setting for rest, relaxation, and bonding.

The boys especially were eager to retreat to the beach once we arrived. They were excited to frolic in the ocean's frigid surf, yet neither knew how to swim, and it was Davi's first time at the beach; Matheus had recalled having been once when he was younger. The serenity of our time together did not last very long, as they befriended the preteen boy who lived at the pousada. George was used to having the run of the small island; he came, went, and did as he pleased. Matheus, especially, would have been most satisfied staying with George and playing his video games or running off wherever on the island without parental presence, to surface only at meal times. Although I was not able to understand most of George's conversations with Matheus, his disregard for adult authority and negative influence on Matheus, as well as on Davi kept me at a distance. As they chattered amongst themselves in Portuguese, sometimes looking in my direction with looks of indifference, I felt suddenly very alone.

I had hopes for this getaway to deepen our bonding via new and relaxed experiences together. Instead, we struggled to bond together as a family as there was heightened friction between brothers that left me feeling completely inadequate in my parenting. George often would seem at times delighted to stir the pot; with perhaps a glint of passive-aggressiveness in his eyes, he would speak in a tone and/or look in my direction as though his intent was to undermine my authority. When George was not around, our relations often were not much better. How was I to know that teaching them a simple card game of War at bedtime, on our last night at the pousada would be eclipsed by my becoming embroiled in the middle of a civil war between two stubbornly sovereign states?

Matheus and Davi's warfare forced a cease-fire by the shared casualty of an early bedtime. Throughout that late afternoon and into the evening Matheus had continued to test my tenacity as a parent that escalated when we attempted to go get something to eat for dinner. It was dark, there were not many places to eat, several places were closed since it was the off-season, and the restaurants were spread out. We had not been walking for five minutes before Matheus abruptly stopped, refusing to budge or cooperate, prompting me to make another call to Lino. Matheus was able to attend only to his own selfish, primal needs; he was *tired* and his *feet hurt*.

After speaking with Lino, Matheus relented, yet he continued to fume that dampened all of our spirits and left a darkened storm cloud of emotional angst suspended above our heads.

Despite my attempts to end the night peacefully with a few rounds of cards, spiteful, mean-spirited words between brothers shot out like bullets; with each shot came the ricochet of another. The situation between them quickly escalated to physical means when Matheus started throwing the shells they collected from the beach; one wayward shell grazed my knuckle. A thin ribbon of blood began to trickle. "*Olhe!*"—" Look!" I yelled to Matheus. Momentarily stunned by the undeniable ramifications of his seething anger, he stopped. With the wind taken out of his sails, I quickly expressed my disappointment about both their behaviors, and their need to work out problems, not make more. They acquiesced easily to their night being cut short and my turning out the lights; the melodious sounds of crickets infused the stillness of the night, cutting through and dispersing the hostile fragments of short tempers and fatigued spirits.

George Orwell once quipped, "The quickest way of ending a war is to lose it". I turned toward an early bedtime as the last resort because I realized there was no point in carrying on. I did not have ready access to the more sophisticated verbiage I would need in Portuguese to sit the two of them down and try to resolve their differences. I was also feeling overwhelmed by the rawness of their emotional vulnerabilities. The boys were unable yet to resort to reason and sensibility, and so I repeatedly relied on the structure and predictability of limits to contain the chaos of their still unprocessed emotions that still would be ominous for a long time to come.

The next evening, safely back in our comforting surroundings of Lar Rogate, I asked the boys to type on the *tradutor* what they liked about our weekend away. Both of them particularly raved about the fun they'd had in the ocean; Matheus also expressed his enthusiasm for wanting to learn how to swim so that he could really get out and take on the sea without fear. There was no mention of George or any of the conflicts among us. The boys slipped right back into our familial routine as if we never left; they held on to positive thoughts and feelings about our time together. The newness of our attachment to each other was still fragile enough that they yet seemed cagey in their relations with me.

* * *

We met with the court social worker later in the week at the courthouse. Matheus's spurt of hostile resentment appeared to be dissipating. Amelia was helpful in further refocusing his negative energy. He appeared calmer, his attitude more pleasant, and he was more patient. However, as Matheus was coming out of his funk, the evenness in Davi's demeanor was now starting to break down as he began to command more attention.

The following morning, I found Davi struggling through a dream-like state, still asleep in his bed. He was muttering, "*Por que?*"—"Why?" over and over again. He seemed to be in distress. I was unable to wake him, even when I pulled him onto my lap and tried to stir him. Shortly after I laid him back down on his bed, he rolled out of it and onto the floor, finally awakened. With the *tradutor's* help, Davi explained that he was "dreaming that I was in a swimming contest," despite his not knowing how to swim in real life. He recalled that in the dream he had gotten "sick, but I was in the water the next day, drowning." He claimed that just as he was about "to die" in the dream, he had rolled out of bed. He did not recall what his muttering "why" was about.

I thought about the potential symbolism his dream represented, reflecting his insecurity about self-preservation in the midst of very real feelings of uncertainty at this time of his life. Davi appeared his natural self through breakfast, yet was relentless throughout the day with bouts of crying, whining, and stubbornness. I gradually took his privileges away and repeatedly enforced limits, climaxing to an early bedtime for both; his obnoxious and disrespectful behavior had eventually rubbed off on his brother.

As I took notice of Davi's unruly behavior that night, I reflected further on his dream. I wondered whether his difficult behavior was a reflection of his feelings of uncertainty about these changes happening all around him. Perhaps he was acting out in an attempt to gain some kind of control over his circumstances. He had so much at stake at this critical juncture of his life, undergoing these drastic life changes in adjusting to his new family life while letting go his family of origin.

The next day, after a night of contemplating about the need to jump start a more proactive way of gaining Matheus and Davi's spirit of cooperation, I started something new with the boys. Instead of relying on warnings about there being consequences of taking away a privilege, such as video games or television, I had them *earn* the privilege as a reward. For every hour that passed where they listened, behaved themselves, and were respectful to each other and to me, another ten minutes was added to their video game playtime for the afternoon. I also kept the morning structured, beginning after breakfast with our thirty-minute English lesson, a long walk to the store, and a stop in the park to play and savor the small treats we bought for their cooperation. We engaged the *tradutor* before lunch to discuss their good behavior. Matheus earned his full forty minutes easily; Davi did fairly well, having earned thirty minutes. He still was fairly cooperative outside of some minor sulking.

The afternoon passed peacefully; the boys played their video games, watched television, and went outside to enjoy the sunshine. Davi continued to have difficulty playing cooperatively, readily erupting into crying outbursts, and assuming the role of victim. However, these episodes were both farther apart and less intense, and he appeared more receptive to discussing his behavior. At such times I often felt Matheus's eyes on me, watching closely how I was handling Davi's outbursts. His protective instincts for his brother were at play, yet I would come to also understand his more specific interests in assessing my parenting skills. How I was handling Davi gave him insight into the parenting he might be able to expect from me, perhaps compared to the parenting he had been used to. Even so, I felt more effective in managing their behavioral issues and hoped that they were seeing me as that kind of father.

Chapter 8

The Simple Pleasures in Life

Looking forward to exposing the boys to the world around us, I had many hopes for the traveling I wanted to experience with them. Michael had already reaped benefits of our travels together. We'd had special bonding experiences during our fall weekends around New England and Pennsylvania, on city escapes to Boston, New York, Seattle, and London, on family trips with Gayle and Jake to Germany and Austria, and on cruises with Grandma and Poppa to Alaska, Hawaii, the Mediterranean, and the Caribbean. I pride myself on having begun early to expand my nephew's worldview, subsequently broadening his perspective on life. I was looking forward to doing the same for Matheus and Davi, starting within the familiarity of their native country.

I hoped to make the most of being able to experience their Brazilian homeland together. I wanted them to get a broader view of their own turf before embarking on their new lives, on terrain that would be foreign to them. With their life's experiences having been marked by the restrictions of poverty and neglect, our treks around Curitiba often proved enlightening for them. With Curitiba's strong Eastern European ties, we visited each of the memorial sites commemorating the city's larger immigrant populations. The Ukrainian memorial complex had a collection of wooden buildings with a replica of St.

Michael the Archangel church and exhibits on Ukrainian life in Brazil. The Bosque do Papa João Paulo II was a complex of wooden houses like those seen in rural Poland, commemorative of Pope Paul John II's visit to Curitiba in 1980. The Hansel and Gretel trail in the German Wood—Bosque do Alemão—led us to a little house in the middle of the woods reminiscent of the Black Forest; there was a library of children's books in the house to peruse by a warm fireplace. We also visited many of the city's recreational parks, walked some of the main shopping streets, and took a popular day-long train ride through tropical rain forests to the small town of Morretes. A guide took us for an authentic Brazilian meal for the region and showed us some of the sights on the way back to Curitiba.

If we had taken the train all the way to the end of the line, past Morretes, we would have ended up on the coast, in the town where the boys were born. Lino cautioned us not to go down there, as many of their family still resided in the town, and that we should not take the chance of running into someone who might recognize the boys. Even so, this didn't stop the impossible from happening on one of our day-trips around Curitiba a few days later; while waiting for the bus after exploring one of the parks, we were stopped by a woman with her husband preparing to start up their motorcycle. She excitedly approached the boys, speaking very fast in Portuguese, claiming that she was an aunt. The boys remembered her, yet politely regarded her rather than expressing the same enthusiasm as she. I stood there, frozen. I was terrified by what she might say, or even do. I knew she understood that I was adopting Matheus and Davi, yet she only looked at me with kindness, and from what I could tell, expressed her happiness for the boys. Later on the *tradutor*, the boys shared with me that she was an aunt by a former marriage, and she was very encouraging to them about how "good it was that we are being adopted," and to "have a good life."

The boys were creatures of habit. They seemed able to handle our outings as long as meal times were not disrupted and the confines of Lar Rogate, our safe haven, were within reach by the day's end. Keeping these cues in mind, I arranged a second weekend getaway. This time we trekked down to Balneário Camboriú in the neighboring state of Santa Catarina. The beach would still be the focus of our recreational pursuits, yet this time amid tall hotels and other buildings, with a plethora of restaurants, shops, and people watching. Not particularly picturesque, yet I hoped the ready access to convenience and sights would suit the boys better.

Having worked a number of years with children in residential treatment settings, I understood how much they became slaves to their routine. I imagined how Matheus's and Davi's everyday lives in the orphanage were fixed, with rigid schedules and lacking in personal choice. There was little, if any need for them to account for themselves. They lived in a reactive mode that manifested itself in their emotional volatility, resistance to activities they were not interested in, and difficulty tolerating frustration in favor of the desire for immediate gratification. They came to rely on these behaviors for their survival, which often were exacerbating our struggles to assimilate life as a family together.

Our relations in Balneário Camboriú were more positive. We laughed together. There was less competition for my affection. Even so, abrupt eruptions of ill-tempered behaviors were frequent. The boys still were prone to becoming easily unsettled when out of their normal routine, and flare-ups of their behavior seemed to appear when I least expected them. Trying to encourage a little walking about so we could make more of an informed choice of place to eat was like asking them to endlessly trudge through the desert with no hope for sustenance of any kind. Their need for structure and making a direct connection between points A and B began to increasingly dictate the way I organized our outings. I took care to ensure that our walking around did not last more than fifteen minutes at a time, a destination point was clearly designated, and any backtracking or sidestepping was minimized to no more than just a few minutes. While I was missing the joys of spontaneity in traveling, we engaged in a more relaxed manner and still enjoyed new sights, different eats, and, most important, enhanced bonding as a family.

* * *

As days turned into weeks, I became less focused on what I thought I needed to do to prepare the boys for leaving Brazil and adapting to their new lives. Rather, our lives together became more about the simple things and experiencing togetherness, such as visiting various parks where we strolled around, played on the swings, observed the animals, and ate a snack. I worried about their transition to the American "ideal," where more tends to be thought of as better. I felt protective of their sense of simplicity and how much they valued the idea that less truly is more.

Maintaining for them the value of what is real, what is honest, and what is from the heart became more the focus of my interactions with them. With their birthdays only a week apart, both were to celebrate while we were still in Brazil. I was struck by how neither boy had any particular request for how he wanted to celebrate his birthday, where he wanted to go, or what he wanted to do—or even what he might have wanted to get for his birthday. After having given it some thought when I first approached him, Matheus came back the next day, and told me he would like a special strawberry cake and soda. It was just a little something special—a simple pleasure of his choosing that would mark this day as different from the others of the year.

As he turned twelve-years-old the following week, Matheus was delighted with the cake the kitchen staff made, covered with whipped cream and dotted with gumdrops over the top. It was our twenty-eighth day together. Balloons circled the table and the few of us sang happy birthday. His smile was broad as he beamed from ear to ear. Davi's ninth birthday was celebrated with the same fanfare a week later; sliced strawberries and bananas appeared on the top of his cake. He had taken notice of his brother's happiness and expressed desires for the same basic frills for his birthday. I found the simplicity of their interests in getting special attention on their birthdays endearing. There were no ties to materialistic, frivolous wants that too often overshadow the significance of a celebrated event.

In hindsight, many months later, I saw how Matheus's lack of concern for materialistic desires seemed more a camouflage for truer concerns. He would not dare seek out what he thought was not within his reach, simply because he felt undeserving of happiness. Just about a week into our cohabitation period, Matheus began to use my laptop to express random thoughts of his, seemingly in a free-flowing manner for fun. At first he seemed more interested in the aesthetics of the exercise, spending a lot of time playing with different fonts, sizes, styles, and images that gave some innovative depth to his words. He soon began to save his work in a separate folder, titled *Matheus Privado*, then made clear to both Davi and me his wish for his privacy to be respected.

After the boys retired to bed, I reserved my parental rights to stay informed of my son's activities and held my own private viewings of *Matheus Privado* on those days he worked on expressing his thoughts and feelings. I had first thought nothing of his interests in using my laptop, yet when seeing how much care and time he was putting into his writing, I wondered whether I might be missing out on some important pieces of his life's puzzle. I had not specifically agreed that I would stay out of his *privado* file, nor did I tell him that I was reading his material; I was afraid that if he knew, the spontaneity of his expressions would be lost, spoiling a chance for me to connect with his emotional psyche. After a few months into our first year together I felt better able to assert my parental authority more frankly. I informed him my need as his parent to ensure his safety by monitoring his activities, yet still being respectful of his privacy when there was no cause for concern that would forever seem like a balancing act with him.

It did not take long before his random writings took on a more focused, serious tone. With his errors in grammar and spelling, as well as problems with literal translations, much of his thoughts got lost in the translation from Portuguese to English on the *tradutor*. Nonetheless, I immediately took notice of his beginning title, referring to himself as a "bad boy." I felt tremendous sadness stirring inside me to think that Matheus thought of himself so severely. I was encouraged by his later references to having a "good heart" and his regard for keeping up with his schooling and his professed dedication to become educated. I had been told by the court social worker how his mother educated herself, having taught herself to read and write and instilling the importance of education in both boys.

I wondered whether, somewhere deep down inside, Matheus blamed himself for his mother's relinquishment of her parental rights. I had come to regard her decision to give him and his brother up as coming from the heart, filled with her love and courage. Hoping to safeguard their future, she made the ultimate sacrifice for them. With bated breath, I read on, finding him abruptly referring to being adopted by an American, and writing that he was now happy and no longer bad. Seeing how fragile his sense of himself was, I began better to understand his angry flare-ups as a reaction to hurt feelings. I would increasingly encounter Matheus's difficulties reconciling with his self-perceived "bad boy" image whenever he felt under attack, struggling to defend against feelings of worthlessness.

Trying to pave the way toward a stronger sense of self for both boys, I took any opportunity I could to praise them for whatever positive moves they made. For Matheus, especially, I made it a point to refer to him as being a "good boy." From the first day, I was attracted to his innate goodness that emanated with the radiance of his smile. It became my job to help both of them grow more comfortable with who they were, as the good boys they truly aspired to be.

As we closed out the final night of our thirty days together, we subtly acknowledged the next day's trip to the courthouse that would legally finalize our becoming a family. It just did not seem real that the thirty days were over. I still was somewhat fearful that something would go wrong and all of this would have been for naught. We settled into our nightly read with a sense of peace after a routine-filled day of togetherness at the park, the store, and out and about around Lar Rogate. After dinner, the boys were delighted to unwrap their special candies we brought back from the store. Afterward, they both took their turns on the laptop; Davi had recently started his own *Davi Privado,* with his efforts being more simplistic and narrowly focused, and he readily made them public to both of us in his eagerness to share his thoughts and ideas. Perhaps more telling of his excitement for the next day, he brought me over to show how he typed, next to a solo picture of me, *My father, the best father in the world.*

* * *

The judge capped it off with the flourish of a signature, in a small room devoid of any adornment save for a plain wooden cross hanging above where she presided. The signing of the adoption papers were conducted without any fanfare beyond her warm smiles and tips on what to see when we got to Rio de Janeiro, and to make sure to frequent the infamous juice bars. In the movie, *Yentl*, Barbra Streisand sings, "There are moments you remember all your life—there are moments you wait for and dream of all your life—this is one of those moments . . ." If I'd dared to blink, I would have missed the moment it became official, the moment that legally defined me as a father, what I always wanted to be.

Suddenly, in the eyes of the law, I was a father to two beautiful boys who could only think at the time, *When are we leaving so we can get something to eat?* In hindsight, I really don't know what it was I expected from that moment, yet what I had not expected was how natural it felt. I still had to remind the boys on several occasions to mind their behavior, such as not sliding down the banister at the courthouse. The boys' chatter mostly consisted of what had happened just five minutes before or what was going to happen in the next five minutes, rather than the bigger, life-altering events they had been experiencing—or what was yet to come.

As we walked the hallways, each boy would sometimes slip a hand in mine for holding as they had since our first day together. It felt rather ordinary, yet quite satisfying. For some time, the boys had been identifying with me as their father. They seemed accepting of the radical change their lives were taking. They also seemed open to embracing their new extended family waiting for them in the *Estados Unidos*. I thought that I really did not need that all-defining moment reminiscent of a Lifetime movie of the week. I had my boys and they had me. We were a family. As we move ahead in life, those ordinary moments of life together are those I will cherish and desperately miss when they all too soon grow up and move on to lives of their own someday.

Chapter 9

You Can't Go Home Again

Once the adoption was finalized in the courts, there was a rush to get the rest of the paperwork completed in time for our departure for Rio de Janeiro. Together we went for the issuing of the boys' new birth certificates the next morning, decisively proclaiming their new surname, permanently indicating their new family identity. Each expressed his unique awareness of what it meant to now permanently assume his new father's name in accordance with his new birth certificate.

On the way to the registry bureau, Davi innocently asked whether they were going to have their DNA tested. When I questioned him further, he specifically expressed his interest in knowing whether some of his blood was going to be taken and combined with some of my blood. It was as if performing such a ritual would symbolically link us genetically. It did not seem enough that the new birth certificates would suggest as much to anyone viewing them for identification purposes, not being privy to the fact that they were adopted.

When individually asked by the clerk what their names were, each boy, without a bit of hesitation, proclaimed his full name. With a hint of pride, they imparted their first, middle, and new last names as if they had been introducing themselves as such all their young lives. I was in awe as to how seemingly committed they were in banking on the present as it was continuing to evolve for them. That day they put a significant piece of their past behind them as their new birth certificates replaced their original ones; their former names were now canceled, a mark of their past lives now inaccessible to the public.

As Davi initially did not have a middle name, I was presented with the task of assigning him a name of my choosing. According to Jewish religion, it is customary to name children after a recently deceased relative to honor the dead and keep the dearly departed person's memory alive. The given name is not always identical; it is often changed to reflect a popular name of the time, usually retaining the sound or at least the first initial. On the day of our first meeting, Davi was told he would be given the middle name Paulo. He blindly accepted his new middle name without question, without any clue of the name's significance for me, commemorating the memory of my sister, Pamela. I was touched by how innocently and automatically Davi proudly proclaimed Paulo along with his first and last name to the clerk.

Perhaps as kismet of sorts, it was easy for me to associate Matheus Eduardo with the names of my two dearly beloved grandmothers: my paternal grandma, Marian and maternal *bubbie*, Esther. My sister's only child, Michael was named after my dearly beloved paternal grandpa, Myer. I was named after my maternal *zayde*, George, who died many years before I was born. With all four of my grandparents' names covered, it was easy for me to associate Davi with David, my very best friend from high school who died of leukemia when we were twenty-one years old. I still honor his memory today and I was excited to have a permanent association of his name with my son's name. It would be two years later before I suddenly recalled David's middle name being Edward, associating it with Matheus' middle name, Eduardo.

Later that afternoon, Matheus turned to his privado on my laptop. In starting a new page, he conducted a rather curious exercise with his newly adopted surname. Perhaps as a way to more firmly ingrain his identification with his new surname, he split Matloff in half: *Mat—loff*. Associating *Mat* with Matheus and—*loff* with Matloff, he followed by writing in English, with help from the tradutor, *Okay, we have already seen the significance of the Mat-loff; now let's show the family Matloff*. Underneath, he copied and pasted his treasured picture of my parents with Michael at his induction earlier that month into the National Junior Honor Society. He followed with solo pictures of him, his brother, and me. I was touched by how much to heart he was taking the adoption of his new surname. Building a strong identification with one's name often is parallel to one's sense of security and feeling important in the world. Matheus and Davi appeared to be fast embracing their new namesake, forging a newer, stronger basis for identifying with themselves as persons of distinction, persons who belonged in the world.

* * *

The protagonist of Thomas Wolfe's *You Can't Go Home Again*, George Webber, realizes, "You can't go back home to your family, back home to your childhood . . . back home to a young man's dreams of glory and of fame . . . back home to places in the country . . . back home to the old forms and systems of things which once seemed everlasting but which are changing all the time—back home to the escapes of Time and Memory." A month had barely passed from when we first began our union as a family. It was time to prepare to leave Curitiba for Rio de Janeiro, our last stop before departing Brazilian soil. The day before flying out, we visited the orphanage, the boys' home for the better part of the last two-to-three years, including the times they bounced back and forth between the home and their family of origin before their mother agreed to the termination of her parental rights. I was anxious to get a glimpse of the boys' former lives, wondering how it might contrast with their evolving new lives.

Both seemed happy with the prospect of a return visit to connect with their former caretakers. But I was puzzled by the sense of detachment I noted in their posture once we entered through the home's front gates, as if it were okay for them only to look but not touch their former surroundings. Except for one little girl with whom they had no interest in relating, the other children were still in school. Albeit neat and clean, the home seemed sterile, devoid of life without the sights and sounds of the other children around. There were no distractions for the boys as they began to survey their former stomping grounds.

Upon our first approach at the front door's threshold, Davi pulled me into the house, firmly grasping my hand, keeping me at his side. He introduced me to the house's social mother, primarily communicating to her in the little command of English he had gained over the past month. He refused to speak in his native, Portuguese tongue, unlike his usual chatty self whenever we were out and about among anyone we met. He spoke only a few English words in simple sentences, without concern for being sociable with his former caretakers; he seemed more intent upon expressing himself as one who no longer belonged there. The boys then ushered me into their former bedroom, housing seven beds for seven boys with the girls' bedroom next door. It was then that Davi left my side to dart around with Matheus to the other rooms in the house before disappearing out to the backyard.

Matheus seemed more secure re-entering this piece of his former life. He had hopped out of the car, dashing ahead with a smile and a quick wave to me down the sidewalk, as if eager to reclaim something that perhaps he left behind. Yet I often found him quietly gazing around his former surroundings with a sense of bemused detachment on his face. He sidestepped questions about what he was looking at or thinking about.

Matheus's actions later that evening conveyed a more vulnerable side of his emotionality. In preparing for bed, he pulled on a pair of Davi's pajamas to sleep in. From the first night of our togetherness, he'd favored an old T-shirt and lightweight shorts, promptly abandoning the pair of pajamas he'd brought from the orphanage. Spotting him in Davi's Mickey Mouse pajamas gave me a brief glimpse of a smaller, younger boy from the past. Perhaps he did connect with remnants of that little boy he'd left behind back at the house.

I was so caught up in the boys' reactions to our visit to the orphanage, I was unprepared for what was waiting for me there. After touring the house, I wandered outside to the back and stumbled across the little playhouse where the video of the boys was taken six months before—where I essentially first met them. It was also where it was suggested to them that maybe a family would be found for them. When asked what they thought about this family having only a father, they reportedly responded, without hesitation that such a prospect seemed rather natural to them.

It was a thrill for me to revisit with them this very special little house, perhaps at times a refuge of sorts for them and now a storehouse of those scattered memories of their laughter, tears, loneliness . . . left behind. I believe in Thomas Wolfe's musings—one truly cannot return to what once were the narrow confines of a previous life. The boys had been so focused on the prospects of their new lives ahead that perhaps a visit to the orphanage and a glimpse back into a rather still unsettled piece of their past may have felt somewhat offensive to them. Their behaviors during our visit suggested as if they feared waking from a dream, back to what once were the harsher realities of a past they would rather, at least for now, leave behind.

With the clock on its final countdown to our departure for America's shores, and neglecting to regard the potential impact our tour of the orphanage may have had on the boys, I romanticized the prospect of returning to Brazil one day as a bonded family. Until then, I was hopeful about helping the boys keep their Brazilian identities alive. I looked forward to cooking their favorite Brazilian dishes and taking them to a Brazilian supermarket and the occasional Brazilian festival in nearby neighborhoods heavily populated by Brazilians. Despite my best efforts in the ensuing years, their responses to my sporadic references about returning to Brazil for a visit typically would be limited to its more generic cultural appeal. The potential to reconnect with their personal past would mostly be met with shrugs of indifference.

Brazil will forever be the keeper of a significant part of the boys' past with which they always may struggle to reconcile. I knew that the reality of a meaningful return to Brazil would depend on the development of a healthier detachment with their past.

Chapter 10

How Do You Say Goodbye in Portuguese?

The next evening it was off to the airport and the boys' geographical parting of the ways with their former selves. Rio de Janeiro was the last stop for us before we took our leave from the last traces of what was familiar to them. It was to be a three-day jaunt for us while we waited out the application process with the American consulate for the boys' visas. Once allowed entry into the Estados Unidos with visas in hand, disembarking onto American soil, they could go about assuming their lives as American citizens.

Stress levels were high for the three of us. There was a mad dash to the finish line to make up for last-minute glitches getting the boys' Brazilian passports. Lino did some fast talking to get us past unexpected bureaucratic red tape from recent governmental procedural changes, that threatened to hold us up from leaving as scheduled. Against the backdrop of Brazil's first *futebol* game against North Korea for the World Cup, it was a race around the clock. With the game poised to end in a two-to-one victory for Brazil, the atmosphere was charged with excitement. Random, boisterous festivities were just beginning to spill out into streets fast becoming clogged with people and traffic. Amid the unrelenting sounds of shouts, firecrackers, and horn blasts, the city seemed primed to explode into a cacophony of chaos as we negotiated our way to the airport.

Saying our goodbyes was bittersweet to Lino at the airport. He had been our constant through the last six weeks, a readily available support as we began forging our familial bonds. I was excited to be on our way, yet I felt vulnerable leaving and knowing I would not have him to turn to, as I had become accustomed to. The boys were eager to leave, although they appeared most interested in fighting for the window seat on the airplane rather than grappling with the reality of leaving behind all that was commonplace to them for a new life.

Late into the night, our flight landed at Rio de Janeiro's Galeão airport. The stress of the past forty-eight hours was fast overtaking my senses, as fatigue was setting in amid the throbbing pain of a migraine headache. The boys' demeanor, noticeably calm was in stark contrast to the overall greater intensity of their acting-out behaviors. They had been acutely testing the limits of my newly developing parenting skills, not to mention the very essence of my sanity. The tension spurred by each hostile interchange chipped away further at my sense of parental competence. The boys' anxiety about the intensity of the happenings at the moment was undeniable, yet what about remained a mystery. I could not get past the language barrier, or budge their unwillingness to engage in the labeling of troubling thoughts or feelings, and perhaps the exploding reality of being taken away by a virtual stranger now officially in charge of them. Instead, their feelings of uncertainty as to the turn their lives were taking was thinly disguised by flare-ups of their angry, resentful attitudes, spurring short tempers, obstinacy, and significant communication gaps. Falling over our suitcases, we collapsed into our hotel room in Rio, all too happy to surrender to our beds.

* * *

The next morning as we headed out into the city, the sun shone brightly with not a cloud in the blue skies above. It was on the early side so the crowds had yet to overcome the view at our first stop. The scaffolding that had been up for the better part of a year for restoration work had mostly just come down only the previous week. All that was left were a few bits of metal below the base of the Cristo Redentor at the top of the Corcovado. The Christ statue was pristine in its appearance, and the views of the city, the mountains, and the ocean were awe-inspiring. Yet barely a few minutes passed before I had to contend with the incessant annoyance and drone of their impatience and discontent, "I wanna go down . . ." "I *want* to go down . . ." "I want to go down . . . *now.*"

Being atop of one of the world's most prized viewing spots, I tried ignoring their incessant pleas, hoping they might yield to the majesty of our surroundings. I kept hoping for the one moment that would slow them down, even if for just one moment, just long enough for me to feel the bond that was supposed to be forming between father and sons. I was getting tired of feeling like I was just a kindly, yet embattled activities' director to them, meant just to entertain and appease alongside their proclivity toward impatience, selfishness, and disrespect.

I was reminded of our last effort at a weekend getaway only two weeks before to Iguaçu Falls, another site to behold for its splendor and beauty. What was supposed to be a leisurely stroll along the path straddling the falls turned into a blurring sprint toward the visitors' kiosk. The perpetual rainbows bouncing of the falls' reflection and the butterflies fluttering around us on our way down to the boats did little to slow down the boys' excitement. Even so, their behavior over that weekend had seemed tamer and easier to direct, and allowed for some spontaneity in our enjoyment together.

We were fortunate to have hired a friendly cab driver to remain at our disposal, carting us around and chatting with us for the two days and nights of our stay. We were on the go from the moment we stepped off the plane. The boys' first plane ride had been a thrill in and of itself. We visited with toucans and other native South American birds at the Parque das Aves, toured the engineering marvels of the world's largest hydroelectric plant at the Itaipu Dam, and took pictures at the mark of the three frontiers, designating the meeting of the borders of Brazil, Argentina, and Paraguay. We also took a boat ride up close to the misted, thunderous roar of the falls, getting a feel for the intensity of nature's power. We feasted on flame-grilled meat sliced from skewers, brought around to our table at the ubiquitous *churrascarias*. At one of them, we celebrated different Latin American cultures through song and dance at a dinner show.

I kept that weekend highly structured and dynamic, with a cornucopia of sights and activities requiring the boys' minimal attention and effort. Having a taxi drive us around with a ready and willing companion serving as a constant distraction helped keep their attitudes in check and their vibes positive. Now that we were seemingly able to maintain agreeable relations as a new family, I hoped to replicate this success in Rio.

In between appointments at the U.S. consulate, we stayed out and about, taking in the sights and touring bits and pieces of the city. This time, however, our comings and goings felt more as an obligation rather than a source of enjoyment. Complaints were incessant from the boys. Matheus even refused to get out of the taxi when we pulled up to the famed Escaderia Selarón, leaving Davi and I to walk around and explore the painted, tiled steps without him. The tension in the air shrouded over us throughout our time in Rio, sidetracking me from recognizing the simplicity of their needs. The other bigger thrills of the Corcovado, Sugar Loaf, and Maracanã stadium were mere distractions, eclipsed by simpler, more immediately gratifying stops. Breaks for coconut water alongside the paved walkways and beaches of Ipanema and Copacabana, smoothies at the city's infamous juice bars, and frolicking dips in the Atlantic were the bigger hits.

We also took a personally guided tour of one of the city's notorious favelas, the barrio Rocinha. Its urbanized neighborhood slum, widely stereotyped for its reports of omnipresent poverty, violence, gangs, and drugs seemed to resonate strongly with the boys. Curitiba also has favelas, although not as many; nor are they as large or perhaps even as gritty as those scattered around Rio de Janeiro. I vaguely knew the boys came from a mostly impoverished background, yet they kept their personal experiences and any comparison to what they saw on the tour to themselves.

The few, ill-defined details I learned about the boys' past living conditions implied the kinds of violence and deprivation they were exposed to that stick to one's psyche and color one's perceptions and expectations for life. In hindsight, for Matheus and Davi to see it on display as tourists, somewhat removed from their own backgrounds still fresh and vivid in their consciousness must have felt like a paradoxical exercise in incredulity as to what their new lives promised. With their bright, trendy new clothes on their backs, appetites consistently, routinely satiated, and the ready awareness of their own personal toys, books, and electronics safely stashed away in suitcases, we toured the narrowed, congested back alleyways of the barrio with its impoverished sights and jarring sounds.

* * *

As we prepared to leave for the airport once more, with their U.S. visas in hand, I was constantly distracted by tending to the boys' acting-out, irritable behaviors, putting our papers in order, and ensuring our luggage was all packed and accounted for. I did not realize that I was disregarding the personal implications surrounding my own forthcoming return home. I had been gone for only six weeks, yet the turn my life had taken and how much I had already changed belied the static existence of my former comfort zone. I was unsure about how taking on my new fatherly role would fit into the familiarity of my erstwhile routine of family, work, and friends, virtually unaffected by my relatively short absence. My former life, now covered with a thin layer of dust seemed tenuous; I was afraid that a simple dusting would not be enough to integrate my drastically shifting priorities.

It had been freeing to begin our father-and-son relations over the past six weeks without the distractions of the imposing realities I'd left behind. Although I'd left my own father in relatively stable health, the ups and downs with his health and overall wellbeing since having received his diagnosis of terminal lung cancer continued to beleaguer my consciousness. I remembered after having left him "fine" for a spring break trip to Europe for ten days to find him, upon my return home chained to a ventilator the size of a small refrigerator forcing oxygen into his lungs. For a few days, we had all tiptoed around him, unsure what to make of his condition until surgery a few days later helped increase his lung capacity so that he was able to breathe on his own again. Even though I saw him nearly every day on Skype, I was still nervous about what kind of state I might truly find him in. I felt liberated in having had this time with the boys, away from the daily struggles of watching my father cope with the gradual deterioration of his physical health as it bore on his attitude and frame of mind. I felt very vulnerable and uncertain how I was going to effectively parent from an emotionally sane perspective, as the inevitability of my own father's impending death would be looming over me again.

I also tried telling myself that Michael would warm quickly to the boys entering into his life. My nephew recently began showing off his preteen angst, claiming indifference and testing limits. He was at that in-between stage, starting to pull away toward independence, yet with great trepidation. Upping the ante, the uncertainties surrounding my father's illness competed with what should have been normal preteen angst. Resistance and testing limits became more the norm as Michael strained against the onslaught of his mounting insecurity. It was not enough that he was losing his Poppa, who was his father figure. He was now going to have to share the spotlight. Matheus and Davi were poised to enter into his life, changing it in ways he was not prepared for, threatening to further shake whatever sense of security he might have had.

Like the swinging of a pendulum, my mother vacillated between the needs of both my father and Michael, placating one while nurturing another. Her movements to and fro seemed incessant; the tension inside her was unrelenting and took its toll as she battled fatigue, migraines, and anxiety. She kept the household together, forever the peacemaker over the surly attitudes, hurt feelings, and passive-aggressive behavior of both Michael and my father. As she already was hesitant about the changing dynamics the boys were to bring to our family, I worried about the potential for added stress on my mother. She was anxious to help me with them, yet how much she would be able to help me because of the demands on her already weighed heavily on her shoulders.

I was anxious to go home, yet what home meant to me was in stark contrast to the mixed emotions about what home might mean for the boys. Regardless of our family troubles, I left behind a life marked by emotional stability and support that I still expected to be ready to envelop me upon my return. Matheus and Davi were leaving behind a vast chunk of their respective childhoods, mired by their experiences of poverty, neglect, and violence. Yet they also were leaving behind all that was familiar to them, clinging to hope for what the future would bring, yet struggling to manage their fears over what was in store for them.

Matheus and Davi had reached the point of no return, whereby the lingering impression of never going home, as they had known it to be for them was to be a long-standing, perhaps perpetual source of conflict with which they would have to contend. They were leaving behind everything they knew of as home while I got to return to the familiarity and safety of my home. I was hopeful, yet feeling pressured by having to reframe for them the notion of what home has always meant to me and all that its heart is supposed to embody: security, nurturance, and affection. Indeed, just the sort of place where one belongs, where one can go home to . . . again and again.

Chapter 11

Father's Day

Traversing the various lines at Rio's airport through check-in and customs seemed no less treacherous than dodging the threat of bloodshed in the throes of mortal combat. The boys went after each other any chance they had, with a slap here and a kick there; pushing, shoving, and verbal abuse were slung fast and furious, as if they were engaged in full-fledged warfare. I was bleary eyed, struggling to keep the tears of exhaustion and fear from rolling down. Once past customs, I sat them both down and in my very best Portuguese firmly instructed them to *knock it off*. There were to be no more behavioral insults if they had any expectations of joining in on the fun when meeting up with their new family "tomorrow." I tried my best to reflect their anxiety and validate what they might have been feeling. They listened quietly with stoic looks on their faces. They agreed to a cease-fire.

As we proceeded toward the gate, a forced calm saturated the air, as if we had entered the eye of a hurricane. I knew better than to let my guard down. With the calling of our row number, getting in line, and entering onto the jetway for our plane headed to Miami, I found myself longingly glancing at others boarding a plane to Lisbon next door. For just a few seconds I fantasized over sending the boys ahead while I anonymously slipped onto the plane bound for Portugal; the free spirit of my former life nagged at my consciousness. We made our way to our row and slid into the seats flanked on both sides by the aisle; there were no window seats to fight over. I had thought ahead, and rewarded myself with a smirk of self-satisfaction. As we would be flying through the night, I told them that they would be turning in for bed just as if we were back at Lar Rogate. Our arrival into Miami would be early in the morning. There were to be no movies, no music, no electronics, no snacks . . . I breathed a sigh of relief as they both quickly surrendered to sleep soon after takeoff. The plane climbed higher into the clouds, leaving behind the last traces of their native homeland.

With a screech of the wheels touching down on the tarmac the next morning, we landed ahead of schedule. The boys were already stirring, happily sated from their breakfast trays. I turned on my cell phone, comforted by its familiar chirping noises as it awoke from its six-week hibernation; it was only a few minutes before my father called to check our whereabouts. "We're here, Dad," I said, reassured by his voice. "I'll keep you posted."

We got up from our seats, elbowing for a position in the crowded aisle. I was used to bouncing off the plane, backpack in tow, ready for the sprint to customs and swift re-entry into native territory. This time I stumbled off the plane, several times tripping over the boys' wayward, misguided feet. I struggled to manage our carry-on bags; the boys' little hands and unorganized ways were more of a hindrance than a help. I worried over keeping from leading them astray. We trudged onward toward customs. My gaze anxiously flitted, from side to side as I kept track of the boys' whereabouts. My father called again. I kept my cool as I told him of our approach to customs.

The customs agent promptly pulled us aside to be led to a more secure area behind closed doors for the boys to be fingerprinted, their papers scrutinized, and for them to be registered as new American citizens. I could only imagine that my father must have been beside himself, as my cell phone did not have any reception while we were contained; no outside contact was allowed. I wanted to get a picture of the boys with the American flag, but photography was prohibited. As time passed, I grew slightly uneasy sitting with the boys in the waiting area, not knowing what to expect, wondering what would happen if something were wrong with the paperwork. I did not need to worry; the agent came back with a benevolent smile and welcomed us *home*.

There were no more hurdles to clear. Once more, we gathered our belongings and headed back on the path to our new lives together. I gave my father a quick call, letting him know we were finally on our way out. Bypassing the lines, I handed our stamped entry cards to the customs agent, who ushered us onward. I stopped the boys just short of the closed, opaque doors where the family would be waiting on the other side. I smiled at them, giving them each a stroke on the chin and a tussle of the hair. I held my breath, my insides trembling with a mixture of fear and excitement. We were cleared, yet we had only just begun.

* * *

Our homecoming was eagerly anticipated: My parents and Michael, along with Gayle and Jake, had arrived at the airport at sunrise, gathering in the international waiting area for our arrival, with cameras poised and the ready wave of both an American and Brazilian flag in each hand. Competing with the other onlookers waiting for their loved ones to emerge, my family focused their gazes with each opening of the doors for that first sight of us. The clocks overhead ticked on mercilessly. With no further word about our progress, and after the last of the travelers from our flight had seemingly emerged, their excitement gave way to weariness. It had been more than two hours now. The once crowded, ebullient hall had emptied, the atmosphere drained of its exuberance. The flags in their hands began to droop, flopping over lifelessly.

With the ring of my father's cell phone, the buzz surrounding our impending entry swiftly picked up again as heads turned for the opening of the doors one last time. As we stepped out into the waiting area, Matheus sauntered ahead of Davi and me. With a flash of his award-winning smile, arms outstretched as if he were appearing for some divine deliverance, he ambled over to his new family like a superstar greeting his adoring fans. Davi stayed at my side at first, somewhat hesitant, yet excitement shone on his face. I was overwhelmed at first sight of the family. Michael was the first of the awaiting bunch I had reached; both our eyes glistened with tears of relief as we embraced. It was touching to see how the four boys eagerly, instantly related to one another, keen on getting more familiarly acquainted. It was a jumble of hugs and pleasantries as we were welcomed home and ushered out into the bright, oppressive stickiness of a South Florida summer day.

The four boys were so intent on fraternizing with one another, they did not want to separate, making it easy for Gayle to volunteer to take them all in her car for the ride to my parents' house, leaving me alone to ride with my parents. For a moment I hesitated, feeling peculiar about this first prospect of being separated from Matheus and Davi, even if just for the forty-five-minute car ride. Yet I warmed quickly to the promise of a little peace and solitude. My father did not share my enthusiasm, quickly grumbling his disappointment. "This isn't what I wanted," he groused, not unlike a petulant child. It was not what *he* wanted, and my mother turned to give me "the look," meant to bridge our shared suffering of my father's impatience. He was anxious to revel in my so-called newfound joy of fatherhood, yet he relented when understanding the pleasing prospect of some space and time alone with him and my mother.

At the house, the boys happily played with one another, taking dips in the swimming pool. There was lots of giggling and cavorting. They didn't seem to have any troubles relating with the imposition of a language barrier. The boys took their cues from natural, inborn tendencies to relate, communicating their unconditional positive regard for one another.

Afterward, we were ready to go home to their new home, the house they had up until now seen only in pictures and in a video where Michael and Jake had facilitated a guided tour. We split up into three cars this time; it felt good to get back into the driver's seat of my own car and take on familiar streets. Matheus promptly nodded off in the backseat on the short ride over to the house. With the grass apparently having been freshly cut, the house was neat in its appearance as we turned into the driveway. Michael and Jake led the boys to the front door, ushering them inside. We saved their rooms for last; with tentative steps, each entered his own bedroom, readying themselves to touch what was now theirs to claim. There did not seem to be any one thing in particular that sustained their interest as they randomly explored their rooms, seemingly uncertain how to assert themselves in their own personal spaces.

My parents stayed back at the house with the boys while Gayle took me grocery shopping. Ordinarily, I have always enjoyed grocery shopping, wandering the aisles and contemplating the endless culinary possibilities. This time I was overwhelmed. It did not help to be shopping with Miss Organic, who was all too eager to share her knowledge and beliefs about the importance of adopting a natural way of eating. I tried striking a balance between encouraging healthy eating habits and still invoking familiarity and comfort. My thoughts also turned to balancing the cost of shopping for three as the grocery cart rapidly filled with food geared toward the needs and tastes of the boys. I was fighting their deeply ingrained habits of reckless eating amid environmental deprivation. Coming from the orphanage, where eating was a tightly scheduled affair with choice and privilege missing from the menu, the boys had a constant desire for the immediate gratification of sugary snacks and desserts and other processed foods. This was in spite of mostly having subsisted on a basic diet of grilled meat, rice and beans, bread, and fruit. I was fearful of their fast adopting the over indulgent eating habits too common in the American diet.

Our neighbors from across the street stopped by. They brought balloons, candy, and good cheer, heartily welcoming Matheus and Davi to the neighborhood. We'd been genial acquaintances for many years, and I had no idea then how much they would become intimately involved in our lives, adding credence to the adage, that "It takes a village to raise a child." After the boys' first taste of American pizza for an early dinner, it felt the right time for the rest of the family to head out, leaving the three of us alone together in our home for the first time. Fatigue, framed both by emotional exhaustion and sleep deprivation, was fast pervading my mood. The house was in total disarray: Half-opened suitcases were propped open in the hallways; clothes and toys were strewn about; bags and parcels cluttered up counters and floor space. All of that would keep as the boys quickly settled into their nightly bedtime routine, surrendering to their new beds.

As they laid their heads down on their pillows, both simply expressed their contentment with all they had discovered on this first day of their homecoming. With the boys out from underfoot, I wandered around the house, randomly poking into suitcases, flipping through the mountainous stack of mail, and moving around varying articles of clothes, sundry items, and souvenirs. I did not know what to do with myself. I felt restless, unfocused, and drained of all feeling. Eventually I made it over to my bedroom, but not before I peeked into their rooms, catching a glimpse of the innocence in their resting faces. It was then that I was able to lay my head down, reassured that all was right for the moment.

* * *

With a bit of irony, I awoke on our first morning home to its being Father's Day. The boys had taken out the LEGOs I left out for them, the very same LEGOs I'd stashed away from my own childhood. They were playing cooperatively, interacting with each other pleasantly and with focused efforts. I greeted them with a "Feliz Dia do Pai"—"Happy Father's Day." They looked up and greeted me with their usual, perhaps dutiful kiss, hug, and a smile in return. Brazil recognizes Father's Day and Mother's Day the same as we do here, yet the boys were not overly zealous in their acknowledgment, leaving me feeling discouraged on the outside and a little hurt and disappointed on the inside.

I recalled how the boys used to refer to me by my first name, occasionally slipping and calling me *Pai*, the Portuguese equivalent to *Father*. I had decided not to force the issue with them, letting them come to refer to me however they wished, taking their time as they became accustomed to me as their father and answering to me as such. As we neared the end of our thirty-day cohabitation, I had worried that they continued to refer to my first name rather than having made any concerted efforts otherwise. With Lino's approval, I took advantage of the day our adoption orders were signed in court, legally pairing us as father and sons, to announce that I would no longer answer to my first name. They could call me anything they wished so long as it directly referred to my being their father. They could call me *Pai* if they wanted to keep in the spirit of their Portuguese roots, or call me Dad,

Daddy, Father... whatever. It took only a few days before my first name seemed expunged from their vocabulary. There was a little back and forth between *Pai* and Father, with Father quickly winning out.

I wondered what Father's Day had meant to them in years past without any memory of having had their natural father in their lives, and now on this day. The boys went on with their LEGO playing for the better part of the morning. I went about tackling some of the more usual types of care taking duties: I prepared breakfast, did laundry, tidied up . . . those never-ending chores that brought me pleasure on this Father's Day. It was my first time taking on the everyday bliss of domesticity. Warm wishes from extended family and friends came our way throughout the day, with most recognizing this being my first Father's Day. My parents had the boys sign a card to give to me. Only their names and the simple proclamation, *I love you,* beneath each of their signatures adorned the card and its photo of two golden retrievers contentedly looking out an open window. It seemed to match the card's unpretentious affirmation as if directly uttered by my parents: *Our special wish is sent with love because it's just for you – the wish is meant for Father's Day, but the love's for all year through.*

I thought it rather silly to forcefully regard this day as so very different from any other day. Every day was Father's Day for me now. The few family and friends who'd met Matheus and Davi thus far marveled in how *happy* they appeared. At least for the moment, their being seemingly content with their lot in life was truly all the recognition I needed. It would have been superficial at that point for me to expect that their regard for me was anything much more than as their potential provider of happiness. I sought to love, protect, guide, and mentor my two sons, the hallmark of a good father. I just wanted to be the best father I could be and make every day count, no matter how trivial or daunting.

Part 3

Settling In

Chapter 12

Putting It Together ... Bit by Bit

The honeymoon phase persisted in spite of the overwhelming onslaught of life's ordinary details. I spent an inordinate amount of time deliberating about how to better simplify so our life was not ruled by the monotony of these mundane details. It was back to work only the day after Father's Day, just two days after leaving Brazil. I had long used up my sick leave; the need to resume earning my paycheck was an unavoidable fact of life. The boys were eager to start summer camp, yet I did not share their enthusiasm for returning to work. Because school had let out for the summer the week before, at least I would only have to contend with paperwork rather than worrying about tending to the needs of students, teachers, and administrators. Waking up at five, leaving the boys deep in their slumber for another hour, I stumbled through the darkness of the early morning to get ready. I could not find my hairbrush; my blow-drying efforts were futile, leaving me to feel like an unmade bed my first day. I am not even sure I wore matching socks.

Our efforts to unpack barely scratched the surface; our tossing aside with reckless abandon what was unpacked only added to the house's mounting clutter. I even had trouble managing the clothes the boys had been wearing, as they felt free to abandon them anywhere they happened to take them off. I found clothes and towels strewn about the floor, soaking wet in the shower, straddling counter tops in the kitchen, stuffed into the couch, and tossed under their beds. Surveying the laundry room a week or so later, I took advantage of an empty cart along the wall and popped in two laundry baskets for $2.75 apiece. With the top basket for their clothes and the bottom for their underwear, socks, and towels, the boys now had a concrete point of reference, and so ended much of the nagging and needless frustration.

I had them share a towel each night for their showers; even with two bodies to dry, the lone towel tossed into the laundry basket still had barely a tinge of dampness, helping to keep laundry needs from threatening to consume my every waking moment. It took me a week to put away all the clothes I had laundered from when we first came home . . . just in time for the next loads with which to contend. There were five loads of laundry in all, until I realized I forgot to do my own clothes. I began to streamline the laundry into small, manageable batches throughout the week, requiring only minimal amounts of time. I also assigned the boys the chore of folding and putting away their own underwear and socks. That saved more time to devote to another seemingly unending domestic chore . . . the dishwasher. It was filled and ready to go three times a week, whereas I had been used to it being once every two to three weeks. I blended that chore in with our morning routine, emptying the dishwasher while I got out breakfast, made lunches, and folded laundry, and the boys dressed and made their beds.

The more organized we became, the better our ability to keep stress levels at a minimum. The boys were starting to turn off the lights when leaving a room more times than not, used the same glass for the day, and paid better attention to wearing clothes that matched. They also stopped putting used toilet paper in the wastebasket, as they had in Brazil, with its fragile plumbing. As the honeymoon began to fade, I held onto these smaller successes. I knew it would be important to keep myself from getting caught up in the frustration and setbacks of their bigger behavioral challenges not readily solved by the popping in of a laundry basket.

* * *

The reality of the boys' behavioral challenges, already having made quite the impression during our time in Brazil, seemed to defy anything I was used to handling in my own professional experience. I was able to maintain a realistic perspective on the issues that presented themselves, yet all my training, knowledge, and direct experience often did little to help sustain my objectivity. Matheus seemed determined to challenge my authority, frequently leaving me with more questions than answers as I struggled to keep a grip on my composure.

It had become obvious that he struggled with a great deal of anger as a result of unresolved issues of loss; yet, more at the forefront, he also struggled with holding himself accountable for his own negative actions. No matter how trivial his offensive behavior may have been, the defensiveness of his denial and avoidance would predominate. Only the passing of time would help soothe the savageness of his rage before he was more receptive to reason . . . and even then sometimes he still struggled to reconcile with the truth and his subsequent accountability for his actions. On the flipside, if I caught an infraction of his brother's, he would adamantly dictate how I'd *better* hand his brother the same consequence he might expect to receive if he were to behave similarly.

Sometimes the refereeing was relentless . . . forever over the most trivial of matters. Davi sometimes seemed to make it his mission to unnerve his brother regardless of the expected ramifications. More than once Davi mouthed off farting noises in Matheus's face to get his attention, only to recoil in panic when physically assaulted in return. His brother's enraged eruptions seemed instantaneous. I felt like a broken record, drilling into them their need to reach out to me once the other became bothersome; physical aggression was not acceptable behavior. Would I have to keep them within my sight and earshot every waking moment?

The more we struggled to negate the language barrier and communicate more effectively in the heat of the moment, the greater I feared would be the erosion of their receptivity to my authority and influence. I was afraid that time was running out on my being able to influence them. I recruited an English tutor for the boys, one hour, twice a week lasting about six weeks, to more quickly help them to speak and understand English. They truly enjoyed their lessons with her, and appreciated their chance to learn more functional English with someone from their own Portuguese comfort zone. Soon after the lessons started, I had the tutor stay an additional hour one afternoon so I could just *talk* with the boys about some of the behavioral issues for a more seamless translation than what we were experiencing with the *tradutor.*

When I met with the tutor and Matheus, he rather simply stated he did not like to ask for help, such as asking me to intervene on his behalf should his brother bother him, because he did not believe anyone would help him. Why should he trust me, his new father, after a lifetime of having caretakers, even his own mother not come through for him because they were either not available, unable to respond, or just did not care? Yet he trusted enough to let me in on a bit of how he was feeling. He was noticeably more relaxed in his overall demeanor for quite a while afterwards, more receptive to what I had to say and offer in terms of perspective, and to those dreaded yet necessary consequences for maladaptive behavior.

One evening, I took advantage of his brother's having an earlier bedtime because of a behavioral transgression to spend precious time alone with Matheus. He readily stepped in to help me prepare a meal ahead for dinner later in the week. It was the most innocent of bonding moments with Matheus at the stove. Wearing only his underwear, dotted with tiny cars, trucks, and busses, he stood by my side stirring the meat and vegetables in the skillet. A word here and there passed between us, yet the emotional connection of our togetherness shaped further the bond between father and son. Matheus clearly needed these moments of unconditional positive regard, which lowered his defenses and encouraged him to take more responsibility for his actions.

Something of a breakthrough with Matheus occurred the next day following an incident with his brother, who likely was the instigator with his attention-seeking behavior that tended to grate on the nerves of others. Both came to me, with Davi reporting Matheus hit him; Matheus stayed close by his side, ready to counter whatever Davi was going to say. Neither was hysterical about this transgression, which appeared to me rather normal in brotherly relations, so I could take a step back rather than having to dive right in. Holding off Matheus, I asked Davi what he might have done to irritate his brother. Davi halfway admitted his own irritating behavior, while I insisted on his need to think further about consequences for his behavior. Even though hitting was not acceptable behavior on his brother's part, I stressed to Davi that, once he chose to engage in risk-taking behavior, it was too late for me to help him.

They both retreated, yet Matheus came to me on his own just a few minutes later and matter-of-factly reported that he would not be able to play his video games for the next day. When I asked him why, he simply responded, "For hitting Davi," as he was referring to what has been the consequence.

I immediately praised him for this rather huge step forward in holding himself accountable for his behavior. He was quite pleased when I also told him he could have his LEGOs back a day early after losing them for not cooperating in cleaning up for bedtime. Perhaps feeling that his emotional needs were beginning to be met, Matheus was starting to respond to me as a trusted authority.

* * *

Although Davi was typically a joy to have around, with his quirky sense of humor, inquisitive nature, and fun-loving ways, his hysterical flare-ups and disrespectful retorts were exasperating. He had to have the last word, forsaking any regard for authority—mine, or anyone else's, for that matter. Just trying to get Davi to "stop," or "be quiet" would result in his snapping, "No, you be quiet." I still recalled Lino's insistence on the boys' need for firm limits and structure to counter their earlier experiences of unpredictability and tendency to give into their wild ways when they were all too often left without proper supervision. The only way to respond constructively was to hand down a consequence centered on the here and now. We still were not able to fluently communicate with one another and talk through difficult circumstances; emphasis on reason and mutual understanding was also still a novel prospect. Such consequences as an early bedtime, loss of an ice-cream privilege, and reduced video game time were immediately doled out. So began the gradual chipping away of Davi's misguided resolve in favor of greater forethought and subsequent decrease in his back talking.

Communication gaps only heightened Davi's frustration. Misunderstandings were frequent. Not being able to get others to fully understand his intentions would prove devastating for Davi. He had earned a reputation for being overdramatic and unpredictable. I received several panic-stricken phone calls throughout the summer from his camp counselor. "Davi ran off . . ." "Davi had a meltdow . . ." "Davi shut down . . ." Each time, it seemed the result of one of the other campmates taking advantage of his limited English. Once, in the middle of an outburst, Davi frantically took advantage of a computer in the room and pulled up the *tradutor* for help in communicating with the counselor. So difficult were Davi's behaviors that when it was time the following year to prepare for the summer's camp program, one of the counselors told me of a brief meeting to "get ready" for Davi. It was for naught; he had blended in with the other campers that summer without incident. That first summer barely lingered as a faded memory.

More problematic on the home front was that, although Davi was invested in being heard, it often was for his own selfish intentions rather than in the spirit of cooperation. He was rather quick to say, "*no saber*"- "don't know"—or, "*no entender*"—"don't understand"—when the spotlight was on him for something inappropriate. Davi also was quick to turn on the tears, perhaps a learned reaction to divert attention and avoid the wrath of a past that was riddled with verbal and physical abuse. Still, he was so much easier than Matheus, who also would fret and fume over the littlest of incidents, yet required a seemingly infinite expanse of time before he would allow any interaction. Davi's return to his jovial self was almost instantaneous; he would bounce back with the snapping sharpness of a newly stretched rubber band as if nothing had happened.

Maintaining consistency in my approach yielded greater acquiescence in attitude. Humor especially worked with Davi, as he often was easy to sidetrack away from his tendency to overreact to minor annoyances. I repeatedly threatened consequences in order to reinforce adaptive behavior, especially when the boys were out of the house, such as at camp, or for when they would be starting school. We discussed Davi's need to maintain safe behavior, utilizing alternatives such as counting from one to ten, or retreating to a pre-designated area in the house for a self-imposed time-out. He also began realizing that his "faces" did not work with me, gravitating more toward reinforcement for what did get my positive attention.

One evening Davi proudly showed me how he'd decided to put one of his circular fabric Frisbee disks under his clock radio so it would not scratch the night table's surface in his bedroom. I had pointed out to him only the night before not to slide the checker pieces all over the wood coffee table in the family room so there wouldn't be scratches left behind. It took so little to influence adaptive, positive behavior that manifested itself outside of the teachable moment. It became important to Davi for recognition as a "good kid." I saw how he and his brother thrived when finding themselves in the good graces of a significant adult. When one factors out the negative, disheartening influences of their earlier history, they are no different from any of our children.

Chapter 13

All Roads Lead to Home

The itinerary seemed fairly straightforward. Our first family summer road trip would start with a stop in Atlanta to attend the adoption agency's annual family picnic. We would continue onward with stops to visit old friends and their families in North Carolina, New Jersey, and Connecticut. I was excited to introduce Matheus and Davi to my long-standing friends. Our last stop before the turnaround back to Florida was Bradford, Pennsylvania, for LIMIAR's annual reunion weekend for adoptive families. Ten days of driving . . . and bonding, visiting . . . and bonding, hanging out . . . and bonding some more. I purposely tried to keep this trip as low-key as possible, with little emphasis on touristic, on-the-go activities in favor of hanging out with my friends and playing with their children. The hard driving was saved for the first and last days of the trip, with the remaining drives in between not to last more than half a day at a time.

The best of intentions in planning and forethought did not take into consideration such events as the horrendous traffic accident on the interstate, barely two hours out of our house. Police cars and fire-rescue trucks whizzed by, and a helicopter circled above as we stood at a standstill. We were diverted back south via a detour, with an additional two hours of traveling time. In noting our turnaround south, I could not help but be annoyed when Davi innocently asked, "Are we going home?" Both had expressed interest in our plans, yet neither showed any great enthusiasm for our impending travels. I had hoped they would be more excited.

Trying to keep quick tempers from boiling over in the car often was a challenge. Managing equal playing time for their portable video game system was a constant struggle. The charger for the cigarette lighter did not work, allowing only two and a half hours of video watching on the portable DVD player each driving day. I had to relentlessly referee their turn taking: whose turn it was to pick the movie, use the one set of ear buds, watch on his own . . . Struggling to keep the peace in the face of insults, name-calling, and teasing to each other whenever their fatigue, cabin fever, or hunger set in constantly jangled my nerves.

The few touristy things we did do were spread out few and far between so the boys would not be overwhelmed by feeling dragged around from place to place. Instead of a day pounding the pavements of Manhattan just for a few ten second thrills and the inevitability of ill-tempered spirits and behavior, we spent a relaxed afternoon admiring the animals at the Bronx Zoo and another day checking out the sea animals and ships at the Mystic Seaport and Aquarium. In between, plenty of hanging-out time playing with my friends' children, who always had some cool toys and activities on-hand that seized the boys' attention. When I asked them later what they liked the most about the trip, both related to these times playing with their new friends.

I especially learned the hard way not to play around with mealtimes. It did not matter where we were or what we were doing. Once the roll of the clock signaled the time for lunch or dinner, even a snack to tide them over was not enough. Unless a full meal presented itself, irritability, obstinate behavior, and hot tempers were the repercussions. Some of the sweeter moments involved our fun meal-times at some of my former roadside haunts, and places I found ahead of time on the Internet. The big hits were special desserts, such as ice cream at Stew Leonard's at the Norwalk beach or at a farm near Mystic, a snow-cone in Baltimore, or soft-serve shakes at the Dari Hut in downtown Bradford.

Our drive through Pennsylvania in traveling to our last stop, LIMIAR's reunion picnic, was particularly stressful, as Matheus had a full-blown melt down. He had lost his ice-cream privilege for our planned stop at Penn State's infamous creamery, for which he sulked his way through the chomping of an apple while Davi and I indulged in our ice-cream treats. I was not going to deny him sustenance, yet I was not going to reward him for an instance of disrespectful and uncooperative behavior. Not happy, he still appeared to be accepting of his consequence, until learning that this so-called snack was to substitute for lunch in favor of an early dinner upon arrival in Bradford. "No lunch?" he incredulously asked. My attempts to reason with him quickly fell short; even the slightest of hunger pangs unnerved him, threatening to revive those feelings of deprivation he still struggled to forget.

Matheus stormed off, not giving me enough of a chance to fully process what seemed to be going on for him. In figuring it out and swallowing my injured pride from having reacted impulsively rather than having first thought it through, I reached out to him and conveyed my misunderstanding of his *need* for lunch. By this time he was in tears, claiming that I did not *love* or *care* about him. Good fortune did not follow us along as we went in search of the campus food court, only to find it closed down for the day. Matheus became incensed, seemingly having reached a point of desperation, falling prey to irrational thoughts and fears of starvation. He misunderstood our need to go somewhere else, thinking we would not be getting lunch after all, that perhaps he had been deceived. He refused to get in the car, put on his seat belt, or keep the door locked. My insides trembled as I worked to gain his cooperation so we could make our way to any fast-food place within reach. I never thought a trip to McDonald's would turn out to be a necessity. As he ate his way through his Happy Meal, Matheus slowly calmed down, his indignation gradually wearing away as we continued onward.

* * *

We finally arrived in Bradford, nestled in a valley in the Allegheny Mountains abutting the New York state line. The weather was cool, a welcome relief from the warmer, humid air along the eastern seaboard. I was excited about the picnic the next day, anxious to meet other adoptive families and their children. I also was looking for Matheus and Davi to have a chance to fraternize with the other Brazilian children, at least one or two of whom had adjusted to their new families and life in America.

I'd enjoyed the family picnic in Atlanta earlier in the week, finally meeting face-to-face the adoption agency's director, who had personally handled my adoption preparations. However, it had been difficult to talk with her at length. Her attention understandably was pulled in multiple directions. There also were no other Brazilian adoptions represented and the newly established director of the agency's Brazilian program, along with her adopted Brazilian children had been unable to attend at the last minute. The majority of families there had consisted of children still in their toddler years. I hoped our experience at LIMIAR's picnic would contain more personal relevance for us.

When we arrived at the site of the picnic, on the campus of the University of Pittsburgh, Bradford, the boys did not seem as excited as I thought they would, surrounded by familiar signs of their former homeland. They maintained their indifference no matter how the Brazilian flags were scattered about, who wore Brazilian *futebol* jerseys as the boys were wearing, or the array of typical Brazilian food and their favored guarana soda to feast on at dinner. The boys maintained a reserved demeanor, responding minimally to those adults attempting to converse with them in Portuguese. In Brazil, they had happily chatted with anyone who was responsive to them. Here they seemed disappointed by the quizzical looks from the few Brazilian children they attempted to speak Portuguese to, not understanding the likely loss of their native tongue as they further learned English and became acculturated to American life. The emotional distance they were beginning to place between themselves and their former homeland surprised me.

Interspersed between family activities, there were a few parenting groups where I appreciated the chance to speak and relate with other adoptive parents in various stages of their adoptions. There was one family soon to celebrate a full year having elapsed since returning from Brazil, and other families who had been together somewhere around three to five years or more. There were even older parents who had brought their now grown children leading independent lives. There was a sense of normalcy I hadn't felt since taking on fatherhood. I did not feel as alone in my struggle to deal with the boys' communication and adjustment issues. I found the prospect of soon being able to distinguish the flickering of a light at the end of the proverbial tunnel especially rejuvenating.

The children—even the teenagers—were charming. They were polite, agreeable, and seemingly content and adapted. It especially was surreal for me to hear the majority of them speaking English so fluently. The trace of an accent was undetectable, yet I also was saddened by how English had bulldozed over their former Portuguese roots. A few of the teens conducted a seminar to tell of their personal adoption experiences, holding me captive with the expressiveness of their emotions in recounting their initial adjustment difficulties. I was encouraged by how each appeared to have found a place for him- or herself despite inauspicious beginnings.

Not all of the children at the picnic shone as brightly. A boy kicked Davi during a soccer game, fueling a temper outburst and pulling me out of the Brazilian teens' seminar. When I got out to the fields, LIMIAR's director was with Davi, speaking with him and helping him calm down. He could not praise Davi enough; he seemed to be a "good kid" who just needed to gain more self-control. I gratefully accepted this validation from someone who had only a half day's worth of mostly casual contact with Davi. The director's quick once-over essentially corresponded with my own intimate assessment of my son.

Perhaps to reassure me, the director later told me that this other boy was a "rough kid" with numerous behavioral and emotional issues; a single father, who had been one of the first to welcome me to the picnic, also was raising him. Throughout the day, I had been puzzled by the boy's apparent aloofness to his father's loving gestures. Too often it also seemed his father did not know where he was, who he was with, or what he was doing. His father was open in sharing some of the difficulties he was having with his son, as well as the boy's older sister, who had been living apart from them.

I tried overlooking the waving of some other red flags surrounding this boy's circumstances, yet I could not get over the father's flippant comments about having "to let the house go." Keeping things tidy and orderly was low on his priority list in favor of keeping the peace rather than contending with an ongoing battle of wills. I tried not to judge, especially pertaining to matters that might not be within his control. Yet the father's perspective jarringly contrasted with my emphasis on organization and structure in our household. I could not "let go" such basic priorities as the boys' making their beds every morning, taking care of their clothes rather than treating them as disposable discards, putting away food after finishing whatever they took out . . . These simple acts represented our working together for the common good to make life less demanding and complicated in the long run. I had already lost a lot of ground, having adopted my boys later in their childhood years. I looked to mark our formative beginnings by making life more predictable, countering their earlier negative experiences of variability and chaos.

Perhaps taking them to the picnic was premature; two months had yet to pass since we left Brazil. The boys barely had yet to be influenced by the onslaught of culture shock; the newness of their environs still lacked reality's wear and tear. School had not even begun for them; enhanced expectations to perform academically, socially, and language-wise would soon threaten summer's more freestyle ways. The boys did appreciate their time at the picnic, and expressed interest in coming back another year, the next time schedules and geography were to align compatibly . . . or perhaps when their English was more up to speed.

* * *

As daunting as the road trip was at times, there still were many moments of delight and pleasure. Most surprising to me throughout, yet no longer surprising in hindsight, was how important the trip's ending—to return *home*—was to the boys. It seemed whenever we would get back on the road, making our way to the next stop, one of the boys would invariably ask whether we were "going home now" rather than inquire about the next stop. At the time, I thought it was just their annoying way of expressing displeasure with having to get back into the car.

Even before we'd started out on the road, the boys' regard for their new home quickly grew past those first photographs, and perceptions of it as just a mere collection of rooms, furniture, and function. They remained calm for our last leg of the trip, mostly two straight days of driving, as we made our way home, even when we stalled in trying to pass an unexplainable mass of stopped traffic off the Capital Beltway outside Washington, D.C. They did not seem to care that traffic flowed freely and easily in all other directions with the exception of the particular interstate section we were on. Although I introduced it more for the purpose of combating my own mounting frustration, they bought into my attempts to turn our stroke of bad luck into a game of survival. We relied on creative backtracking to continue south, navigating the traffic lights and commercial traffic on Route 1 until we got out of the metropolitan area.

Neither seemed to provoke the other as much, and they seemed easier to manage overall. Especially endearing was how Matheus fantasized aloud his hope for Grandma and Poppa and Michael waiting to surprise us upon our return home. No matter where we went, whom we visited, what we experienced, what there was to look forward to... what seemed most important to the boys was the expectation, the anticipation that all roads eventually would lead us back home. With a leap of faith, they began realizing their home and family would not abandon them, still remaining theirs to claim.

Chapter 14

Dear Teacher . . .

"WHOSE CHILD IS THIS?"

Author Unknown

"Whose child is this?" I asked one day
Seeing a little one out at play
"Mine," said the parent with a tender smile
"Mine to keep a little while
To bathe his hands and comb his hair
To tell him what he is to wear
To prepare him that he may always be good
And each day do the things he should."

"Whose child is this?" I asked again
As the door opened and someone came in.
"Mine," said the teacher with the same tender smile
"Mine, to keep just for a little while
To teach him how to be gentle and kind
To train and direct his dear little mind
To help him live by every rule
And get the best he can from school."

"Whose child is this?" I asked once more
Just as the little one entered the door
"Ours," said the parent and the teacher as they smiled
And each took the hand of the little child
"Ours to love and train together
Ours this blessed task forever."

Academics aside, with the arrival of the first day of school, I faced having to share the raising of my two conscientious young minds, eager to be intellectually stimulated and coached in their ongoing development of proper values, capacity for empathy, and social consciousness. We'd briefly met both their teachers the Friday before at the school's open house. Davi's third-grade teacher was warm and nurturing, seemingly nonplussed about having a student who had only just started to learn English. As she was of Caribbean descent, I secretly was thrilled with what I knew to be that people's custom to expect children to be obedient, respectful, and submissive to adults of authority. I was leery about Davi's transition to school, his trying behavior from camp still weighing heavily on my mind. I was hopeful for the teacher's guiding hand, within the concrete structure of her classroom and learning environment, to help Davi settle down and respond more adaptively to everyday stressors.

Matheus's fifth-grade teacher, on the other hand, was rather prim and proper as she politely received us. With a bit of awkwardness, she extended her hand to shake, stopping short Matheus's attempt to lean in and embrace her, as he had been used to doing in Brazil. Her classroom was well organized, stocked with tools and paraphernalia collected over the years that suggested the varied seasonings of a veteran teacher. Yet I sensed her diffidence about just what to do with this wild Brazilian child staring at her with sweetness in his innocent brown eyes, waiting for her to take the lead. He spoke barely a lick of English, was essentially two grades behind, and had a past that left one with more questions than answers. I could almost hear echoing in her mind that this was going to be an interesting year. Leaving with Matheus, I prayed the school had made a conscious, deliberate choice of teacher for him based on his needs.

I walked both boys into school that first morning the following Monday. We walked Davi over to the third grade wing first. His teacher was there at the doorway greeting her new students. With a firm, yet nurturing hand she confidently led Davi into the room with the simple statement, "We'll be okay." Feeling as though I was left empty-handed, Davi smiled back at me and, indeed, I then knew it was *okay*. Matheus and I moved onto the fifth-grade wing. His teacher calmly welcomed him into the classroom, this time graciously accepting his hug. She made direct eye contact with Matheus, a basic strategy used for students learning English as a second language (ESOL), before gently telling him, with a few gestures of her hand, "Now, find your desk; unpack your backpack."

I had been concerned about Matheus' transition to school for many weeks. Unlike his brother, he did not express any particular enthusiasm for starting, becoming resistant over the past few weeks to communicating in English. At one point, I overheard Matheus dryly inform Davi, "only talk to me in Portuguese, or I won't answer you." When first speaking with Matheus's teacher the other day, I had briefly mentioned his nervousness about starting, given his being newly arrived from Brazil and feeling handicapped by his limited English proficiency. She seemed sensitive to this upon directing Matheus to his desk, and he, in turn, appeared to perceive her sensitivity. I gave him a thumbs-up and he responded with a slight smile before dutifully searching out his name, seemingly understanding exactly what he'd been directed to do.

* * *

Even before meeting Matheus and Davi, I had ruminated over what to do about their grade placements. Davi was not as difficult once I figured out where he was positioned in the grand scheme of things. Perhaps in keeping tune with the reversal of seasons on the other side of the equator, Brazil's school year cycles from late January to mid December. The boys had recently started the fourth and sixth grades respectively when we began our cohabitation; they were a year ahead of their American counterparts. They were two grades apart, yet three years apart in age. Apparently, Matheus was unexplainably delayed a year from starting school. With Davi's birthday in mid June and the cut-off for grade placement criteria being the end of August, having him repeat the third grade would not seem like much of a retention. He would just be the eldest in his relatively normative grade level group. He never made mention of being bothered by repeating the third grade.

Matheus readily accepted repeating the fifth grade when Lino informed him at our initial meeting. He was so caught up in the moment and eager to please, he would have agreed to anything proposed to him. I was fearful of keeping him back another year, essentially leaving him two years behind, yet I was more fearful of his innocence in the face of starting out in middle school. With him having to contend with learning English, acculturating, adjusting to his new family, and making up for his compromised schooling, I could not bear the thought of throwing him into the mayhem at middle school. I felt his transition to school and life in general would be easier within the context of the more self-contained, controlled structure of an elementary school classroom.

Regardless of the thoughtful reasoning behind my decision to delay Matheus's start at the middle school by a year, none of that mattered to him whenever he grumbled about not liking school. It was my fault he was behind; he was supposed to be in the seventh grade, like Michael. The fact they were only six months apart in age and would have otherwise been together in the same grade was not helpful. Trying to reason with him, getting him to see how much harder the work would have been for him was useless; his narrow mind-set made him refuse to entertain any option other than where he felt he should be. He even ignored my attempts to point out the obvious: I'd had no control over his later start in school, for which there was no going back in time. I stopped responding to his assertions altogether; it took another year or more before he seemed able to give up his struggle with the powerlessness of his school fate in favor of having reached a new comfort zone with his school achievement, personal interests, and peer relations. Maturity-wise, he was right where he needed to be.

Regardless of their resistance in the beginning, both went about their educational pursuits with a serious regard toward achievement. It was my understanding that their mother had taught herself how to read and write and instilled in the boys the importance of study. I took over as their guide, seeking to continue nurturing their self-motivated interests in learning. I also sought to protect their self-confidence from being beaten too much in their struggles to gain English proficiency.

In comparison with some of the other families with whom I became acquainted from the LIMIAR reunion, we had it easy. I heard many parents speak of grappling with learning and attention disorders. To a lesser degree, other more severe emotional and behavioral issues required intensive special education services. Yet what saddened me the most was some of the children's apathy and/or contempt toward school, which I was most fearful of in my own boys. I sought to maintain a constructive partnership with their teachers that first year to hold steady for them the brightest possible beacon of light that radiated promise and hope.

* * *

Homework forever seemed mired in controversy at our house. How much homework was too much? What exactly was I supposed to expect from them? I often was unsure how to handle their homework; I felt learning English was more the priority. In the beginning, I was grateful for the "busy work" of orienting them toward completing their homework and achieving success in the interim. As time passed, I focused more on work meant to supplement what they learned in the classroom, emphasizing practice at applying what they were learning.

I never had a problem getting them to do their homework; both were already conscientious students, as they were known to have been in Brazil. Matheus, especially, was one to sit right down to do his work as soon as he walked in the door from school. He especially appreciated the busy work for its simplicity and subsequent feelings of accomplishment for a job well-done. But when he was expected to leave the safe confines of rote memorization and apply his learning in an unfamiliar, unstructured manner, his frustration began to mount. If I dared try and encourage him to think through what was being asked or presented, he mightily refused in his desperate search for the easy way out. On a few occasions he broke down and cried at the table, his tears of frustration clear signs of the battering of his overall sense of competence and self-esteem.

I struggled with where to draw the line between what I should expect of him and how well he was capable of performing, given his language struggles. Not only were we battling bilingual language issues, but Matheus's speech impediment, with his lisps and tongue misplacements added to his frustration in learning and communicating in English. The swiftness of his brother's increasing proficiency with English also unsettled Matheus, at times fueling extra hostility and resentment toward Davi.

Davi's homework did not fill me with as much trepidation. Spelling words mostly consisted of those spelled phonetically; most of his words still contained only one vowel sound in the middle. He already knew his times tables fairly well, resulting in mostly 100 percent correct worksheets. He also completed his language arts worksheets with a fair amount of independence when using his Portuguese/English dictionary, usually with only minimal direction.

Matheus, on the other hand, brought spelling words home requiring memorization of those nonsensical rules about how some words are spelled a certain way and others are not when it seemed they should be. He found it dizzying to distinguish ah**ea**d, br**ea**d, and sw**ea**ter from such distinct counterparts as b**e**d, st**e**p, and Fr**e**d. His language arts worksheets required me to first type the reading passages and questions into the *tradutor* so his comprehension of what he was to read would more fairly be assessed; he wrote his responses in English. Math worksheets and their word problems required a heavy dose of translating as well. Many times, I relieved Matheus from completing some of the work, crossing out a section too unreasonable to expect him to do.

With my management of these potential roadblocks and his teacher's support of the lead I took at home, Matheus mostly maintained his conscientiousness and commitment to doing his work. The quality of his work, factoring out significant grammatical and spelling issues, tended to be surprisingly high, and more times than not clearly reflected his comprehension of learned concepts. Matheus preferred handling his work independently so long as the structure was clearly laid out. The English tutor from the summer specifically told me she believed Matheus possessed high intelligence. He impressed as one who tended to think deeply and respond knowledgeably, yet Matheus tended to shy away from asserting himself as one who could compete with the best of them. I let go of making too much of an issue out of his errors and misunderstood perceptions in favor of his tenacity to defer to his teacher for how and what he learned about should be handled. I doubted he had experienced much support with his schooling from his family of origin or at the orphanage; for now, he needed to be the master of his domain, and I had to let him discover for himself the ins and outs toward successful school achievement.

In the beginning, Davi tended to be overly dependent in his need for reassurance. He wanted to work in my presence, stopping after every item to ask whether he was correct or ask for what he clearly could look for on his own with the most minimal of effort. He pitched fits when steered toward greater independence, such as finishing all the items of a segment before I would check it. Once he finally began to get my insistence to try first before coming to me, and give up his crying and whining, though usually not until being countered with several ultimatums, Davi's work also tended to clearly reflect his understanding of presented concepts. His resistance first appeared to come from laziness; yet as it became more obvious later on, his frustration was more a product of his boredom.

Chapter 15

The Arrival of the Great Pumpkin

School and the fall season were in full swing when the Jewish High Holy Days of Rosh Hashanah and Yom Kippur presented themselves. I still was vacillating about how to raise the boys in a Jewish family. Even when I first began contemplating adoption, domestically or internationally, I had expected controversy over the matter of religion; I was aware that so many children available for adoption had Christian roots, albeit with varying degrees of faith and spirituality.

In accepting Matheus and Davi's referral, I knew they identified themselves as Christian, yet did not subscribe to any particular denomination. I knew they enjoyed going to church regularly, sang in its choir, and celebrated the Christian holidays. In the Jewish scheme of things, I have a strong Jewish identity, yet rooted more in our collective culture and heritage as opposed to religious observance of my Jewish faith. I regard attending religious services at synagogue to be a chore, for which I rarely derive much spiritual fulfillment.

Being careful not to force upon the boys an expectation to strip away a highly personal, significant piece of their identity, I briefly explained what the holidays were about and their significance for me as a Jew. They were passive in their acceptance and refrained from asking any questions. Even when I fasted for Yom Kippur, they were not particularly interested other than poking fun at me amid my facetious moans and groans preparing their meals that day. Pushing aside any religious or spiritual relevance, they expressed greater interest in the family's gathering in celebration of the holidays.

For *erev* Rosh Hashanah, the eve preceding the first day of the holiday, they were greatly excited to be having the family over to our house for dinner. They took active interest in our shopping for *comida especial* – special food at the supermarket – tidying up the house for our company, and helping prepare the holiday feast. They also inquired about who would be joining us at the table, running down the hallway with every chime of the doorbell in anticipation of the next arrival to their humble abode. We joined together again at their beloved auntie Gayle's house a week later for Yom Kippur's breaking of the fast. Acceptance by those with whom they were most bonded, further reinforcing the sense of belonging long having been absent in their lives, mattered most to them.

Neither had yet expressed specific interest in pursuing a religious faith. I felt it still was premature to broach it with them; adjusting to their new family took greater precedence. With Christmas fast approaching, Chanukah's early arrival, and Michael's bar mitzvah following a mere two weeks after Christmas, I felt their religious identification might soon be more aptly addressed. I was prepared to take advantage of their natural enthusiasm for and familiarity with Christmas to explore further their religious ties, and blending their Christian roots with those of the family's Jewish religion. But for the fall season, I pushed aside any possible religious significance in favor of enriching their sense of belonging with their new family.

* * *

Autumn has long been my favorite season of the year. After the start of the new school year, summer's heat begins to waver in favor of cooler breezes and crisper air. The varied colors of changing leaves and their crackling sound under feet tingles my senses. Its harvest of nature's bounty teems with the ubiquitous appearance of pumpkins and apples. The thrills of trick-or-treating and the dodging of ghouls and goblins on Halloween brings the season into a frenzy, culminating with the cornucopia of Thanksgiving.

Living in South Florida comes with considerable sacrifices; the arrival of the autumn season always leaves me pining for my beloved New England, where I still hoped one day to return to live again. With four ninety-five dollar round-trip air tickets in hand, it was off to Boston with the three boys, including Michael for Columbus Day weekend. I was excited to introduce Matheus and Davi to their first experience of the colors and smells of autumn, back where I am most content: the area in and around Newburyport, Massachusetts. Clear blue skies above, the sporadic need of a light jacket, and a carefully planned itinerary full of fall activities set the tone for the three days. I hoped that corn mazes, leaf peeping, apple picking, fall fairs and festivals, and Halloween haunts at night would instill family bonding in the most special of ways.

We had our sweet moments, including apple picking just over the state line in New Hampshire. The boys happily cooperated with one another, traipsing from tree to tree in search of those out-of-the-way apples high above, just waiting to be picked. Cider doughnuts and fresh apple cider hit the spot after a hayride and a stroll through a pumpkin patch. Their shrieks of laughter over the frights in the haunted corn maze one night and then again the following night at a fabricated ghost town kept the mood fun and lighthearted. Yet finding myself having to negotiate narrow minded, stubborn perspectives often made getting there an uncertain undertaking.

For the most part, Davi kept himself out of the equation; he maintained rather pleasant, agreeable relations that did not induce resentment or petulance from the others. He also was quick to stop the kinds of irritating behaviors in public that caused unwanted attention, and subjected me to unwanted embarrassment. In contrast, Matheus and Michael would not leave each other alone, hanging on to each other, jostling each other, calling each other *gay* . . . until hostility and contempt took over when one became frustrated with the other for having gone too far. The rigidity of Matheus's mind-set reared its ugly head on a few occasions; he just would not let a perceived slight go when he felt wronged, with which his distorted, narrow-minded thoughts often darkened the mood for all of us.

Having pieced together bits of information shared by both boys over the past few months, I'd surmised that Matheus had been subject to quite a bit of verbal abuse by his birth family. Being left to contend with feelings of worthlessness helped explain why he tended to dig in his heels whenever he felt offended, warding off those unresolved feelings he so badly wanted to leave behind. My trying to explain that to an overheated nephew innocently trying to assert himself only complicated matters. Michael often was unforgiving as well, having trouble understanding the influence of Matheus's past as it still influenced his unreasonable behavior, requiring *everyone's* patience and understanding to remediate.

To prevent a particularly heated episode from escalating further, I forced Matheus to take a time-out to assist with letting go his hurt and resentment, reconnecting him to feeling loved and valued. I physically held him down, drawing him onto my lap after he threw Davi's ice cream to the ground, making other threatening gestures; he'd already lost his ice-cream treat for his ill-mannered behavior. He promptly took it out on his brother, who had been innocently enjoying his ice-cream. I was able to maintain a light hold on him, as he acquiesced rather easily. His tears flowed and he held on tighter as I reflected to him how much we loved and esteemed him. The sincerity of his hurt left Michael wide-eyed, and more open and accepting that there was more to Matheus's rigid stance than could simply be reasoned. At least for the rest of our trip, Michael was noticeably more patient, practiced greater restraint in instigating, and was quick to defend Matheus's position, even when he was clearly in the wrong. Matheus, in turn, was becoming less defensive; as if keeping in tune with the falling of autumn's leaves, he was starting to leave behind the heat of summers past.

* * *

Eagerly anticipating trick-or-treating, the boys were hopeful for the kind of Halloween they had seen on American television shows and movies. The Halloween celebrations started a few days early, with parties in each of their classrooms for early release day. They were eager to show off to me their candied treasures, arts-and-crafts creations, and toy trinkets. I had to stop them short with a discussion about limits on the candy they already were primed to gorge on. Before turning in for bed, we dimmed the lights and tuned in to my all-time favorite, the Halloween adventures of the Peanuts gang in *It's the Great Pumpkin, Charlie Brown.*

The following day, for $3.88 apiece we bought two pumpkins from Walmart to carve our own jack-o'-lanterns. Apart from my newfound budgetary constraints, I was not about to spend more than five times the money for the privilege of snatching a pumpkin from a makeshift patch set up in a parking lot, only for it to collapse into a mildewed mess from the heat and humidity of the Florida sun after just a couple of days. They tore into the guts of their pumpkins and eagerly directed the carving of the facial features. We positioned their finished jack-o-lanterns by the front door with their pumpkins' ghoulish smiles, waiting to greet the trick-or-treaters. As an unknown author composed:

> *An orange pumpkin, fat as can be.*
> *Carve a face so he can see.*
> *Put in a candle, light the light.*
> *A jack-o'-lantern for Halloween night!*

The next night we took out their costumes for a dry run; a classmate's mother from Matheus's class banded with another mother to throw a Halloween party. Matheus decided he wanted to be a pirate, like Jack Sparrow of the *Pirates of the Caribbean,* and Davi wanted to be a policeman. I avoided the sterile, manufactured look of store-bought costumes in favor of original, homespun creations, again keeping in tune with a now tighter budget than I was used to in my single days. Besides, one of my most memorable Halloween experiences concerned a Superman costume my mother fashioned from a sewing kit and articles of matched clothing. It was all about the flowing red cape and the prominent yellow S sewn on a red cable-knit sweater.

I wanted to capture the spirit of making their own costumes, bringing them in on the fun in sorting through a mound of throwaway clothes. Davi quickly gravitated toward black dress pants and a white collared polo shirt to wear with a belt and dressy black shoes. We made a police badge out of cardboard and aluminum foil; Matheus even cut out a yellow P for its cover as a face-saving measure after calling Davi's costume *stupid*. Other accessories we found included a gun and handcuffs from Jake. We found the perfect collared dark blue shirt for Matheus, with a V-neck and grommet holes easily threaded with a cord, making up a series of vertical X's, authenticating the pirate look. We tore off the sleeves of a red fleece jersey, splitting the front to make a vest. We put together the remnants to make a matching belt, threading it through the belt loops of worn, stained gray baseball pants. With shredded pant legs, paired with old black sneakers, the pirate look was nearly complete. We accessorized with a plastic sword and a black-and-white striped sash from Michael to tie around Matheus's head; for another two dollars, I bought a small makeup kit that included a black eye patch and a gold hoop earring.

If only the party had lived up to the anticipation and fun involved in making their costumes. Matheus seemed to enjoy seeing some of his friends out of the classroom, yet I felt bad seeing him regarded more as a mascot as opposed to having any real, meaningful friendships with his classmates. I saw how much his sluggish progress with English still limited him socially. Davi did not know anyone and would have been very happy to leave after half an hour. The music was blaring, courtesy of one of the dads acting as a deejay spinning records. There were no lights on, save for sparkling reflections off a lone disco ball in the middle of the dance floor. Parents mostly sat at long tables eating and watching while the kids milled around on the dance floor. Davi and I were wallflowers, barely even speaking to each other. It was too loud for me to hear someone talking, let alone someone else being able to hear me.

On Halloween morning, I struggled to get out of bed, still reeling from the ill effects of a four a.m. hurling of whatever it was that disagreed with me from the party. I shuffled out of the shower to a handwritten note taped to the mirror from Davi, simply wishing me, *Happy Halloween!!! Today is Halloween . . . please enjoy this day . . . enjoy your family!!! Thank you for everything. I love you.* I mustered through the morning, trying to keep their excitement for the night's trick-or-treating plans from grating too much on my nerves, jangling against my raw, unsettled stomach. Yet how was I to know that a single piece of candy would turn out to be the catalyst for a major meltdown for Matheus?

Becoming more impatient with the limits imposed over not being able to have any more than the one piece of candy with lunch, Matheus grumbled that he should be able to have it any time just because he wanted it. He became incensed when I absentmindedly popped a piece of candy into my mouth, having forgotten for the moment that I was no longer accountable only to myself. Usually having been able to keep my behavior in sync with my word, I should have then recognized my blunder, relenting with good humor and a piece of candy in return. He did not give me a chance. Matheus exploded in a tirade, then stormed around the house, knocking a couple of chairs over when I reinforced Davi with a piece of candy for promptly dropping the issue rather than continuing to harass me.

A prolonged struggle ensued between us as Matheus refused to stay in his room for a time-out, relentlessly attempting to push past me as I stood in the doorway. I backed off and told him that unless we discussed this chain of events, he would not be going trick-or-treating; if he chose not to cooperate by staying behind with Grandma and Poppa, he would not be playing soccer at the start of the season in two weeks. I set the timer for half an hour and told him I would be ready to speak with him then; we were running out of time before it was time to leave for auntie Gayle's house. When I approached him after the timer went off, I found him staring off into space, struggling to contain the build-up of tears as I tried to speak with him. Refusing to engage with me, he left the room.

I went ahead and got Davi ready with his costume, purposely doing so out in the open so we were visible to Matheus. When Davi alerted me that Matheus was crying, I told him I was sorry to hear of his brother's sadness, but it seemed he was making a choice not to problem-solve with me, apparently choosing not to join us for trick-or-treating. I told Davi he was welcome to speak with his brother, which he promptly did. Maybe five minutes later, Matheus showed up at my side, murmuring an apology. He was able to express his frustration with becoming easily angered, fearful of being treated unfairly. He still struggled with his trust in me to care for him, yet I was encouraged that he took advantage of saving face under the guise of his brother's assistance. My structured, impassive guidance, meant to curb his behavior and help him move past the irrelevance of his righteous indignation, was working. With nothing else standing in the way, and their excitement building as we set out, another unknown author's fitting verse came to mind:

> *Jack-o'-lantern smiling bright*
> *Witches flying in the night*
> *Ghosts and goblins, cats and bats*
> *Witches with their funny hats*
> *A full moon can't be beat*
> *As we go out to trick-or-treat.*

Before joining Auntie Gayle and Jake for trick or treating in their neighborhood, the three of us stopped to show off for Grandma, Poppa, and Michael. Claiming he was too mature for trick-or-treating, Michael did not want to go, refusing to come along to at least share in the boys' excitement of their first Halloween. I felt badly that I had overlooked Michael, taking it for granted that he naturally would have wanted to join us, hoping he would come around. I let him maintain his indifference, as he claimed he was "too old" and that he was too "mature" for such frivolity. It was only after we had gotten up to leave my parents' house when Michael weakly expressed his doubts about staying behind, yet I was too caught up in the boys' excitement to notice. He needed his ego stroked and I missed the chance.

The boys were happy to fraternize with Jake and his friends as they made their way from house to house. Excitedly chanting, "Trick-or-treat," they were delighted over the treats they hoped to get with each ring of the doorbell. Davi may have been a little overly enthusiastic, as he was somewhat grabby with the candy before it was handed to him; I reminded him several times not to ask for extra candy, and at one point I chastised him when it almost seemed there were more empty wrappers than candy in his bag. As had been usually the case, Matheus tired easily, being the first to wane in his excitement. His complaints were frequent: "My feet hurt . . . I need water . . . Why do we have to walk so far?" I ignored him, as I determinedly kept the mood light, and my intentions for the evening positive. I was vindicated as he could not bear to miss out on even one house, and despite the afternoon's power struggle, Matheus did not eat one piece of candy along the way.

On our way home, Michael called to ask how the boys did. Perhaps he was calling to find out whether he was missed, yet his genuineness touched me. He still cared, yet having begun to notice how he was becoming more emotionally distant from the three of us, I was becoming more uncertain how to properly answer to his growing discontent.

* * *

Matheus's tendency to maintain his relentlessly black-and-white perspective and his difficulty letting go of whatever might irritate him tended to sour the mood for everybody. Trying to handle his initial outbursts of anger and frustration while maintaining any semblance of rationality, sensibility, and fairness was nerve-racking. Having grown wiser at such times, I began to interact with Matheus only minimally to keep myself in control, until he had calmed down enough to entertain even the slightest shade of gray. In the meantime, I continued to assert myself as his authority by relying on the external forces of limit-setting, consequences, and structure to buffer his feeling out of control on the inside.

Limits could be as simple as withholding a lone privilege, or "Don't ask for anything until . . ." Along with having to comply with whatever was needed, regardless of his insolence before, the expectation of an apology and/or making up for a particular transgression became the standard expectation before more "normal" relations could continue. His petulant attitude could last several days. Sometimes he came around on his own. Other times I would stumble across just the right discourse in passing that would loosen his stubborn resolve. Once he had calmed down and was receptive to what anyone had to say, Matheus usually would express regret and some remorse for his wrongdoing, and become engaging again. As time wore on, his behavioral challenges became less frequent, less intense, and farther spread apart.

Matheus began to meet with an outpatient counselor just before the winter holidays, after a heated outburst in which he ran off to a small neighborhood park nearby. When I reached the perimeter of the park after waiting to see if he would come back on his own, he was just beginning to make his way home; he accepted my outstretched hand and minimal prompt: "Come on; let's go home." We walked back to the house in silence, side by side, holding hands. Back at the house, Matheus had tearfully acknowledged ongoing difficulty with his angry feelings, saying that he felt angry "every day." After a lengthy, torturous process working with the mental health center for an assignment, a stroke of luck matched us with a seasoned therapist who was Brazilian and spoke Portuguese.

I knew we were in for an uphill battle when Matheus steadfastly refused to speak Portuguese to the therapist, claiming he no longer had enough command of the language to speak competently. He at least agreed for her to alternate speaking both English and Portuguese to him. Her meeting with him at the house for his counseling sessions kept the surroundings relaxed and familiar. With a Brazilian flair, Matheus's therapist sought to establish a meaningful rapport with him, framing her relations within the context of cultural familiarity. To the boys' delight, she came on occasion with popular Brazilian cookies and other familiar treats. She also took care to entice Matheus with materials that tapped into his artistic and gaming interests, softening his contempt for counseling. She even utilized a session for all of us to cook together a traditional Brazilian dinner of chicken and rice and beans, fostering family bonding while we all prepared a meal most dearly familiar to them.

Counseling sessions quickly tended to focus on Matheus's need for respect and deference to authority. Therapy sessions sometimes grew heated the narrower and more threatening the focus of the therapeutic work became. On a few occasions I had to firmly remind him of the limits; cooperation was an expectation, not an expendable option. Usually, with his trademark huffing and puffing, he was able to work through his difficulties at the moment with his therapist and return to being more engaging. He began to be more tolerant of the sessions, yet he still kept his therapist at a distance.

Chapter 16

Sibling Rivalry: The Tangled Twisting of Brotherly Ties

My nephew, Michael, had been generous in expressing his enthusiasm about Matheus and Davi's impending arrival, steadfastly claiming they would be his "brothers." Yet his assertions often seemed hollow in contrast to his mounting insecurity over the boys gradually muscling in on his familial territory. I often was too preoccupied, preventing me from paying close attention before I left for Brazil. Usually known to be caring about others' perspectives and feelings, I was hopeful Michael would be unconditional in welcoming the boys into the family. In the beginning, he was.

At first, the three "brothers" played, laughed, and goofed around without a care in the world. Michael seemed eager to share himself, his toys and games, and his time with Matheus and Davi. From the start, they also were eager to relate with Michael, typically greeting him with unbridled enthusiasm. As time elapsed over the course of the first few months, however, patience among the three grew thin. Matheus and Davi became tired of Michael's unrelenting tendency to disparage them for minor indiscretions. He criticized them for chewing with their mouths open and eating too fast, yet he was not one to talk. As they began speaking more English, he also was quick to pick on their mispronunciations; once motivated by benevolence, his corrections seemingly became more aggravated by misguided anger and frustration. The boys were encroaching into his space, gaining the adoration of his grandma and poppa, and taking away his uncle's undivided attention. Life no longer revolved just around him.

Fatherly bonding time I had to give used to be only for Michael. Never mind that as he grew older, he often took it for granted, casually dismissing my attempts to spend time with him. Having to share my attention with two virtual strangers blatantly asserting themselves as two rather needy strangers began to grate on Michael's nerves. Because he had perceived me as a father figure over the years, I can only imagine how much of an insult it might have felt for him to hear Matheus and Davi address me as *Father*, laying claim to me in a way he theoretically could not. Many times I caught Michael jokingly assert his injured pride and counter their assertions in referring to me as "my father" or "my uncle". He would deliberately do so in front of the boys for their ears, and perhaps mine as well, trying to lay the same claim on me that he'd had before they came. I had to ask him several times to stop purposely arousing the boys in such ways that needlessly fueled their insecurity about their sense of belonging.

I was too overwhelmed in the beginning months, often forgetting my need to be more sensitive to the hurt he was harboring inside, manifested by his often unsolicited verbal jabs and, physical pokes, and his poor tolerance of and lack of sensitivity to their emotional needs. Michael was already struggling with the recent passing of his mother, feeling even more adrift than before even though he'd had no acquaintance with her since he was a baby. His father was an unknown entity, and my father's cancer perennially loomed over our family's welfare like a thunderous black cloud.

One evening I pulled Michael aside for a talk, trying to reach out to him. Initially resistant, he conceded in allowing "just ten minutes." I tried to focus more on his feelings and validate how "annoying" he sometimes found Matheus and Davi to be. In turn, he allowed me to reiterate the need for him to remember where they came from. He and I had to contend with their baggage together in helping them adjust to being a part of our family. I realized I had overdone it when his eyes glazed over in mid-sentence. All three boys tended to complain that I talked too much. Michael was more interested in acknowledging his missing our one-on-one time together. "We will never go on another trip just us again," he wistfully claimed.

As we amiably discussed our thoughts further, Michael never strayed past the surface, telling me about how he was really feeling. I made sure to validate him by telling him how much our exclusive one-on-one time meant to me as well. Yet having to manage the pull of multiple priorities, I also often felt the compromise in our relationship. I also felt a sense of loss. I pledged to prioritize better, now that schedules were falling into place and planning was easier with greater stability in our comings and goings. Michael and I would have more alone time together, allowing us to continue the special bond we'd shared over the years. With Matheus and Davi in the mix, I saw that I needed to find a better balance with the closeness of the relationship between Michael and me.

* * *

Back on the home front, I was beginning to feel more skilled at responding to the squabbling between Matheus and Davi in a way that took advantage of the teachable moment rather than just rushing for a Band-Aid. It started innocently enough one early Saturday morning just a few weeks before school was starting, when Davi excitedly roused me awake the one morning I could sleep in a little bit. I hid my discontent behind an emotionless facade, weakly smiling and nodding to him as I sat up. Content that I was getting up, Davi twirled himself out of my room with the carefree energy of a whirling dervish.

It did not take long for the mood to darken. As I was getting ready to blow-dry my hair after a shower, Davi marched into my bathroom and announced, "Matheus bateu"—"Matheus hit." I took a deep breath to keep my wits about me, struggling to maintain a cool, rational mind-set that would lend itself to a resolution. In the absence of any hysteria accompanying Davi's announcement, I deferred to finishing my morning routine before calmly making my way over to Matheus, with an expectant Davi in tow.

I found Matheus in his room on the floor, quietly playing with LEGOs. He matter-of-factly announced, "I no bateu Davi," before I even had a chance to say a word. He refused to say anything further, ignoring my request for his version of what transpired. In between laundry, cooking, and clearing out the dishwasher, I got each of them on the *tradutor* to type out their varying versions of the story. Both were unwavering in the way they presented their perceptions of what occurred. I was starting to feel intimidated about how to proceed as a neutral, authoritative party; both boys clearly were in the wrong, yet neither was willing to entertain personal accountability in favor of blaming the other.

With no peace treaty in sight, we needed to get started with the afternoon's scheduled activities involving haircuts, birthday present shopping, and attending my good friend's son's first birthday party. I could not afford the risk of one, the other, or even both having a meltdown and derailing the day. I commanded a cease-fire, communicating that some of what I had digested seemed understandable while some did not. Unless I got a more complete story both of them could agree on, the prospect of playing their video games in the evening would be put on hold. Once we were out of the house and going about our afternoon's business, I was intrigued by how calm and seemingly unaffected both boys seemed. I also was discouraged by the inevitability of having to take away their video privileges as opposed to having sorted out their problems.

The boys were delighted about getting their first American haircuts, enjoying the full wash, cut, and blow dry experience with my stylist. They were pleased with Michele's personalized, warm, motherly attention. Shopping afterward for Benjamin's birthday present, the boys were eager to scout around for a suitable gift, happily endorsing the final selection. At the party, they were well received by many of the party's guests; several knew beforehand of their adoption from Brazil, and they asked about the boys' adjustment so far.

Both Matheus and Davi were personable, albeit rather cheesy at times; one or the other would invariably stick his face with a broad smile into view wherever a camera should happen to come out, regardless of whether he was meant to be in the picture or not. They also heartily ate as if they had never seen food before, yet with respectable manners intact. They showered Benjamin with lots of attention and seemed genuine in their expressed affection toward him. Both boys had a grand time, leaving the party in positive spirits.

On the way to the store to make a return, they asked about their video gaming time for when we got home, as though nothing had transpired earlier. I continued to maintain a noncommittal stance, reminding them of their need to cooperate with each other toward an agreeable, logical version of what had happened that morning. This time, each began to add more to their original stories, piercing their initially self-professed airtight defenses. We were progressing to another level in our discussions, moving slightly past inflexible mindsets that had us meandering around in circles.

Although both had apparently started out playing cooperatively with each other that morning, each admitted to having disagreed with how the other one wanted to play. Matheus, being the one who typically resisted compromise, promptly ordered Davi out of his room. Davi refused, at which Matheus began to shove him out—"But I no bateu." Davi, in turn, admitted the possibility of an *accident* with the smack of a wayward hand as he was pushed out of the room, rather than its being a purposeful assault against him. Still self-righteous, Davi countered that it may have been an accident, yet Matheus was supposed to "Say he sorry, no?"

As he had been known to do, Davi had clearly overreacted to his own hurt feelings. A simple apology may have spared his feelings, helping him to save face; yet, expecting an apology from his brother, who was all about saving face himself, would not have been realistic. Matheus would regard apologizing as admittance of wrongdoing; he might not even have been aware of accidentally hitting his brother during their heated exchange. If he believed he did not do anything wrong, there would be no meeting his brother half-way for the greater good of their relationship. Upon our return home, I thanked them for their cooperation and honesty. I instructed them to go about their business for the time being. I needed some time to think through their new assertions and how best to respond.

On the *tradutor*, I typed, *Davi, you were asked or told to leave Matheus's room. Matheus has every right to tell you to leave his room when he wants to, even if he might be acting like a little child. You should have left and that would have been it.* I then typed, *Matheus, you should not have used force to get Davi out of your room. You need to keep your hands to yourself, with no pushing, no grabbing—all of that can lead to hitting. You need to come and get me if Davi is not cooperating. I can understand how you may have accidentally hit Davi even though you might not have intended to. You were angry and were not thinking straight.* I concluded, *I like how the two of you worked this out together and came to an agreement on what happened. Because of that, we can go back to normal. Otherwise, I would have had no choice but to wait until tomorrow to start fresh. Play-station or any other privileges would not have been possible this evening. If I have two different sides of the story, it is not right for me to take one side unless I know enough information to do so.*

So rested another fall out between brothers. It was my *Father Knows Best* moment for the day. I wondered whether Jim Anderson ever went off to work still unnerved by the potential ramifications of a tiff between Princess and Bud over breakfast. Parenthood for me did not necessarily fit within the neat confines of a sitcom episode. As I learned that day, too often issues between the boys could not be addressed fully on the spot; time was needed as a way of smoothing out rougher edges before the inner workings of their resolve could be handled. Because I had not been raising them from birth, and instilling in them my values since the beginning of their lives, I felt as though I had achieved a breakthrough in my parenting.

I was able to resolve a conflict between Matheus and Davi that threatened to escalate into the kind of fighting that had gotten them separated into different group homes. I still fumbled my way through the language gaps between my thoughts and what I could verbalize in engaging the boys when trying to negotiate their conflicts. I had been acting on instinct rather than from a strategic standpoint. Yet I maintained my focus on what was logical and reasonable to counter my own fears about the chaos that prevailed in their earlier lives, and its constant, intrusive threat of disruption to our lives together. In turn, the more secure they were becoming, the more trusting they were in letting me handle some of the rougher edges of themselves.

Chapter 17

'Tis the Season

With a drop in humidity and the faint hint of a cool breeze in the air, Winter's muted appearance coincided with Thanksgiving's arrival. The boys came home from school with tidbits of understanding about the meaning of our season of giving thanks. Davi was quite forthright in expressing his gratitude for "my family" and "my father." Matheus tended to refrain from any such verbalizations; he preferred more physical expressions of his gratitude, with his deep hugs, kisses, and the soft, penetrating gaze of his eyes.

Our family gatherings started to become routine for the boys, with their partaking in the fuss over preparing the holiday meal and becoming used to the same core family members in attendance. This time around it was back to Auntie Gayle's house. The four boys played together nonstop; they engaged without apparent conflict among them. Even when frustration cast a slight shadow over Davi's mood, he seemed largely unaffected. He sometimes withdrew briefly to take a self-imposed time-out to collect himself before bouncing back into the fold. It was a free-spirit kind of a day, similar to my childhood days with my cousins; we always looked forward to being together, regardless of whether it was for a specific planned event or a spur-of-the-moment get-together. It always was innocent fun, as we blissfully left the adults behind to their business and idle chatter. I hoped to share that kind of innocence with the boys, countering the unforgiving ruthlessness of their marked past.

* * *

With the boys asleep at Grandma and Poppa's house, I hit the mall at four a.m. on Black Friday with some semblance of an agenda for what to buy. I was determined to balance a tight budget while still fulfilling over-the-top wishes. Chanukah was due to arrive early that year, beginning a mere six nights following Thanksgiving. I had only the weekend to try to make the most of whatever deals I could find and load up our snowflake-decorated fireplace, fronted by a small tree decked out with blue and white lights, otherwise known as our Chanukah bush. We had discussed forgoing a traditional Christmas tree in celebration of Chanukah, but I wanted to acknowledge the season in a comforting way that was respectful of their Christian roots.

The boys met the prospect of eight nights of presents with wide eyes of delirious disbelief that helped distract their focus from Christmas, still another three weeks away. Seeing their wrapped presents decking the fireplace only added to their excitement; I was all too pleased with the fruits of my labor. I'd stayed within a reasonable budget, resisting the urge to spend more money so as to make our first holiday season together as a family grander. Inevitably, at first sight of the presents Matheus quipped, "Davi has five presents and I have four." He eased up on feeling short changed when I informed him that a fifth present was still on its way. Davi quickly countered his brother's self-centeredness by saying the holiday was not supposed to be about the number of presents. Perhaps taking his cue from his self-professed beliefs about Thanksgiving, he remarked that it was about being "grateful for what you got and the family you had." Matheus did not respond.

Neither needed to worry; each received the same number of gifts, including one large package, two midsize ones, and two smaller sized presents. With three of Matheus's presents reflecting his preference for all toys LEGO, I tried broadening Davi's focus onto other toys, seeking to lessen the frequency and intensity of the power struggles between the two over the LEGOs. Other presents focused on Davi's still keen interests in imaginative play and Matheus's seemingly growing interest in artistic expression. I also selected presents for them to open together, where sharing was expected, including video games and each of the three *Lord of the Rings* DVD videos, snatched in a Walmart doorbuster special for $1.96 apiece that especially appealed to my thrifty, bargain hunting ways. The boys' happiness and satisfaction with each present unwrapped was what I'd hoped for, even distracting them from their seemingly unrelenting urge to watch television.

Regardless of how trivial the event might have been, their excitement did not seem to waver over the course of the holiday as they looked forward to the planned celebrations for each night. It did not matter whether the occasion just consisted of a simple dinner of potato latkes and lighting the menorah among the three of us, a family dinner with Grandma, Poppa, and Michael, or a Chanukah party with the family at large. They even got to play in fake snow pumped out from shaved ice on a truck at a Chanukah party hosted by the foster care agency where I still occasionally attended the monthly parent meetings.

Soon after the passing of the eighth night, when our neighbor asked the boys whether they were getting ready for Christmas, I was unprepared for how they promptly responded that they did not celebrate Christmas—"We're Jewish. We celebrated Chanukah." I still had not engaged them in any direct discussion about adopting the Jewish faith; nor was I even sure it should be an expectation for them. I did not want them to automatically subscribe to the Jewish faith just because. I wanted them to make a conscious choice on their own with respect to their religious faith . . . and soon enough they would.

* * *

In preparing for the eighth night of Chanukah, I made a big deal about how the best present was saved for last and that it was too big to put out with the others by the fireplace—and it was for all three boys. I'd already told Michael of the plans to make sure I had his cooperation. He seemed genuinely excited about being a part of the big surprise, eager to be in on the excitement of yet another first-time experience for Matheus and Davi. I marveled to myself how indifferent to his cousins Michael was only just a year ago when first shown the video images of his cousins at Chanukah time. After lighting the menorah, Michael held out the envelope with all three of their names on it, along with three small mesh bags of Chanukah gelt: chocolate coins encased in gold foil. Together, they took out the card and read its printed summons: *The keys to the castle . . . where dreams come true . . . the most magical place on earth . . . is where the Matloff boys will travel . . . to Walt Disney World!*

Throughout the holiday season I could not help but notice that the majority of the cards I received came addressed as a plural . . . to the Matloff *family*, Gary Matloff *and sons*, and so on. Being recognized as a family entity was essentially the meaning of the holidays for us this year. I could not think of any better way to exemplify this than to take the ultimate family vacation to Walt Disney World over the winter break. Michael expressed his excitement in taking on a mentoring role in a place dear and familiar to him, yet magical for the boys, with its being their first time. It was with heavy hearts that we would be leaving my parents behind; my father was not up to going, and he did not take it well. When we lit the menorah for the boys to open their card, he stayed in the family room, too hurt to share in the boys' excitement. He knew he had to save his strength for Michael's bar mitzvah a mere two weeks after our return from Disney World.

All three of the boys were excited about the trip, but Matheus and Davi did not have any real sense of what to expect. If Michael had his way, it would only have been about the thrill rides and skipping out on those that held less excitement for him, rather than for one who had never been to Disney World. His patience sometimes wore thin when he had to tolerate and accommodate the other boys' desire to try every new thing, regardless of how less "mature" it seemed to Michael. I often had to remind Michael about his previously stated desire for Matheus and Davi to feel Disney's magic as first-timers. It was not up to him to decide for the boys what they should like. Albeit with a silent roll of his eyes, Michael stood off to the side without disparaging comment as Matheus and Davi delightfully got to be Jedi Knight trainees, sparring with light sabers in hand against Darth Maul. Most of the time Michael also graced us with his presence for photo opportunities with the Disney characters, even when we had to go out of our way to stand in a line, so long as he had the promise of a more stimulating activity afterward. The boys' genuinely charmed reactions to meeting the characters was endearing.

The weather could not have been more perfect, even if at times a little cold for the boys' comfort levels, yet with clear skies, just like the weather we'd had in Massachusetts two months before. The crowds were manageable, with minimal lines for rides most of the time; the boys easily got to go on their favorite thrill rides several times throughout the day. Being on the dining plan for lunches and dinners, including nightly snacks with reservations prearranged each night for dinner made meal times hassle-free.

All three of the boys' behavior, overall, was improved in comparison to our time in Massachusetts. A newer dynamic started to play out as Matheus and Michael began to bond more with each other, squeezing Davi out of the picture. Even though he seemed content with me as his companion for walking around and going on the rides, it sometimes was at the expense of being excluded, pushed out of the way by the older two. Several times I had to interject, safeguarding the further bruising of his ego.

Matheus and Michael still engaged with each other in a manner that sometimes stood out in public; too much noise, jostling, and chortling required constant redirection. Comparing us with some of the other families with seemingly well-behaved children, I was embarrassed. I struggled to keep my bruised ego from dampening my spirits, and spoiling the boys' fun. Sometimes after I'd had to interject in a firm manner, Matheus would take umbrage, with his typical "don't tell me what to do" mantra. Michael, in turn, sometimes followed Matheus's lead with an "in your face" disrespect. Even so, there still were no blow-ups, and the boys were more responsive to my call for more appropriate behavior. Taking on Disney in a structured way, and using meal times as prolonged down times, helped with the management of the long days. At the very least, the boys gave no resistance to bed once we made our way back to the hotel.

A Disney vacation turned out to be more than suitable for where Matheus and Davi were at that time in their development and how much they had adapted to their new lives. There always was something pleasing to see and/or do to satiate their need for stimulation. Matheus and Davi were open to anything, except when Michael would object to whatever he just knew would be "lame." Like the domino effect, Matheus would follow suit and assert his reticence rather than succumb to his latent interests. My getting the boys onto my old-time favorite Carousel of Progress ride only inspired resentment, thanks to Michael's vociferous objections of how "stupid" the ride was. Unfortunately, neither Michael nor Matheus allowed the ride's whimsy to take over their sour disposition, as they sulked their way through it. Not until we moved on to the next distraction did their mood lighten.

Visiting Disney during the winter break makes it difficult for anyone to overlook the festive ambience that characterized the park, as it was all-decked out for the holidays. Growing up, I resented being Jewish because we did not partake in holiday decorating. I used to love being invited to our friends' house across the street to help decorate their Christmas tree. One year I rebelled, buying Christmas lights with my allowance and stringing them up in my bedroom. My parents did not say a word, feeling secure that it was not about my dissatisfaction with my Jewish faith, but just the desire for more of the holiday spirit.

Trying to keep up with some of the familiar rituals of their Christian upbringing, I did not want Matheus and Davi to look back to this first year as something of a sterilized version of the holidays. Even before the start of Chanukah, we strung up blinking blue and white snowflake lights about the fireplace, decorated a Chanukah bush, and watched the holiday DVD standards, including A Charlie Brown Christmas, How the Grinch Stole Christmas, and Frosty the Snowman. We also took walks around the neighborhood at night to check out the lights and decorations of the other houses. It was timely that one of our days at Disney was on Christmas, where we were away from any direct pressure to acknowledge the day in its more religious form. Still, while waiting for our dinner reservations at the Animal Kingdom Lodge on Christmas Eve, Matheus and Davi were delighted with the chance to sit on Santa's lap. I could not help but wonder what they asked for from *Papai Noel* this time, and what it was they had asked for the previous year—and whether they had gotten what they wanted.

Chapter 18

Passage to Manhood

Life is full of changes, passages, and growth. The day of Michael's bar mitzvah finally arrived, marking the symbolic passage from boyhood to manhood. Up until now, Matheus and Davi had been observers, watching from the sidelines as Michael progressed in his training. They patiently waited at the synagogue many afternoons for Michael to finish with his Hebrew tutor, tolerated the impromptu practicing of his prayers and his Haftorah and Torah portions, and schlepped with me to different jewelry stores to pick out the right Chai . . . "Life" or Star of David charm and complementary gold chain. They questioned me from time to time, engaging me in conversation about what a bar mitzvah was, and Judaism in general. We also attended several Friday-night services, for which they dutifully sat with prayer books open, trying to follow along. One day in the midst of the frenzy surrounding the preparations, Davi abruptly came over to me, ready to proclaim what he apparently had been thinking through on his own for quite some time.

"Father, I have good news and bad news," Davi declared in a playful tone. Fearing the worst, I asked him what it was he wanted to tell me.

"The good news is . . . I am going to be Jewish." After taking a moment to get over the shock of the abruptness of his statement, I asked what made him come to such a realization. He promptly replied, "Jewish is my family and I am part of the family, so I will be Jewish . . . and the bad news is that I want to do . . . I don't know what you call that, what Michael is learning. I want to do that."

"You mean you want to go to Hebrew school?" I asked, trying to hide the incredulity in my tone, and refraining from asking him whether he should become more proficient in English first.

"Yes, Father, I want to do that."

"Why is that bad news?"

"Because you have to pay for it."

I was unable to stifle a laugh, reassuring Davi that it did not matter what he and his brother wanted to become involved in. If they were serious and committed to making the most of whatever endeavor they wanted to pursue, paying for it would not be an issue in spite of my spendthrift ways.

I also took a step back and marveled how Davi and I were suddenly having meaningful dialogues in English. He was speaking with very little trace of an accent, and was rather fluent in his fitting use of vocabulary and phrasing. Matheus and I still relied on the *tradutor* for assistance in communicating; he was more hesitant, and subsequently slower in adapting to English as his preferred means to communicate. I still had to mix Portuguese wording in with my English phrasing for him, yet Davi maintained a preference for communicating only in English, earnestly asking what a particular word meant or how to say something. Matheus still refrained from showing a committed interest in speaking English. I did not wonder so much how Matheus's resistance still was influenced by his speech impairment, but perhaps now more so his insecurity and emotional constraints.

Matheus remained noncommittal to adopting the Jewish faith, not professing any interest with his brother's choices.

Still, he willingly attended services at synagogue, carefully following along, reading through the English wording of the Hebrew prayers, and I often spied him moving his mouth as if singing along with the repetitive parts of the chants. Even so, at one of the jewelry stores, when we were surveying the charms, his eyes drifted away from the Jewish symbols and he wistfully stated his desire for a cross "with the man on it," still feeling beholden to his Christian roots. I repeatedly reassured him that his choice of religion would not dictate how I felt about him, yet how pleased I was with his willingness to participate and be involved in the holidays and other rituals involving the family's Jewish faith. More simply, I communicated to him that his religious convictions would always be his choice, and I would be respectful and supportive no matter his interests.

My experience thus far with Matheus taught me not to push him; he was one who must be in control over his destiny, and no one was to tell him otherwise. Just the mere thought of his feeling directed in a certain way was enough to result in the digging in of his heels. His religious preference would be his choice. As much as Davi expressed his desires to embrace Judaism as an integral part of his personal identity, I knew it to be more a function of his desire to align with his new family than anything else at this point. Though I knew Matheus did not yet feel as connected with his new family to make such personal choices for himself, I also felt that his interest in choosing a path for his spirituality was not as straightforward as it was for Davi. The more I validated Matheus for his *choice*, the more he was feeling in control—and feeling freer to align with me as his father and us as his family. This was more important at this point than his religious preference.

At the conclusion of the morning's bar mitzvah service, I spoke to the congregation in my speech about how in the eyes of G-d, Michael was called to the Torah to become "responsible for observing the commandments of the Torah. The purpose of which is to keep his life focused on what is truly important: family, community, and spiritual relationship with G-d." I firmly believe keeping one's life focused on these tenets of an adaptive and connected lifestyle is the true pathway toward passage into manhood, transcending any one's choice of an organized religion.

* * *

Michael's bar mitzvah performance was a standout; he chanted his prayers and readings in a manner seemingly effortlessly. Michael was poised and emanated confidence and humility as he stood up at the bema, the platform from which services are conducted in a synagogue. Indeed, consistent with my speech to the congregation, he conducted himself in a manner that was reflective of my expressed hopes for him for the future: to "affirm himself positively and act in a manner that reflects pride, dignity, and self-esteem." I was so focused on his moment, I didn't pay as close attention as usual to my sons. I did not need to worry, as they fended for themselves quite well; they were well behaved, sociable, and sincere in their interest in supporting Michael.

When I was called up to recite the beginning and concluding Hebrew prayers for one of Michael's Torah portions, the boys came up with me to the bema. They stood alongside me, neatly groomed and dapper in their brand-new suits. I wondered how the three of us, together as a family, might have looked to our family and friends, many of whom were first seeing and personally meeting the boys on this day. The curiosity factor was quite high. Being respectful and congenial to all who approached them, Matheus and Davi appeared more real and subsequently normal than what family and friends may have expected . . . pitiable discards acquired off the racks from some clearance sale.

At the reception following the ceremony, the boys seemed to endear themselves to those who interacted with them, or even just viewed them from afar. Davi was the life of the party. He was everywhere, freely mingling here and there, all the while maintaining appropriate behavior. He danced, sated his hearty appetite, played all the games, and chatted with the adults. Many especially could not get over how fluent he already was in English. Matheus also obviously enjoyed joining in on the festivities. Despite adamantly stating that he did not like to dance and therefore would not be dancing at the party, I was stunned when he approached both Gayle's mother and later her mother-in-law to usher them onto the dance floor. He had grown quite fond of his aunt Ina and Grandma Connie. Connie was a retired elementary school art teacher who was generous with her attention to his artistic interests, and Matheus especially enjoyed interacting with her. Although perhaps not so much with other adults, Matheus also freely mingled with Michael's friends.

The candle-lighting ceremony proved to be an emotional highlight of the celebrations. In one of the most notable aspects of a bar mitzvah's celebration, those family and friends most important to Michael in his life were recognized and honored as to the significance of their relationship with him. I wrote up the personalized narratives and chose the appropriate song to coordinate with Michael's expressed thoughts and feelings for each honoree's candle to be lit. I left the candle designated for myself and the boys to Michael and my mother; I was not comfortable knowing ahead of time what might be in his mind and heart about us; nor did I want to influence him.

When our turn came up to light a candle, Michael imparted a poignant narrative, emphasizing the love and affection he attributed to us in his life. "I know there are times when we have our disagreements, but I love you and know that I am making a difference in your life . . . but the truth is you have made an even bigger difference in my life. Our family has been made stronger by your presence." As we got up to light our candle at the end of his narrative, to the tune of Barbra Streisand's "People"—"People who need people . . ." I could barely see two paces in front of me, struggling to hold back tears. It was just the right emotional punch as I caught sight of Matheus's tear stained face; he was openly sobbing as we stood to light the candle. Davi also was teary-eyed. When I bent down to him afterward, Matheus told me, "Michael touched my heart," and I felt as though his loving words left behind a reverberating echo offsetting years of sorrow in the face of rejection and abandonment. Matheus's reaction touched everybody's hearts. He felt connected in a way he likely had been missing out on for a very long time.

Michael had previously asked the boys their favorite Brazilian song, intending to have something played just for them at the party. When called onto the dance floor toward the party's end, they were hesitant at first but sang along with Bruno e Marrone's "Dormi na Praça" – "I Slept in the Square" with obvious pride in their hearts. Upon engaging the *tradutor* for a direct translation, I found the song's lyrics to be rather soulful in their regard for a lone, innocent figure with a troubled past. He slept on a bench in the square, dreaming of one who loved him as expressed through "a sweet kiss and a hug," wanting to stay in the moment rather than be woken up to the lonesome reality of the day. Indeed, although not understood by anyone else at the party, the boys' genuine outpouring of emotion in their singing captivated the room.

Both Matheus and Davi shone on this day; they reveled in feeling accepted, validated, and *wanted* as true members of their claimed family. It was real, not some kind of wish experienced only in a dream, as depicted in the song. This was Michael's day, yet he was generous in sharing of himself in a way that signified the true beginnings of his departure from the self-centered perceptions of childhood toward a gracious passage into manhood.

* * *

Standing on the sidelines, I felt somewhat intimidated seeing the other teammates on Matheus's first venture into American soccer. Matheus might have been signed up to play on the twelve-to-thirteen-year-old league, yet more than a few of these boys towered over him, and were more mature as if they were in their later years of middle school. He was the smallest in size, and the other boys on the team had been playing in the city's league for several years. Lucky enough to be placed on the same team as one of Michael's oldest friends, Matheus appeared comfortable being led out onto the field the night of his first practice.

I informed his coach about the possibility of a language barrier, yet reassuring him of Matheus's good, receptive understanding even if he might not verbally respond. I also made a joke about Matheus's being from Brazil, and that the coach might have a future soccer star on his hands. As he did all season long, Matheus came out of practice that first night all smiles. He was part of what he loved, in an arena comfortably familiar to him. He did not appear to relate to any particular boy throughout the season, yet he blended in, seemingly respected as a fellow player.

Given his difficulties with frustration when feeling provoked and/or unfairly treated, I wondered how Matheus would fare in this highly competitive venture; the potential for temper flare-ups is all too real in any contact sport, especially soccer. Matheus often teasingly complained about how much the coach always seemed to be *yelling* at him to run this way or that way, stay with the ball, and keep his focus. Whenever I heard his coach shout his name in a manner that would surely have unnerved him off the field, Matheus moved as ordered. On the field he was alert, followed directions, and always seemed on the go. During the games, I even heard some of the parents specifically cheer him on. In the words of famous soccer player Pelé, who won three World Cups, "Success is no accident. It is hard work, perseverance, learning, studying, sacrifice and most of all, love of what you are doing or learning to do."

Matheus played well, conscientious of playing as part of the team; he always seemed calm on the field. Occasionally shoved aside by one of the opposing team's players, he remained unflappable, maintaining his focus on the game. He mostly played offense, yet seemed uncomfortable taking a more assertive role shooting the ball for the goal in favor of setting up a play for another to attempt a goal shot. One way or the other, it did not really seem to matter to Matheus, as he always expressed pride in the team's success. Matheus's team, the Crew came into the championship game leading the division with nine wins, three ties, and no losses.

I appreciate the role sports play in a boy's maturation into manhood, with its regard for teamwork and enhancing one's self-discipline, self-esteem, and sportsmanship. Matheus appeared to embody all of these potential benefits of playing sports, unlike the coach's son, an older, seasoned player who ordinarily appeared to be a rather mature, nice young man. He had trouble deferring to unfavorable calls of the referee, however, for which he earned yellow cards that left him vulnerable for ejection from the game. He also seemed to lack a conscientious attitude, resulting in a performance that was jaded, failing to match his potential.

After witnessing the first (and only) goal late in the championship game, after Matheus moved the ball closer in range toward the winning shot, I was touched by the shooter's ecstatically running after Matheus to hug him in a victory romp. Matheus, in turn, greeted his team member with just as much zeal. Mia Hamm, the famous soccer player who had won two World Cups and an Olympic gold medal once said, "I am a member of a team, and I rely on the team, I defer to it and sacrifice for it, because the team, not the individual, is the ultimate champion."

What a lucky break for Matheus's first experience to have been with a coach who was generally fair-minded in his direction and guidance and sincere in his interest in each of his players' success. He also found himself with a group of boys who largely seemed unpretentious, lending itself to agreeable, cohesive group relations. After such a winning season, culminating with achieving the championship for the division league made it all that much sweeter. Saying simply that Matheus was proud of his trophy and his part in the team's success would be an understatement. In the words of Denis Waitley, "Winners take time to relish their work, knowing that scaling the mountain is what makes the view from the top so exhilarating."

Their victory would result in an incredible boost to Matheus's self-esteem, which had long been a vulnerable spot for him. Matheus was eager to share his victory, showing off his trophy and pictures to his teacher and classmates, our family, our neighbors, and Lino by e-mail in Brazil. Not only did he feel a sense of accomplishment, he felt valued, and part of something bigger than his individual self; he wanted to celebrate with those who meant the most to him. Even more, his accomplishment reflected a sense of belonging. Matheus continued to progress toward a more stable sense of who he was as a valued player in life.

Chapter 19

The Circle of Life

Just three months after Michael's Bar Mitzvah, my father passed away, peacefully, after a long, nearly seven year battle with stage four lung cancer. I initially delayed more concerted efforts toward realizing my adoption goals to *wait and see* with my father's health; I was wary bringing a child into the family fold with whom loss was likely already going to be embedded strongly into the fabric of his being. My father defied the near immediacy of the expected . . . he outlived his bleak prognosis at least three times over. He maintained significance in his patriarchal role in our family despite unrelenting struggles to manage the aches and pain, fatigue, moodiness, and restrictions in mobility and independence. He was a proud, rather stoic man who struggled with his inability to emotionally provide for our family in the *take-charge* kind of way for which he was accustomed. Yet, he had living to do. He was going to do so however way it was meant so as not to miss out any more than he had to.

Given my father's determination, I questioned the point of further stalling the adoption process, subsequently compromising the extent of his involvement in my adoption plans, this most momentous occasion in my life. I wanted him to share in my joy and excitement, get to know his new grandchild and he be known to him. I shared some of how this truly meant to me in my concluding remarks of the eulogy I gave at his funeral. ...*Of late, one of the greatest gifts I could ever have received is having this last year to share with my father the starting out of my new role in life as father to my own two sons, Matheus and Davi. In the grand Circle of Life scheme of things, if I become even half the man and source of inspiration to my sons as he was to me, then I shall continue to honor my father's presence in my mind and in my heart. Dad your guiding hand on my shoulder will remain with me forever.*

A bond developed between my father and his new grandchildren, even though they often had to tip toe around his proclivity to petulance. They were sensitive to the often fragility of his condition and always greeted him warmly, typically with a gentle hug and a kiss for which he returned in kind. Going over to grandma and poppa's house was a frequent occurrence, typically with expectations of finding poppa stationed at his desk in the office, sitting on the couch in the family room watching television, or laying down in the bedroom resting. They were aware poppa was *sick* and he needed special care, yet the seriousness of his condition and his impending death mostly eluded them.

Michael mostly maintained a comfortable emotional distance from the inevitable, seemingly fostered by a mix of denial and optimism; whenever there was a dip in his physical condition, it was with the expectation that poppa would get better and, indeed, he did . . . time and time again . . . until this last time. As explained by Matheus' counselor, who was Brazilian and spoke Portuguese, with whom he recently began meeting weekly before my father's passing, Brazilians regard death as somewhat taboo. Death is not mentioned in the direct sense Americans are accustomed; there is no discussion beforehand about someone's impending death, even with the person who may be stricken with a terminal illness. There is no forewarning of how long someone may have to live. Not much different than the Jewish custom, once someone passes on, the funeral and burial process usually is completed swiftly, within 24 hours. Her clarity helped negate some of the frustration I felt with Matheus and Davi's apparent nonchalance toward my difficulties coping the days preceding my father's passing

On that last day with my father in the hospital, I had to leave him in the afternoon and make arrangements for the boys for after school. I was protective of potentially exposing them to any situation that would needlessly traumatize them. In telling them of poppa's impending passing, Matheus silently cried, shedding a waterfall of tears. Although used to Davi's crying jags, typically overreactions to minor instances, he loudly, incessantly wailed in a way I had never heard from him before.

Struggling to cope and being distracted with the rush to retrieve Michael and get him to the hospital, I was blessed being able to take them over to the protective folds of our neighbors, where they would stay the night. I was hopeful in keeping them connected to the stability of their routine. Being strongly rooted to this structure would at least for now negate whatever sensitive spots associated with their past losses. They would expect to go to school the next day, be with their friends and beloved teachers, and perhaps most importantly, still expect me to pick them up from aftercare as I have every afternoon since the start of school.

My father passed away with my mother, Michael, and myself at his side in the hospital early in the evening. When I left him early in the afternoon, we had been engaging with each other, unaware that he had only just a few hours left. Although he did not appear to be conscious when Michael and I made it to the hospital, I knew he knew we were there with him. So that he may finally go at peace, it was as if he was waiting for myself and Michael to get there and join my mother; the moment the three of us gathered at his bedside, the numbers on the monitors began to steadily drop and he was gone a mere fifteen minutes later. With the boys safely at the neighbors, I slept over my parents' house with my mother and Michael. We proceeded the next day to follow through with confirming the arrangements for the funeral and sitting Shiva. Traditionally lasting seven days, we shortened our sitting Shiva to three days. The two main purposes, honoring the loved one who had passed and helping the mourners deal with their loss still would prevail. Upon picking up the boys later that day from aftercare, denial was readily apparent as Davi innocently asked if poppa was "feeling better." I was scared having to tell them poppa had passed, yet they already knew and just needed the official word. There were tears, a passive acceptance of life's providence.

Gathering together as a community, we were sheltered by the strength and support of family, friends, neighbors, and synagogue congregants. The days flew by in a blur. Following the funeral, we sat Shiva the rest of that Sunday, Monday, and Tuesday. Michael stayed with us throughout, although I had the boys maintain their school routines; they joined us at the house afterwards. It did not help that the state's series of standardized FCAT testing was to be held starting that Monday for four consecutive days. I felt it was important the boys maintain the momentum they had been building over the course of the year and take the test with their classmates. I informed both their teachers about the circumstances and asked them to judge for themselves the boys' emotional state on each of those days and whether they may need to defer taking the test.

I received an e-mail from Davi's teacher of his wish to defer taking the test on that first day because he was *too sad*; he promptly was scheduled to make up the session later in the week. Always eager to show off what he knew and not having expressed any such sadness that morning in getting ready for school, I also knew of Davi's proclivity for attention and probably having seized the opportunity for a little extra coddling from his teacher. Matheus, on the other hand, seemed to prefer delaying any need for such attention, reporting to me afterwards how he "wanted to take the test... I don't want to sit up in the office and do work." Instead, he sought extra attention from his teacher by asking if he could invite her to the house the next day to join in on the festivities, taking the trouble to ask for the address to be written down. As it often does, sitting Shiva for Matheus seemed to have taken on the tone of a party with its bounty of food, soda, playing, and hanging out. He may have seen this as an opportunity to share with his teacher more of himself in a positive light while having someone special come to the house just for him. When she graciously accepted his invitation and stopped by later in the evening, Matheus obviously was pleased. With his teacher's guidance and direction, he was delighted in making the introductions to grandma, Michael, and other important family members. Playing the gracious host, he offered her something to eat and drink, showed her some of the family pictures adorning the walls, and engaged with her in casual chitchat.

Shiva concluded each evening with the minyan, a public prayer whereby a quorum of ten male Jewish adults are required to be in attendance as required for certain religious obligations. The rabbi officiated the minyan in which all the children, mostly Michael's friends who came with their parents routinely gathered with the adults to pray on my father's behalf. Both Davi and Matheus were observed following along; as directed by the rabbi, Davi read aloud from the prayer book. Again, it seemed as though Matheus and Davi were very much considered part of the inner circle, often inquired about and checked in on. Feedback about how they *seemed* with respect to their adjustments and overall personalities was overflowing, overshadowing their behavioral challenges that typically do not present themselves in the public forum.

Many comments were made about how much more self-confidence Matheus was exuding and how much more *out of his shell* he seemed to be; indeed, the extent I saw him comfortably interacting with some of the more familiar adults, regardless of their inconsistency in our lives was endearing. Davi was praised for the extent of his bright intellect and how pleasurable it was to engage with him. The quickness of his grasp of concepts, fluency in his command of English, curious nature, and assertiveness in expressing his thoughts and ideas were standard comments.

With the conclusion of Shiva, Matheus and Davi quickly seemed to revert back to going about their business. Poppa's passing continued to impress upon them, albeit mostly in subtle ways. Davi was more forthright in making direct mention of poppa's memory, noting his absence now and then. Matheus was tenacious in not wanting to *talk about poppa*, yet periods of moodiness would last for several days. Rather than have the spotlight shine directly on him, he also held his counselor at bay, only expressing his concern for grandma and myself when witness to signs of our grieving. I constantly reassured them how any expressions of grief were *okay* and a normal part of mourning; their patience, caring, and sensitivity was all that was expected.

My father was an inspiration in his determination to live despite unrelenting odds; keeping the fire burning became symbolic of how one should persevere no matter how ominous the blowing winds may be. In so doing, I saw a sense of greater purpose to the recovery of my own grief. I sought to model for the boys more appropriate ways to express and cope with loss, countering maladaptive ways for which they push aside their own feelings about loss in their life.

* * *

Barely two weeks following my father's funeral, the Passover holiday was upon us. My favorite of the Jewish holidays, I was looking forward to sharing it with the boys. It did not seem meant to be that year, as we were not up to taking on the pageantry surrounding the richness of the holiday. We were grateful for having been invited by a family with whom we had been friendly since Michael's early elementary school years; he and his friend went to the same school and played together on several sporting teams. His friend's family was actively involved with the temple and devotedly observant of the Jewish religion. We were promised a traditional Seder, the ritual feast integral to the Jewish faith and celebratory of the Jewish people's freedom from Egyptian slavery over 3,000 years ago. As told in the biblical Book of Exodus, the Passover Seder serves as an occasion for praise and thanksgiving of the Jews' liberation.

As is tradition, guests are invited to share the festivities with the host family; the family's interest in helping my boys experience the rituals embedded in the story of Passover in a relaxed setting was most appealing. Indeed, the boys enjoyed following along with the holiday's rituals and, thankfully, only a minimal amount of reminders for appropriate table manners was needed. Earlier in the day, I read to them how Moses lead the Jews to freedom so they would be familiar with the concept of Passover. Matheus affirmed his familiarity with the story from his bible study days. At the Seder, both participated in the celebration of the 7 symbolic foods on the Seder plate, asking of the 4 questions and encouraging discussion of the symbols' significance in the meal, singing *Dayenu* in joyous recognition of the Jews' freedom from slavery, and searching for the hidden matzo, the *Afikoman* for a small token reward eventually secured by Davi. The boys continued to positively be regarded by all those who were in attendance and appeared comfortable in spite of the unfamiliar surroundings and circumstances.

With five days to go before Easter Sunday, I was unsure how to recognize this bit of Christianity for the boys. In a random conversation, Davi perceptively pointed out how perhaps Moses for the Jewish people and Jesus for the Christian people were similar in that both were regarded as a savior of sorts. Awhile back, Davi expressed interest in why the Jewish people did not recognize Jesus Christ as their savior. He accepted being told the Jewish people still believed Jesus existed, but as an ordinary Jewish man and preacher executed by the Romans for speaking out against their authority and abuse in the Holy Land.

Neither of the boys expressed interest in attending church to formally recognize Easter. Rather, they were more interested in getting Easter candy, yet I could not pull myself together enough to fill a couple of Easter baskets with the celebrated candies and treats as I had wanted to. Instead, I had them each pick out a chocolate Easter Bunny when we were doing our grocery shopping the day before. Matheus' therapist also brought over for each of them a giant, hollowed chocolate egg, containing four wrapped chocolates inside, popular in Brazil for Easter. We visited a nearby Brazilian *supermercado* with these chocolate Easter eggs hanging over people's heads, affectionately known as the *Easter egg tunnel* and seemed a popular tradition in Brazil this time of year. These simple bits of recognition seemed enough to garner their excitement over reconnecting with an important piece of what they had been used to in Easters past.

As many may regard Jesus or Moses as leader over a set of loyal followers . . . I now had two such followers of my own. Davi clearly looked to follow my lead, choosing to take on my religious ideals and beliefs . . . and adopting my tastes in food, clothing, sense of wanderlust, and preference for all things

New England. Matheus still was resistant to clearly committing himself with that of the Jewish faith, or any religion for that matter. It seemed more to do with his burgeoning identity development like any pre-adolescent at this stage in his development. Despite his intermittent problems deferring to my authority, he still looked to my lead as his father, even when using me as the target of his still unresolved, and still largely unknown issues over life's furtive transgressions from his past.

Chapter 20

Feliz Aniversário . . . Happy Anniversary

For several days, weeks even, I was in awe about the impending arrival of May 7, the one-year anniversary of our first meeting and uniting as a family. Although the boys expressed interest in the anniversary, they seemed most interested with the day's planned activities: taking in the aptly timed release of the animated movie *Rio*, taking care of odds and ends to prepare for a Mother's Day celebration at our house the next day, and trying out a recommended Brazilian restaurant for dinner. We started out the day with an impromptu trip to a neighborhood comic book store in honor of Free Comic Book Day, for comics of our choosing. Even though the boys were eager to delve into the stories and pictures of their new comics and get on with the day, conflicts, albeit minor, still occasionally reared their ugly heads.

Though they protested, "Please, I want to have a good day . . ." "It's our anniversary . . ." I still needed to impart the reality of life's lessons. At the bike shop, Davi objected when I informed him there was to be less of a birthday present next month because of the expense in replacing his bike's front tire rim, a Chanukah present from just a few months ago. I promptly countered his, "It's no fair," with his need to care for his own property; having to pay for his rough handling of his bike was yet another example of the ramifications he should expect for his carelessness. In the movie theater, Matheus abruptly went off to sulk by himself on the other side of the aisle when I would not allow him to use his allowance money for popcorn; we'd just had lunch and he chose not to eat. Popcorn was not meant to be a substitute for healthier mainstays.

Parenting is not for the weak in mind; I had learned over that first year what it actually meant to take on the responsibility of child rearing, especially older children with a past I often felt forever competing against. Even so, I was pleased and amazed with the strength of our bond when we'd started out as strangers. As a family, we were operating more in sync with one another, with a better understanding of our needs and wants, and an improved ability to meet them and better prioritize accordingly so that family life felt more natural.

The simpler moments of our time together seemed to be the most satisfying for us as a bonded family. After the craziness that ensued with the younger cousins visiting the following afternoon for Mother's Day, for the better part of an hour afterward, we peacefully congregated around the kitchen island counter. Matheus was drawing and Davi was tinkering with a toy, simultaneously expressing interest in his brother's drawing. I was doing odd jobs: making lunches for school, preparing dinner, folding laundry . . . the usual. We fed off one another, seemingly enjoying just being together in a manner that conveyed mutual interest, respect, and care for one another. I felt no sense of competition for one another's attention, particularly mine, as each boy seemed at ease sharing the spotlight.

They both continued to express disbelief over the rather difficult behaviors of their younger cousins, and their stress over the kids' invasion of their personal spaces, seemingly without any care for proper boundaries. I'd prepared the boys ahead of time by having them put certain prized possessions out of reach. But they were *not* fully prepared for the tsunami of wreckage and chaos the children left in their wake.

I took advantage of an observation they'd made as to disrespectful sibling relations between the girls. I pointed out that as much as they "might fight" with each other, they did not usually go so far as being "so mean" to each other that it was "hurtful", and unforgiving as they'd noticed with the girls. I praised them for how much less they had been "beating up" on each other as they had been resorting to earlier this first year, as well as in comparison to their more volatile outbursts toward each other from their orphanage days. They were even more "flexible" with each other, and how they were more agreeable with each other, sometimes deferring to the needs and wants of the other rather than their own selfish interests.

Especially outside of our home life, I marveled how well they had adapted thus far. Both were faring well with their English, with Davi especially clearly fluent, both in verbal and written expression. Matheus seemed to be responding positively to his speech therapy at school, verbally asserting himself more. We rarely had trouble communicating with one another and we hardly ever used the *tradutor* anymore. They'd also been faring well at school, and although homework still presented its challenges, they'd been completing it without as much fanfare as in the beginning months. Both of their teachers raved over how well they had adapted academically, behaviorally, and socially.

There were many times in the beginning when I'd heavily depended on others' assurances that we would get to a point where it did not seem to be a perennial struggle to get through the day. I was amazed when I'd looked back at the notes I jotted down in an online blog from just after our first twenty-four hours together and compared them to where we were a year later. I still was very much enchanted with Matheus's "soulful side and artistic talents and interests and Davi's fun loving personality and bright intellect." Only now I'd had more of a direct impact in nurturing and fostering their gifts. We were in this as a family for the long haul, and my efforts on their behalf were beginning to register with them. They had begun to show greater faith in what their future was promising them, simply because of how stable their lives had become. What a year it had been, with the promise of many more together . . . It was a happy anniversary, indeed.

* * *

Since the passing of my father, I had been asked by friends and family several times about what I was doing for myself, as far as taking care of my own personal emotional needs in the wake of having to continue carrying on with the demands of caring for others . . . parenting my sons mostly, but also attending to my mother and Michael, counseling my schoolkids, and relating with family, friends, and colleagues. I was mystified by how my eyes would suddenly become teary for no particular reason, even though I was not necessarily feeling sad or even consciously thinking of anything in particular. I had difficulty maintaining my attention in meetings, or anywhere else requiring my concentrated focus. Sometimes I was so preoccupied by random thoughts and/or concerns that I had to be directly jostled back to consciousness by someone competing for my attention. Although I felt pretty much back in the swing of things, carrying on with the everyday routines of my life, I still felt less than complete.

Without a concrete answer as to how I was taking care of myself, I began to realize the potential for emotional exhaustion and how much I needed to do *something* to heed my mental health. I turned to the idea of taking a trip; I was used to having in my arsenal plans of an escape to look forward to as a way of balancing out any stresses of the moment. I would have time away to recharge and regroup. I needed to "run away" and obtain some personal space and time for myself. Our neighbors readily offered to keep the boys for a weekend and encouraged me to go. Yet I still had to work through the guilt quickly surrounding any thought about planning a getaway . . . away from the boys. It had only been a year.

Having trouble reconciling with the idea of taking time away from them, fearing it to be a frivolous reflection of self-centeredness, I thought of how common it was for married parents to go away on holiday together, without their children. Reconnecting with each other as a couple with what bonded them as a couple long before children came into the mix, so they could return back into the fold of family life as stronger partners made sense. Especially as a single parent, with no partner with whom to "trade off" responsibilities, I felt it was just as important for me to reconnect with myself with who I was before parenting became the dominant priority in my life. I felt more ready to take advantage of my neighbors' generous offer and knew the boys would be content spending the weekend with them. My mother was not up to taking in the boys; handling Michael alone was more than enough for her. All that was left for me to figure out was where to go.

I decided I needed a distraction of the big kind, where I could lose myself in the attractions of a big city. I stayed away from my beloved Northeast: Boston, New York, or Baltimore. The idea of returning to places I was most intimately familiar with did not feel terribly invigorating. I felt I needed to go to less memorable surroundings, which held a fresh source of excitement, where I did not know anyone in particular and would not feel an obligation to make any personal connections. I'd visited Chicago five years earlier, and had wanted an excuse to take another trip there. Big-city amenities and distractions, and being able to simply walk off the airplane and onto the elevated train system to go anywhere I wanted at any time, seemed the right fit for me.

I sat the boys down, softening the blow a bit by informing them I was going to a meeting for work, and since I was going all the way out to Chicago, I was going to stay a few days. They both expressed excitement about going across the street for the weekend. Ever perceptive, Davi even took it upon himself to tell me he understood that I needed a break, and it was all right with him. It especially was endearing how both boys selflessly expressed interest in what I was going to do while I was in Chicago. While Matheus jokingly referred to the fun I would be having *without* him, Davi was more forthright in anticipating the pictures I would take to share with him what I had seen and experienced.

I felt a sense of relief soon after I was airborne, watching the receding South Florida shoreline gradually be taken over by the clouds. After landing and deplaning, I recalled only two months before walking through the same terminal, one of a party of six on the way to and from Seattle for a spring break trip with the boys, Michael, and Gayle and Jake. This time, I walked alone, past security and out from the bustle of the airport to the L-train and the anonymity of the big city.

Davi had promised to call and check up on me, but I'd had yet to reach my hotel room upon arrival when he first reached out after being picked up from school. Although still a man of few words, Matheus even got on the phone to check in with me. I spoke to them again later that first evening before they turned in for bed. In between, I stopped to take a picture with my cell phone of the pizza restaurant I went to, and sent it to my neighbor's phone for them to see. Davi enthusiastically told my neighbor, "Father's eating pizza!" To help them keep a live track of my activities, I continued to take pictures throughout the trip and sent them from my cell phone.

When I accidentally left my phone at the hotel the following day, I felt vulnerable not being directly accessible to the boys. I especially was disappointed not to be able to continue with the picture taking, sharing with them my goings-on as they were happening. I missed feeling connected to them as though they were sharing my experiences right alongside me. Borrowing a cell phone to call them, I felt guilt when Matheus declared, "Oh, that's why we couldn't call you this morning when we tried to call." I wondered whether I was missing the boys more throughout the day because I was restricted from having contact with them, yet the forced solitude also freed me further from any sense of direct responsibility for them and my life back home in general.

I spent three days checking out varying sights, strolling through Millennium and Grant parks, touring the Polish and Ukrainian neighborhoods with a Chicago Greeter guide, riding through the Gold Coast, Old Town, and Lincoln Park, and along Lakeshore Drive on a bicycle tour, and taking a tour of the Chicago Cubs' Wrigley Field stadium. I even took in a London theater production of *Peter Pan*. In between the sights were the food stops to get my fill of the infamous deep-dish pizza, hot dogs, Polish pierogies, and frozen custard.

To fill in the gaps, as I treasure every time I travel, I spent time losing myself in the world of the latest novel I painstakingly chose to accompany me . . . this time Brunonia Barry's *The Map of True Places*. I do not think I could have related to a better title at the time, even though it did not seem to strongly complement the story that unfolded; it was still an absorbing read with characters of depth and interest.

Before I knew it, Friday disappeared, Saturday night gave way to Sunday morning, and it was time to get to the airport to fly home. Perhaps it was fatigue from having been on the go for three days straight, perhaps it was the return to the oppressive South Florida heat, or perhaps it was the rather lukewarm reception of all three of the boys upon being picked up at the airport, but I had concerns about not feeling all that much invigorated, not terribly delighted to be back. As the day quietly faded away into the next day, and we resumed our routine, I felt more of the feeling of rejuvenation I had sought. The three of us did seem to relate with one another rather harmoniously. Better yet, I found myself feeling freer to absorb and expound on each of the boys' inner goodness and intentions, rather than harping on minor annoyances. I felt somewhat more balanced, able to juggle our regular routine more proficiently again . . . just in time to get in gear for the end of the school year and the summer.

Chapter 21

Jumpin' June

The arrival of the last day of school came with quite a bit of fanfare, building for several weeks. The challenges surrounding homework had become something of a distant memory around the time the boys took their state FCAT exams in early April. Matheus was getting little to no homework, and Davi brought home the same work he had from the beginning of the year. At least he was not making the same mistakes. There were a few field trips, and although they were to nowhere all that special, the boys were excited about the breaks from the regular routine of the school day. Matheus's class was also busy preparing for their play about the signing of the Declaration of Independence. Initially hesitant, Matheus became excited about his small speaking role and part in a square dancing demonstration.

Matheus took special delight in fashioning a costume reminiscent of what any one of the signers wore at the time, retrieving items from all our closets. Along with a tri-cornered hat furnished by his teacher, a pair of blue sweat-pants, knee-high white athletic socks, dressy black shoes, a blue button down shirt, and a gray farmer's jacket with its hem dropping down past the knees and large, circular buttons lining the front transported Matheus back in time. He graced the stage with confidence, handling his small part flawlessly and confidently. He seemed especially pleased to see me there, afterward happily pointing out his closest friends from class. The big end-of-the-year fifth-grade dance party took place a week later, the day before the last day of school. Matheus decked himself out in his suit ensemble from what he wore to Michael's bar mitzvah, proudly showing off his flair for style. He happily took pictures with the new camera he got for his birthday, danced, ate, and got a kiss on the cheek from his yearlong crush. Matheus also appeared pleased with his end-of-the-year grades, with an A popping up for science and a lone C, for reading.

Davi's end of the school year was subtler, without the pomp surrounding the exiting fifth graders. Davi's teacher continued to rave about his solid academic gains, enthusiasm and inquisitive nature, maturity, keen sense of perception, and sharp memory, with telling me, "Nothing gets by him." She concurred with my push to have him tested for eligibility in the schools' gifted program. Pushing Davi past his tendency toward sloppiness and toward being more accountable for his success, I matter-of-factly informed him that C grades in reading would no longer be acceptable when he brought his report card home for the third quarter; he needed to get a B for the last quarter.

Davi already had impressed me with his reading and language skills; the thrill of learning in and of itself was intrinsic for him. He clearly enjoyed reading, quickly devouring whatever books he checked out from the library and taking delight in bending my ear about whatever tidbits of interest he read about. His reading comprehension was unquestionable. I countered his questions about what would happen if he did not earn a B for the last quarter by saying I was very confident of his ability and that there was no reason to expect otherwise. I had inquired on occasion throughout the last few weeks of school how he was faring toward this goal, but otherwise left it up to him. When I picked him up on the last day, he proudly announced having earned his B in reading, and ended the year making the A/B Honor Roll, exactly the kind of recognition he thrived on.

For the last day, both boys were pleased to bring their teachers fresh-baked chocolate-chip cookies they wanted to make themselves. Rather than settle on a randomly bought store item void of any real personal investment, they made their gratitude more meaningful through the cookies. Both boys clearly adored their teachers, hanging on their every word as though their teachings were the gospel; I knew it was important for the boys to have the chance to express their good-byes on a positive note. I tried countering some of their past negative experiences of loss by emphasizing their teachers' positive impact in their new life and their having contributed to the boys' personal growth.

Both ended the school year on an affirmative note. Davi was squarely invested in putting himself out there for all to see, blazing a trail all his own to travel along. Harking back to his favored "Dormi na Praça " song, Matheus seemed less prone to lying around on a park bench, crippled by troubled events of the past. Indeed, happier trails seemed more the norm; both dared to look ahead, even if for now just as far enough ahead as summer vacation.

* * *

Barely two months since my father's passing, Father's Day unexpectedly took on a new dimension for me that year. I had a hard time gearing up for the big day, no longer able to regard this day as one of direct gratitude to my own father. I put my feelings into perspective by reminding myself of the paradox of this being my first year fatherless while the boys had been adjusting to now having a father in their life after previously not having one. Both intimated on a few occasions that they might have been planning something for me, yet keeping any details a secret from me. Last year's Father's Day occurred only the day after we arrived home from Brazil; we still were too newly established as father and sons to more intimately appreciate the day. Now, I took to heart a close family friend's observation that this year I'd "earned" it.

Special day or not, it started off with a minor verbal altercation between boys, requiring me to immediately separate them and remind them to be more respectful to avoid any further escalations. It blew over quickly, yet not before I huffily retreated to the laundry room, mumbling to myself, "Just great . . . what a way to start Father's Day . . ." They swiftly followed after me, each thrusting a wrapped present and card into my face, ready to put some significance onto the day. Although I had some prior suspicions thanks to some less than subtle comments, they officially told me that our neighbor, Miss Mary, took them to the dollar store over the weekend I was in Chicago and gave them some pocket money to buy presents, in exchange for completing some chores.

I unwrapped an original Matheus oil painting of a beautiful waterfall scene on a small canvas; its vibrant colors and brush stroke style unintentionally, unknowingly bore a striking resemblance to van Gogh's *Starry Night*. I also was struck by how his waterfall painting was reminiscent of Iguaçu Falls, for which he denied any direct intention, modestly shrugging his shoulders. His card also was rather poignant, albeit with Christian overtones, acknowledging our Lord as the Father, with relevant biblical references on the front of the card: *He tends his flock like a shepherd . . . and carries them close to his heart . . . Set an example in speech, in life, in love . . . The glory of the Lord is streaming from you.* Still, Matheus referred to the inside of the card as what he had been thinking to say on his own: *Father, you've been there for me in every possible way, and I'm proud that so much of my life has been shaped by your wonderful example. I love you* . . . adding on his own at the end, *I always did.*

On a more lighthearted note, without sacrificing thought or sentiment, Davi's present was more practical. He was eager to see me use the coupon organizer he bought for me so I could have ready access to all those money-saving opportunities he knew I valued. His card, humorous in tone, was rather affecting in its tongue-in-cheek reference to his tendency to repeatedly ask me questions, pushing my sanity to the brink: *asking you the same stuff over and over until I drove you nuts . . . doesn't it seem just like yesterday . . . it must have driven you nuts, huh . . . until you went nuts, right?*

As for my oldest, my nephew, Michael, I expected him to have a hard time with the significance of today. He'd only asked my mother just that morning to take him for a Father's Day card on the way over for our annual Father's Day brunch. He balked at my mother's insistence that he should pay for it with his own allowance money; he relented only because they were in line and he wanted to avoid embarrassment. His sign-off on his *Happy Father's Day, Uncle* card simply, rather stoically hinted at his desperate need for validation of his own feelings. *I know today might be very hard for you, but I wish you a happy Father's Day and I love you.*

As we sat down at the table for brunch, with a bit of a forlorn look on his face Michael casually waved a hand to the empty chair at the head of the table. Up until that time I had been avoiding any direct glance in that direction. Though Michael later offered, I decided not to go to the cemetery with him and my mother afterward; I was not up to it. I did not want to force the observance of my father's absence by insulting Matheus and Davi's apparent need to perhaps regard today as an appreciation for their father in the present tense. I also did not want to insult Michael's sincere wish to grieve, fearing he might mistake their indifference for insensitivity. Instead, Matheus and Davi made it a point to remind me that today also was significant in marking the one-year anniversary of their arrival in America. How fitting it was to celebrate this day on Father's Day, as it was their new father who brought them home.

* * *

June used to be a mere blip on the radar of life for me, with brief mention in passing of just my birthday toward the end of the month. Forever changed, June became a hotbed of activity with the relentless stream of all our birthdays. Matheus's birthday on the fourth begins the birthday cycle, followed by Davi's birthday a week later on the eleventh. My birthday follows promptly two weeks later, on the twenty-fifth, with Father's Day sandwiched in between. With so much competition for distinctive attention, what to do with the boys' birthdays this go-around proved quite the challenge.

No matter how I mulled it over, there was no justification for having two separate parties. As much as I would have liked having a big house party, the threat of the craziness of an endless stream of ill-mannered children running around the house reminiscent of the gathering for Mother's Day was not an attractive prospect for any of us. I sat down with the boys and queried them about any friends they would like to invite; since they had only a few select friends of interest, formulating a short list was not terribly difficult. After assembling the guest list, we decided on the place . . . one of those indoor arenas with giant inflatable slides, bounce houses, and obstacle courses. I resigned myself to a lack of personal intimacy and flair for the party, and the two hours quickly elapsed as we were systematically shepherded like a herd of cattle from the first "fun jump zone," to the second "fun jump zone," and then onto the party room for cake. The boys were thrilled with the attention and fuss, even if only one of their friends apiece showed up.

Weeks before, Davi had expressed sadness about not ever having had a birthday party, as his family became too poor to afford such a luxury; past birthdays sounded as if they'd been simple. Even their birthday celebrations in Brazil at Lar Rogate the previous year, with their big cake, soda, and balloons, seemed more elaborate than what they were used to. Davi related that their mother made them a banana cake with "nothing on it" to mark their special day. For their party, Davi wanted to have their cake decorated with clowns, but Matheus scoffed at the immature thought; both settled on festive frosted decorations of balloons to adorn the cake's top.

We continued the festivities with a smaller party back at the house that evening, with those family, friends, and neighbors most significant in the boys' lives. It was nothing fancy... just a few pizzas, baked ziti, garlic rolls, salad, and leftover cake. I did not want to overdo it and risk overwhelming the boys, spoiling their rather simplistic need for affirmation of being loved and valued among family and friends.

Individually, I wanted to recognize each of the boys' birthdays in a restrained, subtle manner, bestowing just enough special attention. The week before their party, Matheus had popped up on the birthday assembly line first. We lit a few candles atop a giant birthday chocolate-chip cookie and sang happy birthday. I gave him a camera, its symbolic value rooted in the memory of his having lost their shared camera on a bus in Brazil.

His absentmindedness at the time could have been dismissed with an "oh, well" shrug of the shoulders if it were not for his staunch defensiveness, stubborn indifference, and lack of remorse. Only with assistance from the court's social worker the next day did his tears come, and he was able to acknowledge his regret over his carelessness. Matheus clearly enjoyed pursuing the art of photography, happily snapping photos of whatever struck his interest, experimenting with different angles and subjects. I saw that a camera was a wonderful artistic outlet for him, and I'd felt so bad about that lost opportunity for him when he lost the camera. The time was ripe for a renewal in faith and trust as represented by this second camera. He got to work immediately, impressively figuring out all the ins and outs of the camera's different features and happily taking pictures, taking care to keep the camera within his reach.

As their big party was scheduled for later in the afternoon on Davi's actual birthday, I surprised him with a specially decorated birthday cupcake for lunch to individually commemorate his special day. We sang "Happy Birthday" and he opened his special birthday present. Although he kept in mind expectations of *less* for his improper handling of his bicycle, he seemed no less excited about his present. For months Davi had been very direct, consistently expressing his desire for a watch; I was as anxious for him to have one, becoming weary of forever being asked what time it was, what day it was, what the date was. Knowing his tendency to be rather careless and rough in his handling of whatever might come within his grasp, I settled on a Timex, keeping in mind its "It takes a licking and keeps on ticking" motto.

The last on the birthday assembly line, somewhat overtaken by the attention of Father's Day the week before, my special day was a subdued affair. The heralding of my birthday two weeks later was a subdued commemoration, with the glaring absence of my father's company. We went out to dinner with Grandma and Michael, followed by a smattering of presents and cards. It was a simple recognition of my being. I did not need anything more than that. I believe our birthdays are symbolic as validation of our identity and existence. Perhaps more so for adults, birthdays compel us to think about who we are, where we have been, and where we may be headed. At this middle stage of my life, fatherhood became a most extraordinary life-defining experience, forever shaping my identity as a person and dictating my life's course for the future.

Part 4

**Looking Toward the Future . . .
One Day at a Time**

Chapter 22

Macho, Macho, Man . . .

Culturally, I was reminded more than once how Matheus's attitude often was reminiscent of machismo, a prevalent practice across Latin America. The idea that a man does not let anything detract from his image of himself as a "man's man" helped explain Matheus's often steadfast refusal to reveal his true feelings, lest he be taken advantage of and his manhood be questioned or deprecated. In the not so distant past, Matheus was used to aggressively throwing his weight around; practicing self-restraint gradually was becoming more the norm. That summer I was taken aback when coming across Lino's rather telling introductory description of Matheus: *He considers himself as the best one; "he's the man." He thinks he's always right, does not lower his head to people. Matheus needs rules and limits and you've got to be firm with him from the beginning. He's not a difficult kid at all but you need to be clear how things are going to be, make him realize he's the son and not the father.* I had been approaching him as such all along, instinctively becoming more proactive and constructive in fostering in him a securer sense of himself in our relationship and his place in the world.

Now, a year into our developing father-and-son relationship, Matheus threw a curve ball in taking it upon himself to acknowledge when he was wrong, promptly apologizing for having interfered in a mildly contentious verbal exchange between Davi and me. As we drove home from camp one afternoon, Davi told me he was hungry, "Because I didn't get lunch today . . . because I got to the lunch-room too late." He claimed the entire group was late from the gym. When I pressed for further information, he claimed he "don't remember" any other details. Smelling something suspicious and not appreciating his dodging of the truth, I called his bluff and stated that unless he "remembered" the details, dinner would not include dessert for him. I had "been there, done that" with him. I knew what I was doing, yet Matheus interfered and started disparaging my authority, ignoring prompts "to mind your own business" and let me be the parent. Davi suddenly piped up about how he had "a little salad, but that's all," to which I quickly pointed out that he'd lied to me, attempting to make me think he'd had nothing to eat. Matheus promptly, rather incredulously exclaimed, "Oh, wow . . . you lied?" As it had been Davi's choice not to eat, I expressed my disappointment in his lying to avoid possibly angering me. Still expressing disbelief, Matheus promptly apologized for his interference, and then nodded in agreement to my telling him how he needed to trust me more as the knowing parent.

Over time, I came to understand Matheus's hostile actions as a rather thin veil for his fear of his emotional vulnerability becoming exposed. Not being able to suppress the tenderness of old hurts and disappointments from the past was a threatening prospect for him. More time still was needed for him to become more secure with himself, without so much the nagging constraints of yesterday's baggage. Learning the hard way did not come without its lessons of prudence, humility, and sensitivity.

* * *

In packing for his weeklong sojourn with Michael and his camp group to the Poconos toward the end of the summer, Matheus asked me to check over what he'd packed on his own in his duffel bag and ensure that the packing list was properly taken care of. At first glance, I was dismayed to find a wet bathing suit and towel used earlier in the day neatly folded away in the bag, placed atop his other packed clothing without regard for it being wet. I lightly tossed them out, frostily pointing out how the shorts underneath were now wet because of his lack of thought. He quickly took offense, and became impatient and rude in response to further questions about his packing. When he ignored my warnings about his "attitude," I left the room and told him to let me know when he was ready to "try again."

He followed after me, only to sulk on the couch in the family room. I calmly asked him to please bring the wet towel and bathing suit to the laundry room, to which he snappily replied, "You threw it out." I repeated my request, adding that it was his bathing suit and towel to take care of, for which he ignored me. I gave him a "last chance" to comply. He refused to budge. I promptly informed him the loss of his video game privileges for the day, and that unless he complied within the next five minutes, according to the oven timer, another day of punishment would be added. He stormed into his room, then stomped back out and to the laundry room with his towel and bathing suit. No sooner had he turned to leave the laundry room after I had thanked him for his cooperation, and I proceeded down the hallway in the opposite direction than a loud crashing sound came from the family room. Matheus had flung three filled plastic bags of LEGOs around the room, with the pieces having scattered everywhere. Maintaining my composure, I informed him, "The timer is still going. You need to start cleaning up the pieces before it goes off." He complied, angrily throwing the pieces in the direction of the bucket, with most bouncing against the wall or back out of the bucket. He ignored my request for calmer behavior, as I hoped to deflect his anger by communicating my understanding of his frustration.

I let him be. He was complying with the initial direction. They were only pieces of plastic, not being used in any particularly destructive manner. I refrained from saying anything further, hoping his anger would abate. I stayed in the room, watching until the last of the pieces had made it into the storage bin. I was blinded by fear and confusion, but I should have stepped in and more assertively assisted with his gaining greater self-control. My maintaining a bystander status only seemed to prolong and perhaps further escalate Matheus's anger. I still could not leave well enough alone, as I pointed out to him his need to throw away the plastic bags from the LEGOs on the floor. He retorted in a steely tone, "They are not mine." Trying not to respond to his nastiness, I replied, "Since it was your choice to throw them around and mess up the room with the LEGOs, you need to now throw the bags away," still biting my tongue and keeping myself steady from wanting to have screamed back at him. He viciously shredded the bags into pieces, stomping off to the trash bin in the kitchen with the scraps in hand.

Being on the other side of the kitchen island, I did not see Matheus violently fling open the cabinet door, ripping it off its hinges, leaving it to crash onto the floor. It was doubtful he intended to tear the door off, yet he was caught off guard by the force of his own aggression. I ordered him into his room until he was ready to talk; he responded by stomping off, his hasty retreat likely motivated by fear and his need to escape. But the intensity of his anger continued to escalate, demanding further his release to the tune of more banging coming from his room. I swallowed hard, trying to contain the incessant, fearful beats of my heart.

I went in just as he began to kick the closet door, prompting me to assertively approach him; with a raised voice, calling it like it was I pointed out, "You are not in control . . ." I took hold of his arm and pulled him down toward the floor, intending to physically restrain him as might be necessary. He did not resist the light grasp of my arms encircling his chest, his back straight up against my chest. His angry, silent tears began to dot the hairs of my arm. As I struggled to orient myself, my eyes flitted about the room, falling on a spot on the opposite wall with a newly punched indentation in the drywall, and several smaller pockmarks within its vicinity.

As I held him, I tried to communicate my understanding what he might be angry about, and appealing to some sense of reason for what truly was going on that had so incensed him beyond becoming miffed about the wet towel and bathing suit. The muscles in his arms and legs pulsed involuntarily. Agitated breaths marked the uneven rise and fall of his chest. As he was calming down, I asked whether he could keep himself together on his own; he mournfully shook his head no. I kept my hold on him, stroking his hair and speaking to him in hushed tones, trying also to calm the thrashing around of my own insides in the interim. After a few more minutes, Matheus let me retreat, leaving him alone with his thoughts.

I was left shaken by his extreme behavior, yet more so as a result of my feeling how badly I had handled him. I should have been more proactive and less defensive in response to his offensiveness. Yet it was not too long before I heard a meek voice make it known that Matheus was ready to talk. We had a mostly one-sided discussion; he was still not willing to look past the surface surrounding his hurt feelings and how I "threw them out of the bag like that." I had grown accustomed to Matheus being a man of few words, yet his willingness to begin expressing his feelings, however superficial, still was relatively unchartered territory in our travels together.

* * *

A week later, we sat down to watch the movie adaptation of *Where the Wild Things Are* for our Saturday movie-and-pizza night ritual. The movie seemed true to the book's rather simplistic story line, yet its adaptation was very detailed in its story-telling. Still reeling from the effects of his angry outburst, both Matheus and I were mesmerized by the protagonist's escalation of aggressive behaviors and then running away in reaction to his mother's self-serving attempts to assert her control over his insubordination. Midway into the movie, Matheus professed his difficulty understanding the incidents with Max and the aggressive behaviors of the wild things. It seemed he was more perplexed by watching how out-of-control the expression of aggression could become, the destructiveness one's aggressive actions could lead to, and the resultant isolation from those one might feel closest to, as portrayed by Max and the wild things.

The movie's ending also seemed to have resonated with Matheus. How one's committed love still remained regardless of whatever ugliness may have transpired was shown in Max's unconditional return home to his mother's nourishing sustenance and care. Discussing their thoughts and feelings about how anger was portrayed by Max and the wild things started off promisingly enough. Matheus was receptive to open discussion, until Davi had to interject a, "Yeah, Matheus..." Matheus promptly responded with a slam of his hand down on the couch and an angry scowl on his face. Yet Matheus resisted further comment, allowing me to address his brother's immature, insensitive taunting as being unnecessary and mean-spirited. Wherever it came from, it was not the time or place. Davi promptly apologized and Matheus quietly accepted in return.

In putting Matheus to bed that night, I refrained from overdoing it with more jibber- jabber about the movie.

Instead, I traced with my finger the shape of a heart on his chest, symbolically mimicking what Max left behind for his wild thing friend at the movie's end. It was a token of Max's forgiveness for his friend's destructive lashing out. Perhaps Max also had on his mind hope for his mother's forgiveness for lashing out at her. I wondered to what extent Matheus was bothered by any still negative impact his angry outburst had on our emerging father-son relationship.

I had caught Matheus sometimes stopping to stare on occasion at the cabinet over the coming days, with its gaping hole and door left purposely lying flat on the counter above. Before arrangements were made to fix the cabinet, Matheus intermittently would wonder aloud at the cost of the damage, what he would or could do to pay off the debt, how long it might take, and what it meant not to be able to use his money for other purposes until the debt was paid. He was eager to earn extra money, being conscientious about taking on extra chores to pay off his debt. I believe he was just as eager to repent for his actions, even though he refused to discuss anything more about it. I used the traced heart as a metaphor to both verbally and figuratively communicate to him how love remains, just like the love expressed between Max and his mother and Max and his wild thing friend. Matheus's facial expressions, with somewhat of a raised eyebrow and a softening in his eyes intimated that he got it; forgiveness for anyone, even for him can travel a long way with the hope of learning the hard lessons of life

* * *

During the time of the outburst, I had forgotten that we had been reading together Chalise Miner's *Rain Forest Girl: More Than an Adoption Story.* An American adoptive mother wrote this story of a girl she and her husband had taken out of the Brazilian rain forest, where she had been living under extremely impoverished conditions. The story was told from the girl's perspective in a simplistic manner, appropriate for a young reader. Daiane's story reflected many parallels to the boys' life circumstances. She was unable to live with her ailing mother, lived in poverty with her grandmother, who treated her harshly, and was separated from her sibling. The story also detailed her difficulties adjusting to the American way of life and learning English.

Both boys stayed largely silent as I read aloud, seemingly absorbed in her story. Even Davi was not up for any in-depth discussion about Daiane. Matheus seemed especially quiet. Daiane's story must have hit a nerve with him. He may have been hypersensitive to the stirring of his emotions at the time of his explosion, as he struggled to keep at bay memories of past hurts and disappointments. There is a heart beating strongly underneath that macho bravado of his . . . I knew I would get better at encouraging more of it to rise from beneath the surface.

Chapter 23

Checks and Balances

Fairly soon after our homecoming, I attempted to foster more favorable relations between brothers, targeting Matheus's aggressive behavior toward Davi and the passive-aggressive ways Davi instigated conflict. Neither was thrilled about the idea of a contract that there were to be *expectations* of them to change in ways they had become all too used to relating with each other. *O Contrato de Respeito*—The Respect Contract—outlined in both Portuguese and English just a few conditions:

1. If my brother is bothering me, I will not hit or kick—this is *never* a choice;
2. I will tell my father and let him handle it when my brother is bothering me;
3. When I am given a direction to leave my brother alone, I will obey. I will trust my father to handle the problem;
4. I will let my brother have his space when he wants or needs it;
5. I know I cannot be first all the time or be the only one to get to do special things—I will share with my brother.

Davi appeared receptive, willingly signing off on the contract's conditions. Matheus reacted angrily at the prospect of having to be held more directly accountable for his aggressive behavior, ignoring the focus on harmonious family relations. Signing off on the contract, he huffily declared Davi's need to watch out for himself if I did not punish him for any wrongdoing.

Perhaps the contract leaned more heavily toward protecting Davi's interests. I tended to have a softer spot toward Davi whenever there was the slightest threat of a run in between he and Matheus. I felt his vulnerability in the face of Matheus's rage. His safety was the more immediate priority in these beginning stages of our familial bonding, yet I also had underestimated his passive-aggressive influence over his brother's overtly aggressive reactions, which helped me several months later to better understand that Matheus's position was not necessarily without blind cause. It took only a few days before Matheus angrily tore the contract in pieces when disciplined for aggression in response to Davi's teasing him. There was no reasoning with him about his need to ignore Davi's minor provocations and annoyances; he needed immediate satisfaction to preserve his fragile self-esteem at the time.

I did away with resolutions geared toward superficial, quick-fix solutions. I kept at it, insisting on more positive, at the very least civil brotherly relations. I assigned consequences for any type of verbal or physical act of aggression, even when the boys merely made references in jest to hitting. I also broadened their understanding of what constituted as aggressive behavior to include Davi's passive-aggressive "hit and run" provocations specifically intended to unnerve his brother.

I emphasized reinforcement, including praise, physical affection, and a piece of chocolate here, a cookie there, whenever I caught them in the act of positive relations. As time wore on, the flame of aggressiveness in how they got along gradually dwindled to more of a flicker. I even caught Matheus modeling after me, calmly asking Davi to stop his annoying behavior. I became more practiced in consistently staying on Davi's case, not letting him any leeway about his passive-aggressiveness. The proverbial jig was up.

For a while, it seemed as though the more in control Matheus became refraining from physical aggression, the more problematic Davi's behavior was. Perhaps he was experiencing some symptoms of withdrawal from being deprived of a reliable source of attention from his brother, or he was testing Matheus, challenging him to prove his self-restraint. But eventually, the pokes and prods of his offenses lessened, leaving Matheus feeling even more in control over life's circumstances.

* * *

With brotherly relations having become more positive, their physical aggressiveness had nearly extinguished; even the tongue-in-cheek verbal references to hitting significantly decreased. However, the boys' improved behavior appeared mostly only when we were home and when just the three of us were out together. More often than not, whenever there was a changing dynamic—especially when Michael would enter the fold—their relations quickly soured. I needed them to behave any time, and anywhere, and I knew I had a better shot in getting them to do so by depersonalizing their tendency to annoy and reinforce their cooperative behavior.

I also thought about how to instill appreciation for not only the value of earning money, but also prioritizing and developing responsible spending habits. The boys were well acquainted with my thriftiness for the sake of conserving our family's financial resources. Even in our very early days in Brazil, they were excited to take on the challenge of picking out the cheaper bargains, scrutinizing the different choices out on display and getting good value for their efforts. They even looked forward to riffling through the Sunday newspaper for good coupons, getting excited by the mysterious prospect of special treats, or where we might eat out depending on whatever deals or specials were on hand. It was time for them to move from learning vicariously to directly experiencing earning, saving, budgeting, and spending money for themselves. Despite having had no concept of what it was to spend money, let alone have any money for themselves, they quickly began asking about chores and earning money to acquire toys and tokens.

I secured a couple of bank savings register books for each to start keeping track of their deposits of money earned and withdrawals from their spending, and I instigated penalties for unacceptable behavior. Matheus was assigned the weekly chore of taking out the garbage cans every Friday morning and bringing them back in the evening. Needing the repetitiveness of a daily task, Davi was assigned the chore of bringing in the newspaper every morning. Also expected from both was making their beds every morning, keeping their rooms neat, helping bring in the groceries, folding/putting away washed clothes neatly and in their proper places, and completing their homework on time.

To respect their differences in age and supposed maturity, Matheus was set up to earn seventy-five cents per day and Davi would earn fifty cents. In the beginning, I handled allowance matters daily, so that we could review everyday their progress in meeting their behavioral expectations. With some input from them, we incorporated a response cost system via a short set of penalties: ten cents apiece, tailored according to individual goals. Davi's infractions included his now infamous fresh mouth, teasing his brother, not being truthful or doing as told, not minding his own business, and properly taking care of his clothes. Matheus' infractions included disrespect or back-talking, hurting property, not following a direction or warning, the threat or joke of hitting or putting hands on *anyone*, rude comments, and not minding his own business. I upped the ante with the threat of a twenty-cent penalty, dramatically halting Matheus's inane, obnoxious behavior with Michael, including inappropriate, sexualized gestures and butt smacks.

This time around, both boys enthusiastically greeted this prospect of behavior modification and were eager to start the climb toward financial independence. However, as much as Davi was eager to dart out of the starting gate, his initial efforts were slow as he stumbled around in circles. Penalties came fast and furious for him; he was not yet ready to let go of his uncooperative behavior. I had hoped he would start noting the slow growth in his earnings and become more conscious in avoiding penalties by restraining his offensive, mouthy backtalk.

Matheus also was consistently responsible with his chores, even when on restriction for a week from favored toys and activities for his refusal to accompany us to Davi's dentist appointment. During his week of restriction, his assets were also frozen; he was not able to earn any money or make a withdrawal. He was angry about feeling he should be trusted to stay home alone, and I told him trust needed to be earned, the same way one earned money; the harder one worked to earn money—just as in proving one's trustworthiness—the greater the building of one's bankability, and their reliability, dependability, and respectability. When regaining his banking privileges, he was eager to take on additional chores and increase his earning potential, thereby being more responsible for himself, and subsequently trustworthy.

Soon after, Matheus was excited to go out shopping for his first desired reward: a mechanical pencil he had been pining for. I stood quietly and watched him study the array of pencils carefully, regard the color choices, how many came in a package, and the price relative to each offering. When in line to pay, Matheus proudly commented, "This is a good deal." Given that this was his first successful foray into earning, saving, and keeping track of his money, then carefully choosing how to spend it, I could not agree more. It was a proud moment for me to have taught my son a life lesson that resonated strongly with him.

* * *

Shortly before school was to start back up again after the summer, I noticed that the boys' gains in behaving more respectfully had reached a plateau. The sole use of money was not effective in gaining their cooperation consistently. I came up with yet another ploy to gain further their cooperation; I downgraded my expectations for their allowance to serve primarily as a motivator for responsible behavior: doing their chores, making their beds every morning, and taking care of their clothes. I sat each of them down separately and unveiled a renewed, tailor-made behavioral plan. I still targeted their increased respectfulness toward my authority by targeting their mouthy backtalk and obstinacy. I explained how such privileges as their video games needed to be earned, not taken for granted.

For Matheus, I kept what was expected simple: He was not to backtalk when told to do something or stop something, use appropriate language, stop calling everything's "stupid" and use positive, encouraging comments or not say anything at all, and stop his "whatever" comments and attitude. Even more specifically, hoping to instill growth in his maturity, I emphasized that the need to fart was not funny. "Try to control it, go somewhere else, or at least keep quiet about it," I told him. I tried balancing the need for consequences for his uncooperative behavior and recognition for his compliant behavior with positive reinforcement. When caught "doing good," such as making a positive comment, he'd earn a check: an infraction would garner an X.

For him to earn the week's worth of video gaming privileges, the ratio between checks and Xs needed to be 75:25; at least 75 percent of the tallies for the week needed to be checks. I also highlighted the responsibility factor to encourage greater accountability so he could be trusted to handle desired, age-appropriate privileges. I told him the privileges he was expecting for middle school would need to be earned, such as staying up later on a school night, riding his bike to school, and having a cell phone. After two weeks in a row of his earning 75 percent, I would raise his target level to 80 percent, and after another two successful weeks in a row, the responsibility factor could start figuring in with the extra privileges that coincided with an 85 percent target level. He was on board as he enthusiastically and rather confidently calculated how many weeks without interruption it would take for him to get a cell phone.

Davi's greater deference to my authority continued to yield more responsibility for his behavior by telling the truth the *first* time, doing something when told to do it, without stalling or making derogatory comments, minding his own business, and responding more seriously when being addressed for an infraction and not mocking or making funny faces. Again, Davi was receptive, even reporting on his brother for "doing good" and subsequently deserving a check. Matheus, in kind, started doing the same. They took to heart my emphasis on the positive, reinforcing rather than bringing each other down.

I felt more empowered having a system in place where accountability was fairly straightforward. Although it was daunting to be on the constant alert for marking a check or X the moment something transpired, I hoped we wouldn't have to rely on the plan for too long. I had hoped for more natural relations as the boys became used to behaving in a more positive and respectful manner.

Matheus had very little trouble the first week, being conscientious about his behavior, which most days didn't warrant any Xs at all. However, whenever he did receive an X for a transgression, it usually was not without a stormy backlash of resentment. The first challenge arose a mere two weeks into our new system, when returning home from the grocery store resulted in an X for both that they could easily have averted by cooperating with each other. After I had checked in with our neighbor, I found Davi leaning up against the car and Matheus sitting down at the front door of our house, instead of bringing in the groceries as normal. Davi told me he gave the keys to Matheus to open the door, yet he threw them on the ground. Given how cooperative and responsive Matheus had been the past two weeks, I was not ready to believe Davi's story. Matheus denied Davi's accusation; he said the keys fell out of his hand because his arms were full of books and bags.

I emphasized my disappointment in their not cooperating over something so very simple as getting the front door open, for which I had to dole out an X to each of them. Matheus stomped through the kitchen, dropping the grocery bags on the counter and knocking over an empty water bottle that fell to the floor; he promptly plopped it back onto the counter, proclaiming, "I didn't mean to do that," before disappearing into his room. Davi came in with his bags, telling me that Matheus told him he wished he didn't have a brother, garnering another X for Matheus, as he had made such comments before, and I had told him that he would receive a consequence "the next time."

About an hour later, Matheus came back out of his room, cooperating with the both of us as if nothing had transpired. I prompted both of them for further discussion about what happened in the driveway, and Matheus was surprisingly calm and receptive. With a few more details about what transpired, it was more apparent that Davi ignored Matheus's inability to take the keys at the time and exaggerated the situation. I commented to Matheus that he still could have gone over to put his things at the door and come back for the keys in spite of his brother's jerkiness; since he'd still exercised self-restraint, I felt it was fair to take back the first X, yet Matheus still was out of line in his meanness toward Davi afterward, for which the second X remained. Again, surprisingly, Matheus accepted that without another mention.

Matheus was getting it, yet Davi had ongoing trouble moving past his passive-aggressive tendencies, with X's far exceeding his checks. But still there were times I was able to reinforce him when restraining the impulse to backtalk. Matheus and Davi also were getting along better, being more conscientious in relating with each other agreeably. I saw how Matheus's improved self-control and Davi's decrease in his annoying behavior went hand-in-hand toward improving their brotherly relations. Even so, Davi was fighting tooth and nail all the way, complaining bitterly how he did not want the checks and Xs in his life. I knew I had to hang tough and wait for his frustration at not being able to play his video games start fueling his motivation to change.

* * *

Several months had passed. The checks and Xs prevailed, yet I had a hard time determining the plan's success in changing the boys' behavior and attitude. I thought I was specific about what would garner an X, yet each one would invariably be challenged. It was always was the same: One or the other would try to finagle his way out of a consequence by feigning innocence, pretending to not understand, or proclaiming, "I didn't know!" For the rare X he did get, Matheus still struggled to cope with a roller coaster of emotions. The initial shock of his vulnerability would give way to hurt and unbridled, defensive anger, along with a sprinkling of insistent pleas for mercy. He then would retreat in a huff, perhaps not speak to me for the evening, putting himself to bed and withholding our typical bedtime routine of hugs and kisses; by morning all was forgotten, or at least not mentioned again. On a few occasions we had been able to talk it through, and he showed a quieter acceptance of the X.

On one particular occasion when having garnered an X, Matheus abruptly came out of his room after retreating to sulk and requested his counselor's phone number. I was excited that he wanted to speak with her in the heat of the moment. He wanted to express himself further and perhaps engage in a problem-solving mode that was in stark contrast to his usual tendency of shutting down and cutting himself off from contact with anyone. Not having been able to get her on the phone, I let him stew for another half hour before acting on his apparent need to reach out. I needed to be his father, suck it up, and try my hand in working it out with him. He was surprisingly receptive to speaking with me, accepting my pointing out to him that I saw his anger, and that he seemed disappointed with himself for his expressed hostility toward me. As I turned to leave, with gruff yet disarming sincerity, Matheus asked, "Can I have a hug?"

I felt even more satisfied when his therapist called just a few minutes afterward; Matheus pleasantly told her, "There was a problem, but it's fixed now," and that he could wait until his next appointment to speak further about it. Still, for every step forward, falling back two steps seemed inevitable. The next X a week or so later Matheus crossed the line; Matheus was so angry, he dared the receipt of a second X for continuing to backtalk. He then swiftly ripped up his checks and Xs chart when I doled out the second X, claiming he would not cooperate any further, and how "stupid everything" was.

I kept interacting with him in a matter-of-fact tone, informing him that all privileges were revoked for the remainder of the week, as well as the following week. Since he could not earn checks because he had torn up the sheet to record them on, he would be unable to earn the next week's privileges. Only if he chose to reengage in his program at the start of the following week could he begin earning back his privileges. At the end of the week, with not having mentioned anything further about it, he coyly informed me that he thought I *knew* he had full intentions of starting the program back up at week's end when I was readying up Davi's new chart.

Davi's progress was exceedingly slower. After making it through a particularly rough spell with his attitude, disrespect, and refusal to hold himself accountable for his behavior, I sat him down with a rather definitive ultimatum. Perhaps out of desperation, yet more to structure him in a concrete, straightforward manner, I gave him the two weeks before Chanukah to get it together: Unless he earned at least a 75 percent by the end of the second week, there would be no Chanukah for him. All his presents would be donated to a local foster care agency.

He claimed, "You can't do that . . . what if someone else was to give me a present . . .?" I informed him, "Yes, I *can* when you don't deserve it." I added, "all of your presents will be donated to children who are less privileged and don't have a family who loves them and cares for them like you do." I could no longer tolerate his inane excuses or unnecessary, oftentimes rude comments that kept him from holding himself accountable for his behavior and attitude.

Despite his initial protests, Davi got down to business. He managed to claw his way up to a 70 percent for the first week, including a check a few days into the second week for telling the truth about an incident where he "accidentally" threw a ball into his after-care counselor's face. After I discussed the incident with one of the supervisors a few days later, I believed that he had not been paying attention, and she had not seen it coming. She made nothing more out of it; nor did any of the other children in his group speak of it.

Perhaps more encouraged, Davi seemed to have an easier time the second week. He made it to Thursday morning before being struck with two Xs for slipping in an unnecessary, rude comment subtly aimed toward hurting Matheus, and then made an inane excuse for his rudeness. I reminded him what he had been working toward and awarded him a check for stopping rather than fussing further, as was typical. It was rough the final two days of the week, when we were on our family vacation to Legoland and Universal Studios. I needed to constantly remind Davi of his rude tendencies that were making it increasingly difficult for me to ignore. With difficulty seizing opportunities to reinforce appropriate behavior to offset the Xs, maneuvering to the end of the week seemed even tighter than walking the proverbial thin line . . . until he crawled over the finish line at the week's end with a 76 percent.

The checks and Xs were making headway in raising the boys' awareness about their behavior relative to what was expected of them. Matheus continued to covet the definitive 100 percent, striving for perfection in the spirit of competition. Davi, on the other hand, having finally achieved success in reaching his goal of at least 75 percent, found a new resolve. He became more conscientious and forthright in accepting accountability for his behavior; more empowered, he was more invested in doing what was right, what was expected of him.

The checks and X's still prevailed a little while longer. Matheus was fast outgrowing their purpose, yet I still needed to redirect some of his offensive behavior. I also found it difficult to concentrate on rewarding Davi for his positive behavior without penalizing him for his negative behavior, which threatened to bury him in a perpetual state of despondency. The boys still needed structure. They still were rooted in having experienced a past life filled with chaos and unpredictability, yet they were starting to let go and bank more on the present and future rather than staying stuck in the past.

Chapter 24

That's the Way the Cookie Crumbles

I did not start out with children who experienced a secure attachment, with core beliefs of themselves as "I am good, wanted, worthwhile, competent, and lovable" as a function of caregivers who were appropriately responsive to their needs by being sensitive, dependable, caring, and trustworthy. The world around them did not offer a safe haven with the promise of a life worth living. Rather, their core beliefs resembled a compromised attachment from the lack of consistency in the emotional or physical availability of caregivers, with beliefs of themselves as "I am bad, unwanted, worthless, helpless, and unlovable." Their world felt unsafe, their lives painful and burdensome. I needed to whittle away at their negative core beliefs, those hard and fast beliefs driven by their need for self-protection and survival.

One Sunday morning, newly into our checks and Xs system, I woke up to find them sitting together on the couch in the game room with the top to my laptop on the desk closed and a mouse newly attached. I knew I should have shut the laptop down at night, but thought to leave it up in case Matheus wanted to get a head start on his history web page project. Without a word exchanged, I strolled over to the laptop, flipping it open to discover that *somebody* was on a gory video gaming website; both boys steadfastly denied any knowledge of the sort. I kept my composure, simply stating that it was clear at least one of them was involved, yet each got an X for holding back the truth. A deadline was set for nine o'clock that morning. If the truth did not come out, there would be further consequences for both of them.

I left them to take my shower, using the time and space to defuse my anger and frustration seething inside. I prepared myself to hang tough if there was no admission of wrongdoing. As I was getting dressed, Davi came over, wanting only to tell me why the mouse was attached to the laptop. I stopped him short, informing him the only details I was interested in was who went into my laptop without permission, as it was off limits to both boys; he quietly began to retreat but only to turn back around and claim he had done it. Matheus supposedly did not even know Davi had been on the laptop; he went online while Matheus was still in his room and put down the top before Matheus came in. He only showed Matheus the mouse and how it could be attached. "So, you can take away Matheus's X . . . I don't want him to get in trouble for something I did."

I was not so sure I was ready to accept Matheus's complete lack of involvement; for whatever reason Davi might have sought to protect his brother, it would have to wait for further exploration at a more opportune time. I thanked Davi for being truthful. When he asked whether he could get a check for telling the truth, I told him he'd *could have* if he told me the truth from the start. Regardless, consequences would have to be handed out. It seemed as though he'd broken all of the cardinal rules. He was not allowed to touch my laptop, play video games, or go online without my supervision, let alone go to inappropriate websites.

For his willful defiance and complete disregard for my authority, he was grounded to his room for the day. Returning home from our Hebrew school and Sunday Bible study run,

Davi went into his room; we were not to hear from him other than when I came to check on him. I brought him a simple lunch of a peanut butter-and-jelly sandwich with a glass of water. Throughout the day and evening, whenever a request was made or a meager complaint uttered, I responded, "When you are grounded, you do not have the privilege of choice."

Davi pretty much kept to himself, staying in his room without his usual attention-seeking ways. He seemed all too pleased to hang out, ignore the increasing pile of his laundered clothes in need of folding and putting away, and leaving bits and pieces of toys and other sundries strewn around his room as if a tornado had blown through. He gave me a dirty look when I told him he needed to take care of his room before turning in for bed or he would be grounded again the next day. As I was preparing dinner, he rather meekly peered around the corner to ask whether he would be allowed to join us for dinner. I wanted to relent, but knew I couldn't: "When you are grounded, you do not have the privilege of joining us." He silently retreated back into his room.

When he was officially granted his release orders to shower and get ready for bed, he had already put back his room together and neatly put away his clothes. He seemed relieved the day had passed and all could return to normal. I did not make more of the incident other than to ask why he was grounded, reassure him of my love with a hug, and inform him that perhaps he would be grounded for longer, without his toys and other trinkets to help pass the time if there was a next time he chose to go into something when he knew he was not supposed to.

* * *

Many years ago as part of my graduate studies, I gained clinical experience through a year-long practicum at a day treatment school. I still vividly recall a family therapy session with my ten-year-old client, his parents, and his eight-year-old brother. The entire session's sole focus was on who had left a green cup in the bathtub, ending without anything being resolved, let alone a clear culprit identified. I was dumbfounded at how much emotional energy was wasted. My client was the family's scapegoat; his disturbing behaviors and emotional angst seemed a larger-than-life reflection of his family's overall dysfunction that slowly unfolded in his therapy.

I had flashbacks to that green cup another Sunday morning when something did not look quite right upon opening the refrigerator; though it looked as if it was tucked away in its proper place, I took out a supposedly unopened roll of cookies for a closer inspection. Not only was one cookie missing, but someone took the trouble to tape around the roll as if it were not yet opened. I was impressed by the care and precision of the culprit's handiwork. It was easy to dismiss Davi as a possible suspect, as there was no way he was capable of such neatness in his work. Yet I still had to start off from an unbiased vantage point.

I sat them down and asked for the truth, yet got only shrugs of the shoulders and refusals of accountability for the deed. While disposing of the rest of the cookies in the roll down the garbage disposal, I simply stated how disappointed I was about this act of mistrust, and that until the truth came out, no desserts would make an appearance, in addition to an X for each. Once again, it was off to their Hebrew and Sunday schools. Throughout the car ride, Matheus was noticeably grumpy, giving greater credence to his having done the deed, with his conscience taking a beating.

After dropping Davi off at the temple, I challenged Matheus by stating, "Just so you know, not that I will know who did it until I am told, but the cookie roll had been taped up with such neatness, with such perfection, that I have a hard time believing Davi could have done it. He is not capable of such neat work." Matheus angrily retorted that there was "no point to that," and that I had "no proof" of who could have done it, and how dared I make any such accusations of him. I was seething inside over his unrelenting stubbornness, yet puzzled by what kept him on the defensive, willing to let it snowball no matter the cost. His brother had been forthright in wanting to make sure he took all the blame the last time. With the shoe on the other foot, Matheus was willing to throw Davi under the bus rather than fess up to a rather innocent transgression, yet which was now starting to magnify out of proportion with the potential for rather serious implications.

As I dropped him off at church for his Bible study, for which he had only just begun attending, I wished for the convenience of Catholicism and a confessional I could toss him into. He needed an anonymous, nonthreatening mechanism to help him take greater accountability for himself. I liked the premise that anyone who takes advantage of this sacrament of penance in a purposeful manner stands to understand the freedom that can come from confessing our sins to a minister of the Lord and subsequently become absolved. In making the commitment not to sin again, a whole new start in life can be assumed when admitting guilt, and being free from carrying around the burden of the bad choices initially made. As we had previously arranged, I returned an hour later to escort Matheus to Sunday mass with the congregation at large. I had to stifle a rising smirk of self-satisfaction when spotting the most relevant of psalms highlighted on the monitor: John 8:32—*Then you will know the truth and the truth will set you free.*

Even though he remained taciturn, I still derived satisfaction from taking the opportunity to mention the psalm and how true I thought was the sentiment. At one point during the minister's sermon, when forgiveness and unconditional love were referenced, I reached out and took Matheus's hand, and he comfortingly grasped mine in return. Still, there was no admission of his guilt. Back at the house, I took out my baking provisions to start in on the holiday baking with the likes of chocolate-chip cookie bars, butterscotch blondies, white-chocolate-chip oatmeal cookies, and chocolate cheesecake brownies. Perhaps he could not ignore his conscience anymore, or maybe the comforting smells of my baking efforts wafting throughout the house and the threat of no more desserts did him in. Seemingly lacking in contrition, Matheus abruptly appeared, simply confessing that he had taken the cookie. I asked him when he ate the cookie, but he did not remember. I asked him why he ate the cookie: "Because I wanted to." I asked him why he decided to tell me now: "Because I wanted dessert."

Although Mathues had proven capable of higher moral reasoning levels, his social and emotional immaturity still reigned, and he clearly had not yet fully internalized society's conventions of what is right or wrong; instead, he still tended to focus largely on avoiding external consequences. I asked him, "What should we do now?" As expected, he replied, "I don't know," seemingly waiting for the inevitable consequence to be doled out. I surprised him by deemphasizing the doling out of a consequence in favor of my stressing to him the importance of being truthful, and my understanding of how hard it could be for him to do so. I also took the opportunity to point out to him that his surly attitude toward me throughout the day was mostly a reflection of his conscience eating away inside. This could easily have been averted by his having told the truth when first asked rather than letting it snowball, with the threat of being buried by the avalanche of fear and regret.

I informed him that he still would be washing the car that afternoon as he normally did every two weeks, but would not earn his allowance money for it. He, in turn, dared to negotiate: Could he still earn money for washing the car, yet not earn the previously expected same amount for the extra chore of digging a hole and taking out a sprinkler head? Happy to let him hold on to some semblance of control, I relented. None of that proved important, as he simply, lightheartedly declared after finishing with the car, "Father, you don't have to pay me for washing the car . . . I had fun." He had his brother's so-called help, but Davi was really there to provide comic relief and jack up the fun factor. I could clearly hear their squeals of delight from outside. Matheus was able to save face and repent at the same time . . . perhaps another step closer to a securer attachment.

* * *

Just a mere three days later, when I was getting ready for bed, I noticed that a small pile of pants I'd laid out on my chest at the foot of the bed was moved on to the bed as if someone had gone into the chest. Flipping open the lid, I found a Nerf bow-and-arrow set and air gun were missing; I had confiscated them from Matheus more than a year ago. My heart skipped a beat as I recalled taking the toys away from him in the midst of his heated temper tantrum, when he aimed the bow and arrow at me. Feeling overwhelmed with just handling his tantrum at the time, I missed out on engaging him further about his threatening behavior; he never mentioned the toys again, and I did not give the event a second thought; nor had such provocative, threatening behavior resurfaced.

Matheus was the likely culprit; Davi and I had left the house as usual in the morning, with Matheus still at home for another hour before he would go off to school. The three of us did not return home until after Matheus's soccer game late that evening. There was no chance for Davi to even have gone into my room. Several months before, I had found the same exact clues indicating that someone had been in my chest, although nothing had been taken and the bow-and-arrow and air gun still lay there untouched; Matheus had tearfully, steadfastly denied having gone into the chest back then. Meeting up with the brick wall of his emotional defenses, I left it alone other than to spell out to him that if there were any more such "funny things," he would be signed up for his school's before- and after-care program, as he could not be trusted at home alone.

Supposedly in bed, both boys had just gotten up for a glass of water. I hoped to take advantage and resolve this so a new day could begin fresh; I thought that in light of the previous Sunday's events it might not be terribly difficult to deal with it right up front. I simultaneously flipped on both their lights, positioned myself in the small entryway between their rooms and started off once again with "I need the truth . . ." With no response from either of them, I strolled into Matheus's room, and instinctively rolled back the closet doors, to reveal the toys casually placed on the top shelf, in plain sight. He'd made no real effort to hide them, as if he wanted to be caught; yet he steadfastly denied knowing anything about them. He was not willing to engage further, and it was pointless to push. Before turning to leave, I simply told him how disappointed I was, that I expected to be told "the truth" and hoped he would do so "tomorrow."

After another sleepless night, upon emerging from my morning's routine I was taken aback when Matheus greeted me at the kitchen counter with his bright smile, exclaiming "Look, Father, I finished my homework!" I stared at him, incredulous at his detachment from the previous night's unresolved events. I simply replied, "That's nice, but I am still waiting to hear the truth about the Nerf toys." His pearly whites suddenly vanished behind the scowl on his face. With his counselor coming that afternoon, I went about our morning routine.

I reminded Matheus about his counseling appointment that afternoon, and which teachers he needed to speak to, to clarify a few F grades he could not explain why they appeared on his online grade book.

Coming home in the afternoon, he tried passing off another broad smile, exclaiming, "Look, Father. I got a free soda." Again I replied, "That's nice," trying to maintain a balance between neutrality and indifference, all the while doubting his claims of the soda's being free, and wondering how he really got it. Trying to engage with me further, he informed me, "I almost got punched in the face today." I shrugged off this proclamation and informed him that I was glad he was okay and that he could get started on his homework while I picked up Davi from school. With a shrug of his shoulders, he went about his business. When his counselor arrived, I asked for a family therapy session to more directly address Matheus's stalwart ways.

Matheus was overtly cooperative in sitting down with the three of us, yet he maintained his resistance to discussing the matter past assertions of not having committed any wrongdoing. His attitude also was surly toward both his counselor and me; she attempted to enforce limits pertaining to his need for respect while reassuring him that we were not there to persecute him. He swiftly got up, readying himself to leave. She agreed to let him go, to which I countered, "But you are expected to return." His counselor continued working with Davi, maintaining focus on the ramifications of lying, albeit more for Matheus's benefit, still within earshot in his room. After about fifteen minutes, Matheus emerged from his room, still incensed; he nodded his consent when the counselor asked him whether he wanted his alone time with her.

As I was folding laundry, Matheus came over and promptly declared, "I took the guns . . ." and thrust his cell phone at me, further proclaiming, "And here is my punishment." His counselor came up from behind, prompting him to "hold on" for one issue at a time. It was a toss-up for Matheus between worries about his consequences for taking and then lying about the Nerf toys and feeling the sting of the cold shoulder. He became teary when his counselor told me of his concern about being grounded to his room and getting only peanut butter-and jelly-sandwiches as Davi had for lunch when he had been grounded. I had long sensed something connected with his past concerning fears of being confined, isolated, and rejected; being grounded, detained to his room, would only exacerbate his vulnerability. He also had "a very bad day at school today" he'd wanted to share with me. His feelings were hurt when he felt rebuffed. After reassuring him that I had only been following his lead, and that it was his choice to keep me at a distance with his refusal to tell me the truth, I reminded him of his consequence of starting his school's before- and after-care program for the month. A half hour before, he had adamantly refused: "I won't go . . ." "you can't make me"; this time he only weakly protested, "But I don't want to," before dropping it.

After his counselor left, I summoned Matheus over to the couch in my office. He came over, but only to stand, staring back at me with obvious reservation in his eyes and stance. "Come over *here* . . . sit down." As he did so, I wrapped my arm around his shoulders and pulled him toward me. As he laid his head on my chest, I softly asked him to tell me what had happened today. We had a free-flowing interchange of information, ideas, and sentiment without any sense of wariness or air of petulance from him. The moment was all about being connected as father and son, without Matheus worrying of being judged, rebuked, or slighted. For that moment, we were bonded, and I was his safe haven.

Chapter 25

The Truth of the Matter Is . . .

The Jewish High Holy Days took on new meaning for us this second go-around, coinciding with Davi starting Hebrew school. Davi heartily embraced his new teachings of Hebrew, Judaism, and Israel. Counter to the spirit of the holidays, two days before ushering in the Jewish New Year, Davi came home from school with a note in his planner; he was "playing around" during Spanish. He denied having done anything; the other kids, who "pointed at me for no reason" when the teacher had his back turned, had framed him. Knowing better, trying to get him to be more accountable for his actions, I informed him, "This is your chance to tell me the truth." He shrugged, maintaining his stance even after I told him I would check with his teacher for verification.

The next morning, prior to his leaving for school, I showed Davi the e-mail I'd composed to his teacher; he said the note was "perfect" and it was okay to send it, all the while continuing to maintain his innocence. Later that afternoon, I informed him that his teacher wrote back and she would have the Spanish teacher e-mail me directly. Davi waited until later in the evening, while I was preparing dinner, to tell me he did talk out one time, yet he stopped when the teacher addressed him; it was somebody else who talked out the next time, when the others pointed at Davi and he was then sent out of the classroom. I simply thanked him for filling me in, yet I remained cautious over the skimpiness of the details and said I would wait for his teacher's e-mail for further verification.

After Davi had gone to bed following our family's Rosh Hashanah dinner celebrations, I saw that his Spanish teacher had written back; he clearly detailed, *Davi had been disruptive for most of the forty minutes by either talking or laughing out loud. I had given him several warnings but he kept being disruptive as was another student in the class (they don't even sit near each other). After the last time, I gave him a consequence. His teacher told me she is having some behavior problems with him as well. I think he will be better in Spanish next time because he now knows that there will be a consequence.* I felt my cheeks redden, the heat beginning to rise from the soles of my feet.

With services to attend at the temple in the morning, I was conflicted about how to make good on the need to address this second burst of behavioral issues in school; even more important, once again Davi was dodging accountability for his behavior. I did not want to interfere with the symbolic value of the start of a New Year and mar the focus of the service, deciding to wait until after services to address the truth. It was kismet as I found inspiration in the rabbi's concluding remarks the next morning about Teshuvah, literally meaning "return," and associated with the concept of repentance in Judaism. Only by atoning for our sins can we restore balance to our relationship with G-d and with our fellow human beings. In referring to Teshuvah, the rabbi emphasized the need for being truthful so there is genuineness toward others, and seeking forgiveness for wrongs that may have been committed.

The rabbi's sermon neatly followed a discussion the cantor had had with the students the previous week about the need for concerted efforts to apologize for a wrongdoing, even if the person wronged was not accepting. As Davi related to me what he heard, I tried expanding his narrow understanding of what was even more important: the need to be genuine in apologizing for a wrongdoing. Talking was one thing, but taking action was what mattered, in the need to refrain from committing the wrongful act again.

I left Matheus with Michael and my mother while I took Davi home, simply telling him we needed to confer about an e-mail I'd received; he only wanted to know why we had to go all the way home only to look at an e-mail when we could do it at Grandma's house. He played it cool in the car. He was not interested in speaking further about Teshuvah, instead trying to engage me with irrelevant facts and trivia. I coolly feigned a passive interest. At home, I pulled up a website with a child-friendly discussion about Teshuvah that set the tone for the afternoon's work detail.

Davi appeared receptive as we reviewed the different stages concerning Teshuvah. We started with the need to recognize one's wrongdoing and feeling sincerity and remorse, doing everything in one's power to undo any damage caused while also asking for forgiveness. Resolving never to commit the wrongful behavior again rounded out the discussion's focus. I then brought up his Spanish teacher's e-mail. Ignoring the carnival of faces of his feigned disbelief, I asked how he could have been disruptive one time when the teacher told of his being disruptive for nearly the entire forty minutes. He had no answer, standing in silence, impassively waiting for the inevitable consequence. The already sad, tired truth of the matter was that I already knew consequences didn't have much of an effect on Davi.

"You need to be responsible for your behavior . . . you need to be truthful . . . you need to . . ."

Davi did not want to hear it. He was becoming more insubordinate about his passive-aggressive ways, spiraling further into the black hole of empty, insincere, unsatisfying relations with others. Most important, his behavior was taking a toll on our father-son relationship, supposedly the very center of his world, and the jumping-off point for adaptive and emotionally fulfilling relationships with others. I was becoming increasingly stressed by the struggle to nurture a more secure attachment between us as father and son.

* * *

Calvin once said to his imaginary tiger pal, Hobbes, "I can't think of anything to argue ... I'm always right and everybody else is always wrong! What's to argue about?" Davi recently found some of my *Calvin and Hobbes* cartoon collection books. He bulldozed his way through the many similar sentiments of a bright, articulate, yet exceedingly self-absorbed, and at times rather like-minded mischievous youngster. As he chortled along with the antics of his apparent counterpart, he *got* the outrageousness of Calvin's expectations of the world revolving solely around him; thoughts, feelings, and perspectives of anyone else simply did not matter. However, even Calvin stopped in his deference to authority. Davi's relentless pursuit of the last word, serving to maintain his ego seemed mostly a reflection of his misguided intellect and emotional immaturity; he was still in need of direction *and patience.*

Not unlike an exploding pressure cooker, I was increasingly blowing up at inopportune, nonsensical times; sometimes I felt myself turning into a raving lunatic, forsaking logic, rationality, and reason, only to be tuned out and regarded as a nonentity. I began questioning how to effectively allow myself to feel my emotions more sanely, still assert myself as the responsible parent, and avoid erupting like a volcano of unprocessed emotions. Combating the symptoms of Davi's broken cycle of attachment seemed unrelenting; his difficulties being truthful and accountable for his behavior prevented him from adopting an authentic mind-set.

Sitting at the computer with Davi, I quietly laid out for him the afternoon's work detail. I explained he was to start by writing a letter of apology to his Spanish teacher; it was to be specific about what he was sorry for and what he would do differently. It was not to be a quick one-sentence write-off, but a detailed, fully written paragraph, neatly written, and corrected for spelling and grammar. After that, he was assigned to write an essay about telling the truth and what it meant, including both what he thought it meant and what others said it meant. For his reference, I printed out some quickie online, child-friendly excerpts about telling the truth, and stories from a website of fables; each concluded with the moral of the story in relation to lying. Lastly, his essay would conclude with why he thought he had problems telling the truth.

He had all afternoon and was expected to stay in his room working; if he wanted to join Michael, Grandma, and Matheus for dinner that night, the work had to be completed. At first Davi was overwhelmed, yet he tried playing dumb, claiming he did not know what an essay was. I simply explained to him that writing an essay was analogous to what he had been learning from the start of fourth grade, to prepare for the state's critical writing test at that year's end. It was no different from when he'd recently had to write about a favorite memory. Having run out of stalling tactics, he disappeared into his room, mostly appearing to sustain due diligence in his work. The house took on a calm, peaceful atmosphere.

He had to make a few rewrites, and we discussed in between his genuine, conscientious expression of the key components of telling the truth. The end result was a full page, front and back, aptly titled, "Don't Lie." Davi started off strongly, subscribing to thoughts of avoiding the ill regard of others in having someone "you lie to thinking you're lying even when you tell the truth." Davi's later points reflected less mature thoughts with concerns about being truthful simply for the sake of not getting into "more trouble." His conclusion reflected greater maturity in his thinking as he expressed concern over interpersonal discord, feeling bad as a result of his consequences for lying. *I cannot play with my brother and I like spending time with him.* He further wrote, *I don't like when people don't believe me, or when I get into a lot of trouble, and when Father does not feel so much excited about me.* His conclusion even reached higher levels of mature thinking, adhering to a law-and-order mentality in his deference to authority. He warned, *You should not hang out with liars... you'll get in big trouble, because other people will think you might have done something with the liar. Not only will you get in more trouble you lied, than if you did and think you'll feel guilty. So, think again... don't lie.* I was finally able to relax a bit; remorse figured into the equation after all.

* * *

The Greek philosopher, Epictetus fittingly noted, "When you are offended at any man's fault, turn to yourself and study your own failings. Then you will forget your anger." The idea is much easier said than done, yet keeping the focus onto the heart—or truth—of the matter helped me stay more objective about Davi's difficult behavior. To continue modeling more appropriate and controlled expressions of emotion, I put myself on a checks and Xs chart, with my publicized goal to stop yelling for a month. I gave myself a check each time I would like to have yelled, highlighting to the boys how I could handle a situation in a calm, impassive manner simply because I was motivated to do so. Davi even sometimes took it upon himself to tell me when I earned a check for having handled a problem in an apparently fair-minded, rational way.

Over the course of the first two weeks, I ended up garnering two Xs, both of which were on Yom Kippur, the Jewish holiday for atonement and remembrance. I was struggling to cope with yet another first occasion of significance with my father's absence in our lives. I felt particularly vulnerable in having to light my very first *Yahrzeit* memorial candle on *erev* Yom Kippur. It seemed no accident that it was also my father's birthday. Having to watch the candle's flickering glow throughout the next day, with its flame softly fading away late into the evening, I was held captive by the constant reminder that my father was no longer with us. Fasting the next day, engaging in the Jewish ritual of cleansing the spirit, didn't help stabilize my mood. The boys and I muddled through the day and moved on to the next day, apologizing to one another for our short tempers and uncooperative, insensitive attitudes.

Another incident with the Spanish teacher occurred only the day before Yom Kippur, yet truth and accountability seemed more at the forefront this time around. Davi told me about the conflict straightway when I picked him up from after-care, and was forthright about the details. His account appeared mostly credible in comparison to another email contact with the Spanish teacher, which seemed to highlight an overreaction on the teacher's part: *I was talking to another student when Davi said something and of course it gets the class going. I then told Davi I still had your e-mail address. At that point he put his head down. Mind you, we were in the middle of an explanation of Spanish material and I had no time to waste, so I asked Davi to sit up and he did not. I asked him several times, but he seemed to be crying and I told him there weren't any babies in here so he shouldn't be crying. I don't think he was crying so I asked him one more time to pay attention, and when he refused I asked him to leave the classroom. He ended up chatting with another third-grade teacher with whom he was familiar from the year before and told her he was sad because his grandfather had died. I think it was more relevant to my mentioning I still had your e-mail.*

I alerted the teacher that my father's still-recent death had been affecting all of us, in light of its having been his birthday on that day, as well as the Jewish holiday of remembrance. Though Davi's loss of emotional control was still not appropriate, I felt it was important to highlight our need for our greater sensitivity at this time. The teacher responded, *I'm sorry for your loss. I will speak to Davi alone to make sure we are on the same page so that he can talk to me about things like that . . .* I praised Davi up, down, and all around upon his earning a check for being truthful and responsible for his behavior. At week's end, as Davi and I converged for the tally of the week's balance of checks and Xs, a positive change was in the air. The long-coveted reverse in the graphing pattern was noted; its raised line of checks finally crisscrossed away from the lowered line of Xs. Having achieved a 61 percent, after a full month of being away from the television, Davi was pleased to finally have shown the improvement he needed to have gotten his TV privileges.

Even further encouraged, Davi also began to ask whether he could start earning his allowance again, which had long been frozen for lack of his sincere interest in consistently carrying out his one daily chore of bringing in the morning newspaper. He claimed he was motivated to earn money for an upcoming weekend trip, and he wanted to be more responsible, and was ready to renegotiate. To make it as simple as possible to keep track, I decided that just one missed newspaper would void his allowance for the week. Matheus could relate, having had his weekly allowance voided for the week on the few occasions he "forgot" to take out the garbage cans on Friday.

* * *

This new drive Davi had to earn privileges as a function of hard work, manifested by the spirit and integrity of honor and trustworthiness, would be short-lived. I caught Davi in his room one morning later in the week playing the Nintendo DS without permission; he had yet to earn the privilege according to his performance with the checks and Xs. Feeling betrayed, yet maintaining my composure, I snatched the DS out of his hands. Ignoring his look of generic disbelief, I told him he was grounded to his room for the day. Still, he had his basketball game that morning, and there were team pictures, and haircuts that were scheduled that afternoon, and we needed to make it to the library to return some books due that day. While he was in his room throughout the spurts we were home, I gave him the work detail of organizing all his clothes, neatly folding and putting them away, as well as cleaning out his closet. There would be no time for reading or playing.

Davi immediately responded, "I'm not going to do it," to which I countered, "Fine. You will be grounded to your room until you do what you need to do." Perhaps feeling this was too harsh, or again not trusting my parental judgment, Matheus began to interfere. He claimed it was "not fair" for Davi to have to do his clothes, telling his brother, "You only need to do your pants," the only articles of clothing strewn about the floor in the closet at the time. Matheus might also have been reacting to having lost his own videogame privileges at the same time for playing the other DS system in his room without permission.

Perhaps I was a bit extreme, but I relied on trying to overcorrect his behavior by requiring Davi to restore the loss of trust by inconveniencing him, and discouraging his repetition of this rule-breaking behavior. I had hoped to inconvenience him with having him to refold, reorganize, and clean up, yet also symbolically relate to the act of repentance for his wrongful behavior, not unlike the tenets of Teshuvah. My intention was to continue instilling in both Davi directly and Matheus vicariously the need to take responsibility for their actions.

When he was explicitly directed, Davi's performance tended to be impeccable, reflecting a great deal of care and sincerity; after several hours had passed and he maintained due diligence in his work, he had neatly folded all his clothes and put them away in drawers and in the closet with nary the chance for a crease or furrow. Hence, I promptly praised Davi for his hard work, essentially reinforcing the kind of positive behavior that contrasted with lying and contempt for authority. Even Matheus appeared somewhat contrite later that day, sincerely reporting to me that he felt badly for angering me about also playing the DS that morning.

Clearly, apologies are important, and it does matter whether a person asks for forgiveness. Yet words do not mean anything without the action that attests to one's sincerity, which apparently was lost on the boys from an earlier time in their lives, ruled by chaos and unpredictability. As instilled in Hebrew school, G-d wants us to truly feel remorse and regret; subjugation is in and of itself humbling. Although fumbling the week with a 43 percent, Davi rebounded the next week with his strongest performance of a 64 percent. He made concerted effort, yet it would be another two months—and the threat of more repentance with the donation of his Chanukah presents—before he finally got it.

Chapter 26

A House Divided . . .

Only a few months into our first year together, I took a day to meet up with my "little brother," Brandon, who was home on leave from the air force. It was a three-hour drive to get to him, with another three hours to get back home; the boys were to spend the day with our neighbors. It was a Sunday and it meant they also would be going to church. I was leery about them attending church so early into our family's evolution. The Jewish High Holy Days had only recently passed, and I still had yet to think about handling the upcoming Christmas season. We'd yet to have any discussion of significance about religion; both boys seemed fine with the little bit of exposure to Judaism thus far, going along with these strange customs of their new family. They both still made references to their Christian roots, but neither indicated any specific desire to pursue that faith.

I hoped religion would become a non-issue as they continued their acculturation into the family. I was fearful of the unknown and possible influences their visit to church might have, yet holding my breath, I sent them on their way. Later that evening, Matheus was quick to dismiss his experience as boring; it was "just like school." He did not like being separated from the adults in the main sanctuary to participate in religious activities he felt were "just like work." Davi also did not seem to take any of the teachings to heart. It was only a couple of months later, shortly after the Christmas holidays, that he announced his intentions to adopt the Jewish faith, further aligning himself directly with his new family. His brother continued to maintain a passive stance on religious identification.

Once Davi put his intentions out there, he never looked back. He enthusiastically took in the sights and sounds of Judaism, while Matheus gradually asserted his interest in aligning with Christianity. His growing insistence climaxed during the second go-around of the High Holy Days, nearly a year and a half since we'd forged our path as a family. During services, it was obvious he had grown further dissatisfied with, frustrated by, and disconnected from the practice of Judaism. He mindlessly thumbed through prayer books mostly written in Hebrew; contending with the absorption of a third language was not practical for him. Even when trying to attend to the English translations, Matheus still was not relating to the lack of emphasis on accepting Jesus Christ as our savior.

Consumed with the emptiness surrounding the newness of my father's absence, and regenerated by the customs associated with *Yizkor*, Judaism's memorial prayer, I was unprepared for Matheus's tactless approach in the parking lot following the service. With impatience in his tone, he abruptly asked, "Father, when can I go to church?" His ill-timed query obviously was motivated by his growing discontent at feeling forced to assume a religion to which he was not relating. It was brutally apparent that the time had come to frankly take on Matheus's implied Christian convictions, amid the rustlings and groans of my ancestors rolling over in their graves.

I asked Matheus to be patient as I investigated how to get him started in a way that would be meaningful for him. I also needed more time to squarely grapple with my own feelings about the prospect of raising a son who wanted to assume a religious identity contradictory to my beliefs and cultural heritage. For another perspective, I turned to a long-time close family friend of my mother's whom I'd known since elementary school. Her oldest son had converted to Christianity and was the minister of a large church congregation she and her husband attended regularly. Her husband also converted to Christianity. Her other two sons did not expressly follow the Jewish faith, having married non-Jews, and their children were not specifically being raised to follow the Jewish faith. My mother's friend was the lone holdout, maintaining her Jewish identity and beliefs. I asked her thoughts about managing a family with varying belief systems pertaining to religion and G-d; she responded rather poignantly, "I believe in G-d. He is everybody's G-d. I run my life by the ten Commandments, and it is the same no matter whether you are Jewish or Christian ... G-d is G-d; how you get to him is what unites all of us."

I, too, have always felt the need for spirituality in my life. I took to heart the Hindu perspective: For those who dive deep into the inner self, best connects spiritually with one's belief in G-d. It is only through the path of spirituality that enlightenment can be gained and salvation reached. To get to God we need to travel the path of spirituality, the path of absolute wisdom. This was what I hoped for Matheus and Davi; the choice of a particular organized religion did not seem to matter as much anymore.

* * *

For convenience sake, the prospect of bouncing back and forth between two different houses of worship seemed inconceivable. That first Sunday Matheus started to go to church had us out of the house promptly after breakfast, first zipping down south for Davi's nine thirty drop-off at the synagogue for Torah school. With no time to dawdle, it was off to the eastern end of the county for church at ten fifteen. My mother would pick Davi up from Torah school that day so I could stay and attend the church's adult service while Matheus checked out the youth ministry service for middle schoolers; if she hadn't that day, it would have been a hasty turn-around to pick Davi up at eleven thirty before the mad dash to return and pick Matheus up at noon. He was visiting the same church our neighbors attended; we planned to meet there and go in together that first Sunday.

The Friday night before, we attended a special service at the synagogue led by Davi's Torah class. Perhaps in anticipation of his visit to church on Sunday, Matheus appeared more distant, only casually taking a glance at the prayer book during the service. Davi seemed completely in his element, situating himself front and center on the bema. He handled his small solo reading passage flawlessly; his voice rang loud and clear in reciting the Hebrew verses. I wondered how much Matheus might have resented his brother's self-assuredness and his contentment with his chosen religious aspirations. Matheus struggled to find his own personal niche, and his shyness too often held him back from acting on his desires; yet his desire to stake out his claim with the familiar may have motivated him to actively begin re-establishing his Christian roots.

On that first Sunday, Matheus took care in donning his good dress shoes, jeans, and a long-sleeved button-down collared shirt; he did not care to dress as nicely for the Friday-night service, for which I had to direct him to at least wear a collared shirt. When we first arrived at the church, I was taken aback by the gargantuan size of the complex. Golf carts whizzed around, shuttling people from the far reaches of the parking lot. Once inside, I could have been attending a convention as we made our way through crowds of gatherers milling around and moving about in multiple directions.

While waiting for our neighbors to arrive, I took Matheus up to the sanctuary for the middle school-aged kids, taking in a quick tour of a darkened area with two huge video screens blaring Christian rock music. He did not appear to have any reservations upon my leaving him as I joined our neighbors in the main sanctuary.

With all the trappings of a rock concert, the resident band played Christian songs to lift the congregants' spirits before Pastor Bob took the stage. Cameras constantly zigzagged across from above, filming the service for the benefit of the church's satellite campuses. I felt Pastor Bob delivered an intelligent sermon. I connected with many of his comparisons to real-life situations in his emphasis on spirituality, morality, and self-worth . . . until there was the almighty reference to fellowship in accepting Jesus Christ as our savior. I was not comfortable; it was so very different from what I was used to.

When I met up with Matheus afterward, the shine on his face was unmistakable; he clearly appreciated worship with which he was familiar. On the way to pick up Davi, I queried him about his experience and equated Pastor Bob's remarks with what G-d expects from all of us. Regardless of whether debated from a Christian or Jewish perspective, there seemed the universal expectation of being respectful to one another and to oneself, deferring to authority, and knowing right from wrong. Matheus mostly shrugged his way through our conversation, devoid of any particular insights of his own other than a trivial comment about how "you really are not allowed to say 'I am'" in recognition of one's deference to G-d's authority. I teasingly denied knowing another way to say something like "I am proud of you . . . I am pleased how you . . . I am frustrated . . ." If I'd been engaged with Davi, I would have received an entire dissertation leaving nothing to my imagination. Matheus merely shrugged his shoulders again, not willing to engage with me further; nor did his shine endure, as he did not appear enthusiastic about returning the following week.

I was not sure how to proceed. I still was uncomfortable with the pageantry surrounding this church's version of the communication of G-d's word. I sat Matheus down again, this time to entertain trying another church with a different perspective for comparison. He simply stated, "I like this one." I explained that even in Judaism there were different perspectives to consider, starting with reformed, conservative, and orthodox. My parents and me had been to several different synagogues over the years and experienced many assorted ways Judaism is observed. We chose our particular synagogue as a result of an informed decision. Especially since the Christian faith encompassed so many different outlooks, I felt it was important for Matheus to at least gain one other perspective. Bending ever so slightly, he warily responded, "Okay . . . but only this one time." I doubted he had much of an open mind, yet I was surprised I got even that far with him.

Matheus returned to that same church the following Sunday, Thanksgiving weekend; he wanted to go even though Davi had off from Torah school. Matheus was on a mission. I did not know what point he was trying to prove; I doubted he even understood himself. After services this second go-around, Matheus did not at all emanate the same shine as he did the previous week. He commented, "It was the same thing . . . only the songs were different." I did not engage him further, avoiding the potential of a power struggle amid the narrow-minded confines of his tenacity.

* * *

Given the go-ahead to seek out a different church to try, I was mindful to look for a church community offering a smaller, more cohesive congregation in line with what Matheus was used to in Brazil. I first turned to the Unitarian faith. I liked the idea of the diversity of beliefs put into practice via the focus on social justice within the context of a smaller, closely knit congregation. In further discussion with the youth director, I decided they were too small; the youth group was comprised of only five teens in Matheus's age group "if they all showed up."

I turned to another community church more traditional in its practice of Christianity, just three miles down the road from our synagogue. Even more of a coup for me was the convenient timing of the youth's Bible study, sandwiched in between dropping Davi off at the synagogue and picking him up, with enough time for doing the family grocery shopping before picking him back up. Just before leaving Matheus behind for the youth Bible study, I was able to introduce him to the pastor who led the meetings; he bluntly told of his leaving the church in a mere two weeks, with Christmas Day being his last. Pastor Chip would be taking over, an older gentleman who seemed to have an enthusiastic, welcoming persona when we met him in passing.

Seeming to feel awkward in having to fend for himself, Matheus waved me away anyway. I left him there, wondering whether he would give this a genuine try. An hour later, he greeted me with a smile, again claiming, "it was the same thing," with the group covering the same part in the Bible from the previous week, picking up where the other church had left off. He then simply said, "It was smaller," leading me to wrestle aloud with him whether he meant it was *too* small or with the right amount of intimacy he was hoping for. Matheus intimated that he liked it "better." He wanted to come back the following week. He told me everyone clapped when he was introduced as a newcomer. He claimed to have been embarrassed, but I knew he was pleased, feeling positively received.

I accompanied Matheus to mass following Bible study the next week so I could experience firsthand the church's spiritual perspective on Christianity. This church was more intimate in its feel, and I appreciated wholeheartedly the sermon's all too timely focus on the essence of telling the truth. But it was perhaps a little too intimate for my taste; I was taken aback when the pastor called attention to "the new faces today," extending an invitation to "come on, stand up . . ." I played innocent, looking behind me for some other new face in the pews, only to turn back around to Matheus popping up like a jackrabbit. He broadly smiled, flailing his arms around as if trying to land a plane. He proudly called out his name to the pastor when asked who he was, then confidently corrected the pastor for mangling his name, as so many others tend to do. Matheus clearly appeared pleased to be in an environment in which he felt familiar.

I appreciated the time alone with Matheus on the way to get Davi, chatting with him about what the focus of his group meeting was each week. Matheus seemed actively engaged with the group and the topic of the moment, such as the value of spirituality over materialism. He said it was important not to be consumed over having, *needing* the latest, the greatest next best new thing, for fear of losing sight of what is most important: namely, spirituality and fellowship, fueling the fundamental heartbeat of any religion's significance.

* * *

Embracing Matheus's path of worship within the fellowship of our family was daunting. He did not make it easy, and was often quick to throw in my face that I was *Jewish* and could not relate to his Christian beliefs whenever I would try to make a relevant point. I persisted, maintaining my insistence on the practice of sound moral values based on the ten commandments, a cornerstone of our shared religious foundations.

After the weakening of his resolve about a month after he began regularly attending the church, about ten hours from when I first confronted him and he staunchly denied having committed a wrongdoing, despite strong evidence to the contrary, Matheus agreed to respond in writing to a brief series of questions. I hoped this would be a less threatening way of gaining direct accountability for his actions after he'd partially admitted to the bare minimum as to his wrongdoing. We discussed his responses to this series of fact-based questions with the best saved for last. When I asked what made him a good Christian, he simply replied, "Because I believe in Jesus."

I told Matheus my surprise at how he was ready to throw his brother under the bus by accusing him of having stolen the bracelets from my little brother, Sean, who had started living with us only two months before for no reason other than his refusal to hold himself accountable for "something that had nothing to do with Davi." To Grandma's attentive ear, to which Matheus turned after refusing to speak further to me when I first confronted him, he tried claiming an accidental mixing of backpacks that would have implicated Davi. It was not until the next day, after discussing his answers, that I hit on a nerve when I threw out . . . "And Jesus died for *your* sins, and that is how you respect that? You might want to give your actions some more thought." A mere ten minutes later, Matheus dutifully came over to me. "Here," he simply uttered as he dropped the other bracelet he had stolen, still left unaccounted for, into the palm of my hand. It was no longer important why twenty-four hours and much angst, anger, and deceitfulness had to transpire before Matheus was able to step up and own up to taking the bracelets; it was another step forward in the right direction.

Pastor Chip later validated my emphasis on how moral behavior dictated against lying, stealing, and/or cheating, and went along with any one's religious beliefs. I almost had Matheus convinced to speak further with Pastor Chip on his own about the Christian perspective and stealing; I emphasized that it was not about getting into trouble, sustaining the wrath of G-d, or causing the pastor to think ill of him. Rather, it was about consciously gaining a clearer understanding of what it meant to be Christian. Still, he tried for the avoidance route and declared he would not be going to church the next day. Nonetheless, we pulled into the parking lot the following morning, with his hair neatly combed, dressed in his Sunday best, and an air of stoicism in his attitude. He appeared to have given further thought about speaking with Pastor Chip while in the car; there were long pauses in between responses before he gave way to being shy. Rather, he gave permission for me to speak with Pastor Chip over the phone, as "it would be helpful for me" to support Matheus with a clearer understanding of his Christian faith's take on such matters of morality.

After speaking with the pastor, I shared with Matheus the details of our conversation as we waited in line in the temple's car loop to pick up Davi. Pastor Chip validated my own way of already trying to help Matheus with his Christian beliefs; namely, having accepted his salvation in Christ, how he responded to his grace was how he should live his life as a witness to Christ, and draw people to rather than push them away from G-d. I told Matheus that since he was considered saved in accepting Christ as his savior, then he had a duty to live an exemplary life. He accepted this rationale and its importance in his refraining from any temptation to lie, steal, or cheat, and in being accountable for oneself when committing a wrongdoing. By then, Davi slid into the car, munching on Hamantaschen cookies from the evening's celebration of Purim, speaking his thoughts about how Queen Esther saved the Jewish people from annihilation, as recounted in the biblical Book of Esther.

* * *

The following Sunday, Matheus got into the car after church and mumbled, "I don't want to talk about it," rather than get into our usual discourse about the group's focus. For a few seconds I pondered the hopeful relevance of the teachings to his own issues, until he relented and told of a video they watched about a group of white supremacists and their views of the Holocaust. I wrestled with what could possibly be the video's purpose. My concerns about whether the church might be promoting anti-Semitism were relieved when Matheus echoed Pastor Chip's expressed emotion of how "that makes me so angry"; the Jewish people did not deserve the horror inflicted on them. Apparently, the video profiled the way some of the supremacists "changed their minds," and became no longer hateful, or intolerant of others' religious beliefs and cultural practices.

I never did understand what Matheus did not want to talk about, yet he expressed interest in the Holocaust and wanted to see a movie about it. I found a site on the Internet with reviews of Holocaust movies geared toward children. I chose a story set in France, *Miracle at Moreaux,* with a fairly simple plot to follow, gripping in its portrayal of a lone incident during the Holocaust. Transfixed to the television screen, without so much as the flinch of a muscle, Matheus clearly was engrossed in the story.

In the film, three Jewish children are attempting to make their way to the border into Spain and meet up with a pre-arranged guide to lead them to safety. Along the way, a nun takes them into her convent, passing them off as part of her student group at the boarding school, personifying the role of Good Samaritan. She risks her own and the others' lives violating the law in trying to protect these children, simply because it is the right thing to do in the name of G-d. The school's students, fervent Catholics, also are conscious of their Christian obligation to love their neighbor. The students band together and get the children out from under the watchful eyes of the Nazis and through the woods to meet their guide for safe passage into Spain.

Rather than press Matheus into a long, drawn-out dialogue he was not likely to bite into, I kept the spirit alive, and fostered family togetherness by having us make Hamentaschen cookies together. I had Davi tell the story of Purim, making references to how similar the trials and tribulations of the Jews in ancient Persia were to those of the Jews in Europe during the Holocaust. We discussed how G-d loves *everybody*. It's our duty as human beings to respect and revere the almighty by living with enough self-respect to do what is right, like the nun and her students, rather than be paralyzed by self-doubt.

Matheus was starting to part ways with his tendency to disregard others' perspectives in favor of self-preservation. In his relying more on being a G-d fearing individual, his conscientious drive to live a righteous life in the name of G-d as personified by Jesus Christ was influencing greater connectedness to the essence of truth and accountability. Both of their needs for love, faith, and belonging were being validated as we continued to coexist as a family with different religious beliefs.

Chapter 27

Educated Guesses

With the arrival of a second go-around with the first day of school, I was more than ready to leave the lackadaisical days of summer behind in favor of structure, routine, and predictability. Both boys eagerly anticipated the start-up of the new school year now that they had a whole year under their belts. Davi was excited to re-engage in the learning process and find out who his teacher was, and who was in his fourth-grade class. Upon arrival at school that first day, he confidently waved me away; he did not need me to escort him to class, because, "I did not know anything last year; I did not know English and now I do."

Matheus was interested in reconnecting with his "friends" and teasing out an increase in independence and responsibility, a hallmark for the beginning middle school student. Even so, he maintained caution, bordering on indifference, when we walked over to school the Friday before to pick up his schedule and locate his classrooms. The dialogue between the three of us played out like a sitcom script. Stopping to refer to his schedule in the hallway, I asked, "Okay, Matheus, which class do you have next?"

"Ida know," he replied, at which Davi then quickly piped up, "Matheus, you have science next."

"Oh," Matheus mumbled as we continued walking.

Later on in our hallway wanderings: "Matheus, what's the room number?"

"Ida know..."

"Matheus, it's one fifty-four," said Davi.

"Oh..." Matheus dully answered back, glancing down at his schedule.

"Matheus, which direction do we go to get to your math class?" I asked.

"I-da know..."

"Matheus, it's back that way," answered Davi, referring to the school map on the schedule.

"Ohhhh," he lazily answered back.

In the cafeteria, Matheus resisted introducing himself to a burly man sitting all alone in front of a bare table, with a single sheet of paper titled, "Athletics" inconspicuously dangling. Trying to rouse more interests, I asked, "Why don't you go over there and introduce yourself? Just tell him your name, shake his hand, ask him about soccer tryouts?" With a shy glance in the table's direction, Matheus came up with one excuse after another, not wanting to assert himself and grab that all-important competitive edge. He ignored my explaining that if it came down to just him and someone else, because he had been forthright and introduced himself early, the coach might be more likely to pick him, remembering "that nice, mature, young man who introduced himself."

For the first day, as Matheus wanted, after dropping Davi off I came back in time to walk him over to the school; he stopped me at the school property's perimeter, and proceeded on his own, without even a glance backward when reaching past the first fence post. I was home to greet him that afternoon after school. He was in positive spirits, eager to share how his first day went. He promptly thanked me for his lunch, which I'd brought over to school after finding it still in the refrigerator when I returned from the morning's walk; I could not let him go without his lunch on his very first day of middle school. Yet I reminded him in the afternoon that I could not, *would not* operate a delivery service for forgotten lunches, homework, and projects.

Matheus continued to vie for the role of absentminded professor. On the third day, he forgot his lunch again, claiming, "So, I had to walk back to the house to get it. Oh, Father, and you know what? Then I forgot to turn off the TV and the lights, so I had to walk back *again* ... and you know what? I still got to school at the same time!" Thursday morning he left me a message on my cell phone to inform me that he could not find the key to lock the door, "So I have to leave the door unlocked until you can get home to lock it, okay? Bye." At least he set the alarm. Later that afternoon, his wallet was promptly stolen when it fell to the floor as he was reaching into his backpack at dismissal time in the bus loop, with hundreds of students milling around; before he could retrieve the wallet from the ground, some anonymous kid ran off with it. Matheus made a report on his own to the school's resource officer, and the wallet turned up the following day, minus the few dollars he had stashed inside.

Matheus seemingly weathered the series of life's lessons, always eager to return to school the next day, trying his hand at being more attentive to his surroundings ... until the next rash of miscommunications, misinterpretations, and sloppiness in his dealings with the real world. He claimed to look forward to soccer tryouts the following week, yet he did not pay close attention to the morning announcements of when he was supposed to have his cleats and shin guards with him, "So I could not go." I pulled the ESOL (English as a Second Language) card and e-mailed the coach, who invited Matheus to come for the second round of tryouts, although not before informing me, "On the Friday the students picked up their schedules I had a table set up for athletics to answer any questions." I felt vindicated by Matheus's playful facial expressions when I showed him the coach's e-mail; he wouldn't talk about it, but his face told me that he understood the potential importance of speaking to the coach earlier. He did not make the team that year.

Davi also seemed pleased with his first week and how "nice" his teacher was, yet he lacked enthusiasm, as if he were still waiting for the real start of school. When I picked him up from school on the second day, he announced, "We're probably going to do math tomorrow," to which I asked, "What *did* you do today?" He replied, "Oh, we mostly talked about the FCAT," the state's high-stakes testing. Davi went on in great detail about what he needed to pass, how students would randomly be assigned an expository or narrative passage to write, and he wondered how well he could perform relative to specified standards. He spoke with such informed conviction that I wondered whether he'd skipped school in favor of attending a workshop on the FCAT. Disillusioned about the seemingly dismal prospect of a stimulating education, I recalled the famous United Negro College Fund's 1970's campaign slogan: "A mind is a terrible thing to waste."

Over the summer, Davi's intellectual functioning had been tested to see whether his IQ would be high enough for placement in the gifted classroom, taking advantage of his ESOL status and its lower criteria for eligibility than for a native and/or proficient English speaker. His disadvantaged background—in having lived in an orphanage for prolonged periods of time, experienced multiple disruptions in his schooling, and contended with an environment that did not foster the greatest of expectations for the future also justified the special considerations. Davi fared well, but not well enough; I felt he scored well in the right areas where another IQ test I prefer for these purposes would perhaps push him over the line. The school psychologist, who was from Brazil and bilingual in

English and Portuguese, concurred with Davi's bright intellect, curious nature, and quick grasp of concepts. She raved about Davi, clearly enjoying her interactions with him; she was impressed with how far he had come in such a short time, given his background of disrupted life experiences.

When Davi still didn't meet criteria the second go-around, this time coming up short by only four points, the school psychologist and I both lamented our disappointment and frustration at not being able to secure the challenge and stimulation he obviously needed. I feared the potential for boredom and the stifling of his intellectual growth. I did not want him or his brother to regard their schooling as only a means to an end. I always made sure to pick up and enhance where school would leave off. Hence, my push for them to read anything, appreciate humor and irony relative to astute observations, engage in prolonged conversation, participate in extracurricular opportunities to boost particular interests and talents, and go on outings to places and events both stimulating and thought-provoking, all the while promoting familial bonding.

* * *

Davi continued to impress with his wit, intelligence, and memory, as well as how he applied his learning, and used logic and reason in everyday conversation, and displayed an insatiable enthusiasm to learn and absorb whatever tidbit of information there was to share. With only the third week of school in full swing, I shot an e-mail to Davi's teacher to request that she place him in the highest reading group, for fear she would regard only last year's FCAT score. Although he'd scored a respectable level three out of five, his focus was compromised by having taken the test the day after my father's funeral. I feared he might have to suffer the indignation of placement in a reading group where he would find boredom, the breeding ground for behavioral issues when he was not sufficiently challenged. Just two weeks into the year at open house, I could not help notice Davi already amassing the most points on the accelerated-reader chart. I need not have worried, as his teacher replied, *Thank you so much for your communication. I actually made the reading groups last night, and based on my observations and assessments of Davi since the first day, I already put him in the highest reading group. I was actually surprised at the level-three FCAT score, because I can already tell he is an excellent reader and very bright.* He also was placed in the highest math group; his teacher seemed especially to appreciate his eagerness to learn, and his taking the initiative to point out how to solve math problems in different ways.

Davi was more comfortable than his brother in taking on what the future might hold for him, and his success in school was a tremendous catalyst for him. He earned straight A grades throughout fourth grade and improved his FCAT reading score to a level four, while achieving a perfect score for math. His short-lived bout of behavioral problems clowning around in class from the beginning of the year never resurfaced. He seized any opportunity to learn, and excelled in all of his subjects. For a class project on landforms, he devoted extraordinary effort in his conceptualization, organization, command of content, and attention to detail. One Sunday he kept himself engaged in researching and formulating his report for more than four hours, making the most of the maximum allowance of three pages. His teacher marveled at his taking on multiple perspectives of a learned concept and "thinking outside the box" that added to the teaching experience for her.

Prior to the start of fifth grade, I persisted in having Davi privately evaluated for gifted eligibility just once more; this time he passed the minimal criteria. His verbal score increased by a whopping twenty points. Davi's transition into the gifted class seemed effortless, with his smooth adjustment to the different expectations and lessened emphasis on structure. He also settled in with the classroom's group of students, most of whom had been together since the early elementary grades. However, not before having happily taking on a minor food fight in the cafeteria at lunchtime on the second day of school.

Davi's eagerness to show off his intellect and his tendency to dash through his school demands with a total command of what was expected of him contrasted sharply with Matheus's dithering tendencies when he had to apply his learning outside the monotonous, repetitive demands of copying and memorization. Matheus was known by all who had "the pleasure" of teaching him for his impeccable behavior, and handwriting, a neat and organized manner of completing his work, and his focused attention in the classroom. However, if task demands required a step outside his comfort zone, Matheus steadfastly dug in his heels. If he allowed me to help him study for a test, I had to ask him the vocabulary words in the order they appeared in the text; he tended to refuse attempts to discuss the words and broaden his rigid understanding of the definition. Getting him to independently use the dictionary was futile. My encouraging him to think through a particular prompt or add greater detail about initial thoughts and responses quickly gave way to his insistence on continuing to subscribe to the barest minimum.

For fifth grade, Matheus's teacher was instrumental in ensuring that he understood and followed through with task demands, boosting his self confidence to achieve above his own modest expectations of himself. But with six different teachers in middle school, he found it extremely difficult to keep track of each subject's demands; Fs were quick to stack up from the start, but too often because of sitting there and making it look as though he understood, rather than asserting himself and asking for clarification when needed. He didn't complete many assignments, missed due dates, and disregarded important notices. He didn't even bring home the notice for school pictures; there would be no sixth-grade school picture to fill a frame alongside Davi's fourth-grade picture for that year. Along with that loss early in the school year, it was fast threatening to become a lost year.

Each time when I approached him about a hole in his work, he took it as a confrontation, and became defensive. "I didn't know . . ." "I forgot . . ." "The teacher didn't told me." Some issues were relatively easy fixes. His history teacher began keeping me in the loop, e-mailing me her Power Point slides to help me study for upcoming quizzes and tests with him. Most of the time, when I directed him to approach a particular teacher about a misunderstanding, he would comply, and get a second chance. My checking his planner became a daily affair, with the expectation that all assignments and upcoming tests and quizzes were to be written down . . . until he lost the planner, claiming he didn't "remember" where he left it. His history teacher came to his rescue, kindly supplying him with a second one. Other classes would prove daunting on an ongoing basis; I maintained constant communication with both his language arts and reading teachers to help keep track of all of his assignments and their expectations for him.

At the first quarter's conclusion, in a parent/teacher conference he was unanimously praised for his conscientious attitude in spite of his oversights and performance disparities, in which they often dismissed to the tune of its being "the age." I knew all about "the age," yet sitting on the other side of the table for a change was a bit off balance as I was more used to being the one to make the suggestions to parents at my own middle school. The teachers also made many positive comments that Matheus had "come out of his shell," fraternized with a positive set of peers, and seemingly conveyed a sense of belonging and acceptance.

The following week Matheus received two days' internal suspension for his involvement with six of his friends in a rather innocuous peer-devised game of putting one's hand lightly on the shoulder of another; if the hand was felt by the other person, then it was to be smacked away. The longer it took to feel the hand and then smack it away, the more it meant the one with the insensitive shoulder was "gay." Unfortunately, the one who was having fun with Matheus went too far . . . "he was trying to touch my balls!" Matheus promptly kneed the boy crying to the ground. My mother's endearing sentiment about how "wonderful" it was that Matheus was "part of a group," and that he was "accepted" by his peers, was not terribly comforting at the time.

Matheus ended the first quarter earning the A/B Honor Roll distinction . . . pulling in the lowest B possible at the ring of the closing bell for language arts. Although I did not do the work for him, he would readily have lazily taken the back seat, if I had let him. His fears and doubts about navigating the twists and turns in his learning made it a struggle for me to keep him in the driver's seat. I was his seat belt, sometimes as a source of support to lend the feeling of safety and security, and other times a source of restraint, with expectations for his constructive efforts.

I sought to instill in him greater ownership for his learning, so he could proceed independently with confidence and achieve relative to his own personal aspirations and goals in life. With his keen regard for details, ability to focus, and the endearing amounts of care and respect driving his work efforts at moments of conviction, I could see a bright intellect was buried deep within. I constantly reminded myself that providing structure was the key for both boys to help stave off their tendency to become overwhelmed by fleeting memories of a world that once was so chaotic . . . unpredictable, nonsensical, unrewarding. I had to constantly even out the playing field

for Matheus by seizing the opportunity to nurture his inner strength and getting him to "try it," rather than avoid it for fear of failure. The more success that Matheus was experiencing as a result, the brighter he began to envision a future for himself.

* * *

How Matheus managed to lose his science project's paper and giant three-fold poster board will likely remain a mystery. He'd carried it all out with him when he left the house in the morning, yet it never made it into the school building. With the winter break following right after the project's due date, Matheus managed to keep me at bay an entire month, leaving me to believe he turned it in that day; he told me that he did not understand how two zeros popped up on his school's online grade book later that evening on the last day before break. When school started back up, his standard answer to my queries about whether he spoke to his teacher was that "she was not there today," having been out because of heart problems. When he finally told me "She was there today . . . but only for a few minutes," and he had spoken to her, he still was evasive, and the holes in his account began to rival those of a hunk of Swiss cheese. We were locked in a standoff, wherein my repeatedly asking what he did with his science project yielded only his standard, "I don't know." I was mostly concerned about his dodging both his teacher and me, shrugging it off as though he lost a pencil.

Matheus denied any dissatisfaction with his lemon battery project, even though it did not achieve the desired result of lighting the LED light-bulb. The next day his guidance counselor queried whether someone might have taken his project from him, intending to claim it as his or her own. He denied this as well, later telling me he put the project down somewhere when with his friends behind the school, forgetting about it until he went to his science class second period. He was unresponsive, seemingly nonchalant about the waste of his hard work, time, and energy, not to mention mine as well. I had struggled with his preference to keep me in the dark about his project rather than engage me to work *with* him to problem-solve. The harder I scratched the burning itch of desire for some semblance of an understanding why Matheus had not been forthcoming about his project's loss in the first place, and still likely holding out on me about what might have actually happened to it, the more frustrated I felt.

I passed a few days of ignoring his cold shoulder, combating his illogical macho behavior before he was receptive to a more straightforward exchange about responsibility. I pushed my resolve even further, catching Matheus off guard with my pointing out to him my feeling that the checks and X's had gone the way of his lemon battery, no longer capable of generating enough energy to shed light and lead the way. He was pleased with the rationale that I offered in reinforcing his efforts in gaining greater self-control. Although he still experienced difficulties with disrespectful verbalizations, inappropriate language, and impatience, these issues seemed more those of any average pre-teen than anything else, and such instances were happening more intermittently, with his greater receptivity to redirection.

As his self-confidence was growing and Matheus further worked toward gaining greater independence, the constant threat of his being struck down with an X was not the constructive exercise it previously started out to be. In spite of his continued inconsistency with completing and/or turning in his school work, I praised Matheus heartily for having improved in reading, not being as hesitant in working toward being a more fully informed reader. His resistance to reading was gradually wearing down; he was choosing books more to his liking and appropriate for his grade level, and making more concerted efforts to read. We discussed further his likelihood of passing the FCAT this next time around, as he seemed primed to do; indeed, he felt he was doing better. With an increase from level one to level three in reading, as well as from level two to four in math, Matheus more than met statewide curriculum standards; he was excited about not having to take a reading class in favor of a second elective for seventh grade.

Rarely out of sight or earshot, Davi finally begun to absorb the potential for him, asking about the ramifications if he reached that magic 85 percent. He was more vocal about his distaste for the checks and Xs, relentlessly complaining how "unfair," and impossible a task it was. He pleaded for "anything" but the checks and Xs. If only I would do "something different. You're good at that, Father . . . just make something up."

Although he slipped after having finally earned his video gaming and television privileges those first two weeks in a row, Davi agreeably sustained his motivation to pick up where he left off the following week. He easily earned his privileges over another two weeks, moving up from 75 to 80 percent. So much more motivated, he was equally conscientious in controlling his verbalizations, those unnecessary comments and excuses to avert getting an X. He especially kept tabs on when he earned a check . . . "That was the truth, so don't I get a check for that?" "I was responsible for my behavior . . . don't I get a check for that?" "I did what you told me to do . . . right away. Aren't I supposed to get a check for that?" Even when something was not readily determinable, he was quick to contract the earning of a check if a point might be determined later. About nine months after we'd started with the checks and Xs, without any particular fanfare, Davi was finally able to leave the system by the wayside, allowing for more natural relations between father and son.

Chapter 28

What Comes Around Goes Around

With the luck of good timing, both of my "little brothers," Bobby and Brandon were able to make it home at the same time in October, a mere four months after Matheus, Davi and I returned from Brazil. We all converged at a halfway point one evening, about a two and a half hour drive from opposite ends for each of us to get to the restaurant: myself with Matheus and Davi, Bobby and his new wife, Brandon, Sean, and their mother. Regretfully, only Michael was missing; he was grounded for his unrelenting testing of limits, his emerging adolescence now starting to roll in, with the ebb and flow of each wave cresting higher and with greater force than the one preceding it.

That night I straddled the shiny newness of fatherhood and the pleasing familiarity of big brotherhood. At one point, as I slowly shook my head, silently pursing my lips when Davi asked whether he could have a special drink on the menu, Bobby heartily laughed. He recalled my famed frugality and how I also used to refuse him and his brothers when they would ask for extra, unnecessary frills. Matheus now likes to good naturedly chide me at such times: "come on, Father, don't be so *chip*." I snapped some pictures, especially treasuring the one with my "little brothers" alongside me on both ends while my two sons stood squarely in front at my feet.

* * *

For the one week earlier that second summer, when Matheus traveled to the Poconos with Michael, and Davi and I traveled to New England, we missed out on being able to travel to LIMIAR's reunion picnic, having occurred at the same time. I still wanted to take a family vacation together, but I did not have the stamina for a lengthy road trip like the previous summer, and I still reeled with the memory of when I took Matheus and Davi to Seattle and Vancouver with Michael, Gayle, and Jake on our spring break family trip five months before, which proved stressful beyond what Gayle and I were prepared for.

Gayle and I had traveled with Michael and Jake to Germany and Austria during winter break four years ago; we were eager to recapture the magic from that trip with Matheus and Davi. I also had looked forward to having a second parental figure along with whom to bounce off of, lend support for those challenging times, and share those times of wonder and delight. I had already traveled with Michael to Seattle two summers in a row a few years before when he was six-and seven-years-old. He and I stayed with an old high-school friend and her family; we would all be staying with her this time. The challenges and struggles in traveling with four boys between the ages of nine and thirteen-years-old all too often felt unrelenting, without any promise of the type of congenial family bonding we had been most looking forward to.

I was taken aback by the significant amount of behavioral regression that occurred for both Matheus and Davi on this trip; they were overly hostile to each other, serving as the catalyst for Matheus's angry, defiant outbursts and Davi's resistant, oppositional stance. Negative energy frequently permeated the overall mood that made it exceedingly difficult for one, some, or at times even all of us to coexist in harmony.

Especially problematic was how protective Matheus was of his rather comfortable position, wedged snugly in between Michael and Jake age-wise, and maturity level. Being the youngest in the group, Davi simply could not compete; it often felt as though it was three against one.

Desperate to gain their attention, Davi's vindictive behavior in reaction to their rejection spurred all three of the boys' contempt, only exacerbating his obnoxious behavior. Even more frustrating was the extent of Davi's overt insubordination to authority and absolute refusal to hold himself accountable for his behavior. His "fresh mouth" resulted in substantial amounts of time-outs and restrictions from participating in many activities. He lost out on sodas, special desserts, ice-skating on Grouse Mountain, and spending his allowance monies.

Matheus also found himself on the receiving end of consequences and reprimands for his blatant disrespect of my authority and overt refusal to ameliorate an uncompromising, hostile attitude. At one point he had run away from the house in reaction to my reprimanding him for being verbally aggressive toward his brother; Michael and Jake found him quite a ways out in the neighborhood, which bordered woods where coyotes, and sometimes bears were known to frequent. On more than one occasion I found myself helplessly longing for those simpler times when it was just Michael and I traveling together; we certainly had our moments for which we clashed, yet it was never to the point that it was not quickly, more straightforwardly remedied. Even so, Michael and Jake were not innocent in the mix as I found them at times to be catalysts in their own right. I often wondered to what extent they also dared to long for the more harmonious relations of simpler times, as things had been in the past before Matheus and Davi came along.

Sometimes feeling as though they were far and few between, we still did have our enjoyable moments, such as our day out at the Whistler ski resort area. It was all about the snow, and with four Florida kids in tow, it proved quite a memorable diversion. We went zip-lining over snow covered valleys and evergreens, tackled snow tubing, enjoyed Japanese cuisine whereby Matheus had expertly handled and readily developed a fond affinity for chopsticks, had ice cream at Prince Edward Island's *Cow's*, and most important, the boys got their much anticipated snow ball fight with the energetic crew from our zip-lining stint. Upon returning to Vancouver for the evening, we ate heartily at a wonderfully unpretentious Greek restaurant. Our day was highly structured and busy, hit the mark as to readily available food of interest and sustenance, and centered on winter's enchantment that was a mutual source of excitement and inspiration for all of the boys.

Perhaps typical for family vacations, such positive family-bonding moments prevailed in the boys' memory banks, as they'd draw upon them at a whim, time and time again, conjuring up those bonds that keep us emotionally connected to one another. I was happy whenever I heard a "remember when . . ." comment, often followed by the boys' smiles and laughter. We really did achieve our goal in strengthening our family bonding, despite the trials and tribulations that still haunted my memory.

I was hopeful that a shorter family trip would be less stressful of a jaunt, and still achieve more family bonding moments. Through a series of e-mails with Bobby and Brandon's brother, Sean about his plans upon graduating from high school, he dared to express his desire for joining us on a five-day family road trip to Georgia. I toyed with the idea of having him come along and being both the fun loving, older brother playmate for the boys and a mature teenage companion for me. I would have someone to bounce off of, while he'd provide a balance of positive role modeling and comic relief.

With a fully scheduled agenda in place, we hit the road, and picked up Sean in Jacksonville, the halfway point between home and Atlanta. The car ride was pleasantly uneventful; having third-row seating in the back, courtesy of my newly purchased SUV, prevented intrusions into anyone's personal spaces, and Matheus, Davi, and Michael maintained harmonious relations as they shared and played against each other via two Nintendo DS systems. We made it to Atlanta without a major flare-up, although I pulled Matheus aside at the hotel to admonish him for being uncooperative in the car on the outskirts of Atlanta, in the middle of a massive downpour. I declared, "How dare you put us all at risk . . . be so selfish when I needed to focus my full attention to the road." He quietly accepted my reprimand, rather than demand, as he usually did, that I punish Davi for his taunting. Even so, like in Seattle, Matheus frequently was disrespectful, uncooperative, and at times made lewd gestures and used foul language that bore the brunt of my negative attention. Davi also still needed to be reprimanded for his "fresh mouth" and passive-aggressiveness as his way to circumvent my authority. But perhaps because of the lack of intensity in competition for attention that stirred too many behavioral problems in Seattle and Vancouver, he also appeared somewhat more manageable this time around.

Michael's offensive, obnoxious behaviors were kept to a bare minimum, and when he was told to stop, he usually was quick to relent. Perhaps picking up on Sean's influence, he even took it upon himself to try and influence more positive behavior from the other two, encouraging greater maturity and respect. Michael also seemed better able to divide his attention between his two "brothers" that made relations occur as though there was a more even playing field this time around, without Davi forever feeling neglected and pushed aside. As much as I saw how all three of the boys responded favorably to Sean, Michael often appeared on his own to be invested in setting a better example for Matheus and Davi.

* * *

Newly graduated from high school, Sean was uncertain about his future, and we explored his interests and tossed out varying possibilities throughout our road trip. He did not want to follow in his brothers' footsteps into the air force; he was doubtful the armed forces would suit him. He struggled with what he truly wanted in a future for himself. He was excited to explore further the ideas we talked about; we kept in constant e-mail contact afterward as he explored various options, many times checking in for reassurance whenever he had more questions or doubts or felt as though he'd hit a roadblock. Throughout, I teased him about the idea of coming down south to live with us, taking advantage of greater opportunities. Though my invitation had seemingly fallen on deaf ears, Sean abruptly threw it back out there one evening via another series of e-mails, coyly starting with: "How much do you really love me?" I fired back, "When do you want to come down?"

Sean's interest was sincere. He wanted the chance to start out on a new path in life toward self-actualization, where he had some semblance of control, and my guidance to help him along. He also professed to having become attached to Matheus and Davi, in addition to being previously attached to Michael. He was eager to lend a hand to all three as a Big Brother type of mentor to them.

There was much to prepare for Sean's big move-in. He struggled with doubts about whether such a move would be in his best interests; what, where, and how should he start out on the college track; and whether he would be able to obtain gainful employment and sustain himself financially without racking up debt. He also was fearful of starting over, making new friends, and adjusting to a new living situation with his two "little brothers" butting into his personal space and business.

All eyes were on Matheus; it was his bedroom Sean was moving into. He would be sleeping on the spare bed in Davi's room so Sean could have his own space to spread out in at night after the boys were in bed. Matheus's room was expected to remain unchanged, and during the day he could go in and out as he pleased, yet still mindful of being respectful in sharing his room. Matheus did not express any reservations about his personal space being invaded. He proved invaluable in spearheading the redesigning of his room, incorporating two desks and allowing for some separation between his and Sean's possessions. I also knew that deep inside he was thrilled with being relieved of sleeping alone in his room. From the beginning, he had trouble with the darkness and nightmares, as he'd often rouse me awake for comfort in the middle of the night, sometimes trembling with fear from top to bottom, unable to return to his room in favor of sleeping with me. He tended to feel exceedingly vulnerable in the face of those past demons that tended to wail the loudest at night, when he was left alone with his suppressed memories of the past. At Davi's insistence, he even agreed to sleep without the protective glow of a night-light beside him.

* * *

Sean's transition into our house and immediate and extended family seemed remarkably smooth. Matheus and Davi could not get enough of him; they followed him everywhere, and hung on his every action. He, in turn, embraced all of their predilections for goofiness and sometimes frenzied behavior with patience of a saint, and benevolent intentions of being a good "big brother" and role model. Michael at first seemed distant, perhaps harboring jealousy at not having Sean for himself, on his terms and at his convenience. Sean also sought to knock Michael down a few pegs, perhaps playing a little hard to get in hopes of getting him to relate with greater maturity and sincerity.

As time wore on, the honeymoon period began to fade. Matheus balanced on the tightrope between his aching desires to trust and be loved and accepted and his nagging inclination toward mistrust and subsequent expectations of rejection. It was inevitable that a hotbed of repressed emotions erupted one night while I was out. Apparently Sean "yelled" at Matheus when horse-play with Davi went too far and one slap led to another. As Sean tried taking control, Matheus retorted, "You're not family; you can't tell me what to do!" Sean tried to reason with him, unnerved by the intensity of Matheus's hostility, which was free-flowing from all sides of a volcanic explosion of emotions. Each time Sean tried to reason with him, to connect with him emotionally, Matheus only threw back angry retorts.

Not being able to reach me, Sean turned to my mother and, as she likes to recount, "crying hysterically" to her over the phone, expressing his doubts as to why he came down in the first place, and whether he was truly being as helpful as he'd hoped. My mother reassured Sean of his place in our family, his role with the boys, and his own purpose for being here. In the interim, Matheus stormed off into his room, leaving Sean behind with fears of whether he might damage some sentimentally prized possession of his. Matheus soon came out on his own, crying as well, to apologize. When I spoke with Matheus over the phone afterward, he was remarkably calm and unfazed; there was no brooding, no air of hostile discontent, yet he remained tight-lipped about what had really spurred his emotional outrage.

Feeling forced to take the low road, and bulldozing over matters of the heart when I returned home, I clearly stated that

Sean was indeed part of this family. Also, Sean was an adult, and whenever the boys were in his care, his authority was to be respected without question. A week or so later, Matheus let loose another derogatory comment when Sean spoke up in my defense against Matheus's rude attitude toward me. Again, I sternly reminded Matheus not to make Sean feel estranged from our family, and said that if Matheus were to continue to do so, perhaps he might "want to leave." Not having said *that* right, it was too late. I should have been more sensitive, and perhaps not have implied that I did not want him around. Matheus immediately countered, "All right, you don't want me here, then I leave." He ignored my attempts to clarify what I meant, storming around the house in his tank top and shorts after stepping out of the shower. He stuffed a few randomly grabbed clothes and his flashlight into a plastic grocery bag, abruptly stopping to pick up the phone.

"What are you doing?" I asked, protective over whom he was intending to involve.

"I'm calling Grandma to tell her I'm leaving," he replied in a steely tone. I resisted my inclination to keep him from calling, preferring he problem-solve with me. Instead, I recognized that his attempt to reach out to my mother was a reflection of his desire to stay connected to home base.

"Yes, that's a good idea. Grandma would be very upset if you left without saying good-bye."

I heard him ranting and raving to her from the laundry room; my mother spoke to him calmly, encouraging him to consider speaking with his counselor. "I'm not talking to her; she always take Father's side . . . " Or, perhaps he should take a shower and cool off . . . "I already did . . . " Or, get into bed and let the night pass so he could think more clearly in the morning and be more receptive to speaking with his counselor then . . . "Well, okay, but I'm not unpacking." He bade my mother good-bye. Without another word, he slid into bed and shut himself off from any further exchange.

The next morning we carried on, as we'd done so many times before; I let him be, only responding to him impassively, when necessary. This was a familiar dance between him and me, as I waited for him to offer his proverbial apology for his rudeness. He skulked around, slowly, painstakingly working toward the realization and acceptance of his need and latent desire to defer to his father's authority. I left for work, reminding him he needed to be home after school on time to meet with his counselor, with whom I spoke later that afternoon, filling her in so she might lend a strategic hand in their afternoon session. When I got home with Davi, he and his counselor were already in the midst of their meeting; he appeared actively engaged with her, as she confirmed afterward.

With his fully informed consent, his counselor and I met afterward to discuss the overarching contents of their session. She felt he had been readying himself to apologize all along, building up even before she arrived to writing me an apology letter. He declined to share the letter or its specific contents with her, yet told her his purpose to write it was so he could be sure to have a chance to express himself without interruption. He needed to be *heard* by his father; he felt a letter would give him the chance to express his thoughts and feelings without feeling dismissed.

I thought the issue was fairly straightforward, centering on Matheus's feeling somewhat displaced by Sean's being in his room. To complicate matters even further, Davi suddenly became territorial over the space in his room. He announced the embarkation of a cleanup campaign in his room, putting things away, creatively organizing his storage needs; he cleared out a cabinet in his desk, filling it with his important books and proudly declaring it his "personal library." He also tried dictating not only where but how Matheus could have a certain possession placed. I had to stifle myself from snorting too loudly when Davi asserted that Matheus could have his clothes for the next day on the lower shelf of the nightstand, but they had to be neatly folded. This from someone whose space would resemble the inside of a garbage Dumpster if I did not forever get after him to clean up, put away, and organize.

I tried praising Davi for his emphasis on an orderly and tidy space, which certainly would make it easier for both to share the same room, but I had to take a stand when I caught Davi rather ceremoniously attempting to remove Matheus's backpack from his room. With his usual flair for dramatics, Davi held the backpack a full arm's length away, as if it reeked of a vile stench akin to diseased carnage. I sternly turned him back around and return the backpack to his room, pointing out how "rude" he was being to his brother for "absolutely no reason," and that he was "NOT to make your brother feel unwelcome" in his room. Matheus later referred to his brother's actions to his counselor, adding, "But my father fixed that."

Both Matheus's counselor and I were pleased with the extent to which he allowed the processing of recent events and appeared open to multiple perspectives other than his own. He was waiting to offer me his apology letter, but I was not supposed to know about it. After she left, Matheus and I returned to the same degree of indifference in our relations. I waited, wondering when this letter would be presented. Dinner for the four of us was a subdued affair, with Davi happily commanding the attention. It was not until after everything was cleared away when I found a single piece of notebook paper, neatly folded in half, lying flat on my computer's keyboard, simply addressed, *To Father*. My eyes misted at its simplicity, yet Matheus had been emotionally expressive as to his vulnerability. Whether he truly was remorseful from the outset or his apology was at least partly steeped in his feeling a sense of obligation, Matheus started out front and center in asserting that he was *sorry for everything that happened yesterday.* When I read further, it did not seem so much that he felt his personal space was imposed upon, but rather, he felt the very essence of his burgeoning relationship with his father had been encroached upon: *I don't like when Sean get in the middle of our conversation, because it have nothing to do with him,* never mind Sean's intentions being merely to instill in Matheus the idea of more respectful relations with me.

Still problematic for Matheus, his rigid thought processes caused him to become easily overwhelmed; he had yet to fully develop an adaptive filter, being prone to misconstruing a negative interaction and taking it as a personal offense: *Not only Sean feel bad when I say that he is no part of the family, which I didn't, I don't like when you say that I said that Sean is not part of the family, even though I didn't, and then tell me that I can bag myself and leave, that makes me feel that you don't care about me, and you don't want me in your life. So, I am sorry for all of this and I hope that it will never happen again.* I neglected to account beforehand for how *any* shift in the playing field for Matheus could be felt as a threat to his still very fragile sense of emotional security.

He brought his letter to a close, returning to nurture his wounded pride: *Now, the reason I am writing this is so you already know what we are going to talk about. Well, I already said my part, and too, I want you to hear me first without talking when I am talking and that is the answer for every question that you have for me.* Maybe he would listen to what I had to say, but he did not intend for this to be a mutual discourse. As I looked up, knowing Matheus was within sight and earshot, aware of my reading his letter, I summoned him over. We assumed our familiar positions on the couch, next to each other side by side so that face-to-face contact was kept to a minimum in the privacy of my office. I reiterated that I did want him and would always want him in my life, yet his comments and scornful behavior sometimes made it seem as though he did not want to be a part of my life. It was an opportune moment to point out the hurtfulness of his words, how divisive and dismissive they could be, and how misguided they were when focused only on unleashing his inner rage.

As I continued instilling his push for greater accountability for himself, I began to realize how important the role of apologizing for their transgressions was for both of the boys. I came across Dr. Harriet Lerner's *The Dance of Connection*, which seemed to channel my instinctive beliefs as to how one "will not feel accountable and able to apologize—no matter how we communicate—if doing so threatens to define [him] in an unacceptable or intolerable way." For Matheus, especially, the capacity to take responsibility and feel remorse is related to how much self-love and self-respect he has available to draw on." His emotional growth, albeit gradual, had been steady; he was apologizing both more readily and with greater sincerity and conviction than before. After our talk on the couch, just the mere suggestion of offering his apology and speaking with Sean was met without resistance.

Both Matheus and Davi were increasingly allowing for movement toward "a more solid place" as to the preservation of their own "wellbeing and integrity," which had undoubtedly been on a downward spiral when prospects for their future were bleak and unforgiving. In many ways just as expected, Sean's positive spin on life and the genuineness he projected was greatly contributing to the boys' further growth. They were being challenged to conduct themselves and relate to others from an emotionally healthier vantage point. If I had any such influence on Sean and his brothers so long ago, then I believe in the doctrine of karma: All good actions produce good effects. Energy expended through the action of the doer becomes a karmic force and like a boomerang, inevitably comes back to the doer sooner or later.

Chapter 29

Walking the Emotional Tightrope

Perhaps without as much fanfare as his brother's staunch resistance to talking about the past, with his ready assertions of "I don't talk about the past" whenever he might fear the threat of his emotional vulnerability being exposed, Davi, too, tended to refrain from making any direct references to his own or their shared past experiences and memories. In reading aloud a completed writing assignment, Davi caught himself saying, "My mom always said . . ." After an abrupt pause, with an apologetic tone, he continued, "That's what I put, mom, dad . . . I don't know . . ." He seemed at a loss for what to say further. I countered, "I'm glad you still keep your mom in your heart and in your thoughts. That's fine; that's good." Without further comment, he read on. My simple reflection of the authenticity of the moment's devoted thoughts of his mother, a key figure from his past was enough.

Matheus continued to require a great deal more extensive attention and effort to nudge his tolerance of even a single-sentence comment about his possible mind-set whenever there was the threat of exposure of any kind. When I discovered that cash I had yet to run over to the bank had gone missing from my dresser drawer, it seemed obvious who the suspect was. As I predicted, Matheus steadfastly denied having anything to do with the missing money, leaving me to slowly, randomly, over the course of twenty-four hours, piece together a logical scenario about what likely happened with the money.

At one point, responding to a flashing thought, I turned my gaze to Matheus, narrowing my eyes as I silently stared at him. "What?" he asked, his tone reflecting a slight bit of suspicion.

"Oh, I think I just figured something out," I breezily replied.

"What?"

"Oh, I'm not totally sure about everything to talk about it right now."

"Just tell me."

"I can tell you more about it later." With that, I turned back to the stove, tending to my frying potatoes.

With the brilliance of additional thoughts flashing, I mentally noted his school's sudden ceasing of the unrelenting computerized phone calls announcing the default of his cafeteria account by ten cents. Another flash had me recalling the unlikely coincidence of how he'd left or *forgotten* his lunch in the refrigerator three days in a row the previous week. It was obvious he had been spending the money to buy school lunches, along with what I discovered later a dollar here and there for the occasional ice cream, or a muffin at breakfast . . . or soda from the vending machine. I suddenly recalled the empty soda bottle in the outside sleeve of his backpack, which his *friend* supposedly bought for him the day before. I turned back around to face him, feeling like a cat slowly inching his way toward cornering a mouse. I asked, "Um, Matheus, all of a sudden we're not getting those phone calls from school about the ten cents on your lunch account . . . By any chance did you give the lunch lady ten cents?"

Without missing a beat, he replied, "My friend found twenty-five cents and I asked him to give it to that." Nearly choking on a rising chuckle over the preposterous improbability, I momentarily retreated into the cartoon world of my fantasy life. I tried shaking off the feeling of being the cat in a *Tom and Jerry* cartoon, overreacting to being outwitted by the supposedly defenseless mouse. My fantastical thoughts had me imagining myself leaping across the kitchen counter in a single bound, pinning Matheus to the ground to the sight of stars encircling his head.

Taking the high road, still letting well enough alone until I could gather clearer, concrete evidence, yet with hopes he would confess on his own, I tossed out to him, "So, that would mean you have fifteen cents left in the account."

"I don't know."

"Do the math, Matheus. You owed ten cents and you paid twenty-five cents. That leaves fifteen cents, so it makes sense why I am not getting those phone calls anymore."

"I guess so."

"Well, I will call them in the morning . . . first thing . . . before lunch starts."

"Why you have to call?"

"You know how I don't like funny things. When you're an adult, that's what you do. You have to check when something is strange so you don't miss anything, don't get messed up."

He dared to retort testily, "There you go about the money. See, you don't believe me."

"Excuse me," I countered, "I did not say anything about the missing money. You are the one bringing it up." The air hung heavy with his guilt, yet he remained reticent.

I was readily familiar with the school's administration, sixth grade guidance counselor, and his teachers; it now was time to give a shout out to the cafeteria manager. She proved quite the knowledgeable source. Having seen it all throughout her years with middle schoolers and their manipulative ways, she was unfazed by the notion of yet another preteen "stealing money." I was completely vindicated when I obtained a print out of a nearly uninterrupted two-week span of Matheus's buying school lunches, beginning just days after I'd stashed the money in my drawer.

I'd already briefed his counselor earlier the next day, so we all sat down together as I presented Matheus with the print out. He continued to deny stealing any money, first trying to claim the print out was a lie, then quickly reverting to the denial of buying lunch every day, then claiming his "friend" and even a teacher had given him money for lunch. "You know how I forgot my lunch those days..." he unconvincingly proclaimed. None of these "friends" had a name he remembered, and the print-out confirmed that he also bought lunch before the three-day run of leaving his lunch behind at home. As we pressed further, he threw out yet another far-fetched "friend" story about winning a thirty-dollar bet that he would not run up and down the hallway yelling. Maintaining a matter-of-fact tone, I pointed out that that it was a form of bullying and I needed to discuss this with the assistant principal; this so-called friend put him at risk of getting in trouble. "Furthermore, you complain I don't believe you, yet I do believe you would not do such a thing and risk getting yourself into trouble like that. That's why I am not buying this story."

I'd reached a dead end with him, and there was nothing else to do but assign his consequences. He would have to pay back the money, plus the two dollars he took from his teacher, who he declared had told Matheus he didn't have to pay him back. His cafeteria account also was frozen and he was slated to return to the school's before- and after-care program for the rest of the school year.

He unleashed his fury, yelling at his counselor, "I told you I don't like counseling!"

He dared me to make a move as he angrily shoved a book and a set of markers off the table. "What are you going to do?!" he challenged, babbling further that I'd better not touch him or he would "fight back." He proceed to yell at me that he would not cooperate and leave the house for before-care in the morning; he was telling me what he was not going to do, yet I knew he also was acknowledging the inevitability of his consequence.

He seemed somewhat surprised by my controlled, emotionless response. "It is really sad how you're trying to make a point and doing so in the wrong way. That is why you need counseling. You have stuff from the past that keeps getting in the way of what you do, think, and feel. You need to talk about it. Counseling is serious, not just fun and games."

When I'd spoken with his counselor beforehand, she was able to connect to a particular pattern I overlooked. "You see how everything major with the lying, the cheating, and the stealing has to do with food?" With the click of a light switch, it all made sense: the missing food from the refrigerator, his sneaking sodas from the school's vending machine with stolen coins from my room, and now the pilfering of hard cash to buy school lunches. Not so long ago we attempted to discuss with him Sean's discovery in the bedroom closet of a closed box containing two bowls filled with his favorite cereal; a spoon was neatly set alongside each bowl. There was no sense of hostility pervading the air of that discussion; yet Matheus was unwilling or unable to offer any particular reason for his actions, nor how long ago he'd stashed it away. Although he denied it specifically, I still like to think that at least on some subconscious level, he had his brother's interests at heart with having secured two bowls rather than just the one.

I also recalled the intense power struggles that erupted during our earlier days together, as he readily became angrily resentful when we were out and about and he could not eat his expected meal right away for whatever reason. There was no listening to reason at such times; he'd angrily verbalize feeling neglected and uncared for amid the biting forces of his hunger pangs. The week before I discovered the missing money, perhaps prompting his taking the money, Matheus gave me the silent treatment for three days after I took Michael to his counseling appointment and a particularly favored buffet restaurant afterwards. Again, Matheus refused to accept reason and logic; it did not matter it was less costly for just Michael and me to eat there, and that it was convenient, given that it was near Michael's counselor's office and in the same shopping center where I needed to run a quick errand. Never mind also that the restaurant was otherwise more than half an hour from our house, and coupons to make the outing affordable for the three of us were not readily available. In his mind, it was simple: He had been asking to go; I had no right to take Michael over him. The day after having been with Michael, he was still unable to give up his rigid perspective in discussing the matter further, wearing a pained expression on his face that clearly reflected his hurt and perceptions of betrayal.

The focus on food is all too often readily associated with children who come from backgrounds of neglect and institutionalization; taking food can readily be translated as a coping mechanism and/or survival instinct. Whether motivated for something the child specifically desires, or just a matter of *when* he may desire something, he may not ask for food simply because he wants to avoid being told no. Feeling restricted from the availability of food may exacerbate feelings of desperation, and feelings of being unsafe and insecure. Only with the passage of time, never again feeling the rising panic of an inability to reasonably satiate the pangs of hunger can the adopted and/or foster child heal these very deep-seated wounds caused by hardship and trauma.

For both boys, yet especially for Matheus on a deeper level, issues related to the past may not necessarily have been a direct reference to food, but rather about control. Despite conveying a seemingly desperate desire to connect, he still struggled with trusting the significant adults in his life to provide him or his brother with a secure, safe, fulfilling environment. It came back to the ongoing need for me to convey my love and deepest unconditional devotion to combat their still deeper scars of neglect.

* * *

Shortly afterward, as the school year was drawing to a close, Matheus was suspended for six days, which he attended the alternative to suspension school program for fighting. It took time for me to piece together a viable understanding why he would fight another boy for no apparent reason, and neither of the boys even knew each other. I caught sight of the first red flag when the assistant principal informed me that Matheus handed over his cell phone to his friend to videotape the fight for his "cousin," Michael, just before the fight. He had a point to prove; he was not one for anyone, including Michael, to mess around with. I also recalled how somewhat keyed-up he'd seemed to leave the house and get to school that morning; the fight was prearranged from the day before, yet he'd remained tight-lipped the previous evening and that morning about anything going down.

According to the assistant principal, the idea for the fight came up when Matheus was speaking with his friend the previous day, who had newly returned from suspension for fighting. Matheus naively expressed never being in a fight in America before, and that perhaps he would like to find out what it might be like. His friend responded by saying he knew of a kid who wanted to fight Matheus, so he could go after him. Meanwhile, a different kid supposedly filled the other boy in on how Matheus wanted to fight him. Matheus went to school that morning ready, dare I say excited to fight.

It was only during a rather stormy session with his counselor the next day, in which he was largely uncooperative, hostile, and verbally threatening, that he revealed wanting to be "popular" and said, "Now they know me." Throughout the year he endured frequent occurrences of being made fun of for his speech and called gay. Twice on his own he valiantly filed a bullying report with the guidance counselor, with one incident involving a peer sticking a wad of chewed-up gum onto the back of his neck. The class had been managed by a substitute unable to handle the disorderly students. Apparently, Matheus had had enough. Reporting to me and school authorities various incidents as they came up, and restraining himself from aggressive retorts to others' taunts and meanness had not changed the peer environment for him. He seized the opportunity to take matters quite literally into his own hands.

As Matheus had maintained his anonymity nearly the entire school year without so much as a faint blip on the school's radar, the assistant principal's shock over the fight was genuine. "He's a role model!" she exclaimed when I spoke with her over the phone. Matheus's history teacher later confided to me a few weeks later that she wanted to make sure I understood the boy he fought was "bad news. Please don't be mad at Matheus." With Matheus's smaller stature, and having successfully taken this boy on, he was an inspiration to those who felt threatened by this bully. Straight out of the pages of a Judy Blume novel, Matheus became something of a local hero to his peer community.

Clearly, his fight with the other boy was supposed to be dismissed as an isolated, uncharacteristic display of unfortunate behavior. Still, I had needed to apply consequences to discourage Matheus from engaging again in the purposeful, willful choice to fight when there was no overt cause for self defense. Over the weekend following the fight, Matheus displayed ongoing bouts of ill-mannered, disrespectful, and hostile behavior that challenged my sanity. I relied on his counselor to get me through, maintaining phone contact with her on the Friday, Saturday, and Sunday following our heated counseling session with him on Thursday, the day after the fight. Each time, she reminded me of Matheus's need to be accepted and the likely fear in his heart of disappointing me; he was acting out to make up for his inability to be more forthright in expressing his distress.

On Monday I delved deeper into my own feelings of exasperation and disillusionment with my own therapist and shed some of the hurt lurking in the shadows. I had maintained appointments at three and two-week intervals, depending on the acerbic flavors of the moment, with a seasoned clinical social worker since shortly after I'd started the adoption quest so many years ago. My sessions with her were invaluable in providing an objective mirror for me to continue parenting in a logical, reasonable, and protective manner, all the while keeping my balanced stance on their emotional baggage and remaining neutral to their behavioral insults.

Throughout that weekend, I was directed by Matheus's counselor to continue as I had been doing and go about my business, ignoring Matheus and leaving him to fend for himself as he continued the slow, painstaking process of priming himself to approach me. Until then I had to sit back and wait, withhold any comment and watch him bolster his bravado, flaunting his "I don't care" attitude. I could only look on as, like a scene right out of a television sitcom episode, he put a hot dog bun in the microwave for sixty seconds too long and overcook his hot dog on the indoor grill. He made as though he did not care, scarfing down a burned, leathery piece of meat encased in a bun charred all over with large black spots for his lunch. As exasperated I felt with him, I dared not make eye contact with him for fear that I would burst into a fit of laughter.

There were several false starts, with the dip of a toe in waters he feared might still be too frigid to wade in; each time I reminded him that I expected him still to follow through with a sincere apology for his behavior toward me. When he popped up at the kitchen counter just as I laid out the vegetables to be chopped for the evening's dinner, I knew he was gearing himself to approach me yet again. He silently feigned indifference as I chopped an onion, a favorite task of his. As I reached for the second vegetable, he rather forlornly asked, "Do you need help with cutting that?"

I replied, "Oh, that's not what I am looking for, but thank you. I appreciate your offering."

He remained silent as I continued chopping. When I reached over for the third vegetable, he softly offered, "I am sorry for disrespecting you from this morning and being rude to you."

A brief discussion followed before I handed over the rest of the chopping to him. Matheus evaded constructive dialogue in favor of soft, nondescript *okay* responses.

Still angry on the inside, his act of concession was short-lived, lasting not much past dinner; the perennial twenty-four hours was needed once again before he was able to more fully return to his old self, more comfortable within the context of his place with his father and family after school the next day. The days, even weeks that followed were rather blissful. We maintained open dialogue, and his patience and cooperation with his brother was at an all-time high; Matheus's overall mood was positive and amiable. As my therapist had so wisely pointed out at some point in our ramblings over the past year, with my insistence and Matheus's gradual responsiveness, I was a driving force that was pulling my son out of quicksand . . . slowly yet consistently, persistently, resolutely. He was being pulled out of the emotional chaos of his weakened sense of self-worth and self-confidence. He was gravitating toward a healthier, stronger self-perspective with the realization of his worthiness and, therefore, his potential in life.

Yet before that, over the course of that weekend, the likelihood for a particular battle was staged when he refused to change the clothes he'd worn the previous day. The threat of not being taken to a local university art school where he was scheduled to compete for a scholarship to one of their summer camp art programs, did not seem to matter to him. Even with a fifteen- and then five-minute warning about our impending departure time, he did not budge; losing out on spending time in a professional art studio with top-of-the-line art materials, meeting others who shared the same passion for art, and getting to interact with and gain positive feedback from professional artists did not matter to him. He remained wedged in his comfort zone of avoiding his fear of failure, perhaps fearful that he would not be able to compete.

We ended up doing our regular grocery shopping run instead; he begrudgingly decided to cooperate and come along, including having changed his clothes. Only later, after one of his apologies, did Matheus admit he did not want to go to the university at all; as he reasoned, "I couldn't think of what to draw."

"So," I replied, "because you were not feeling very confident in yourself, you thought you could not compete?" He nodded in response.

I asked him why he could not simply tell me this directly so we could have talked it through. He shrugged his shoulders, as Davi swooped in with his input, daring Matheus's contempt: "You said we were going to an art museum, right? Well, we could have gone a little earlier and walked around so Matheus could have gotten some ideas about what to draw."

Although Matheus rolled his eyes, he refrained from further comment, allowing me to praise Davi for his well-thought-out idea as yet another example of how talking through things can help solve problems. I turned to Matheus and pointed out that taking risks was what life was about, and I hoped he would not let such an opportunity pass by again simply because he had fear in his heart. Being an artist was about being a risk taker, as it's not possible to exactly dictate the outcome of one's creative expression.

Later that day, all of a sudden the colored pencils, markers, and pens came out. Matheus set out on a mission to organize his substantial lot, discarding those that were broken or no longer usable. After taking out his drawing books he'd checked out some time earlier from the library, he set out to draw. He alternated between copying out of the books different cats and dogs, going outside to sketch the tree in the backyard, and trying his hand at a self-portrait, with the previous year's fifth-grade school picture as his reference. At week's end, Matheus even traded up from his first set of art books from the library, which were characterized by simplistic, one-dimensional line-drawing techniques to a more sophisticated book that incorporated light, shadow, and shading. It was not just the extent of his artistic endeavors and the output of his focused energy that caught my attention. Even more so was the amount of enthusiasm and pride he expressed in his efforts, reflecting a stronger sense of self-confidence. He "got it" even more when selected by the art teacher for the school's yearlong art elective class highly regarded throughout the county. His artistic talent and self-confidence blossomed further under her intensive tutelage.

It seemed inevitable during the annual review meeting regarding his progress in speech therapy a few weeks later that the altercation would be brought up yet again. His language arts teacher also boldly asserted her support for Matheus's standing up to the bully, concerned that he might have been targeted by the bully rather than the fight seemingly having no direct purpose at the time. Matheus was at the tail end of another one of his bouts of petulant behavior toward my authority; he icily informed me that morning that he was choosing to stay in class rather than participating in the meeting. He later approached his speech therapist to ask her about attending the meeting, ensuring that "only" his speech was talked about.

He treated me with indifference upon walking in and sitting down with us at the table, yet I was unprepared for the show he put on otherwise, confirming a side of him I did not ordinarily get to see outside our familial context. He was assertive, confident, charming, and spoke clearly, matched by the steady gaze of his eyes. I needlessly held my breath when his speech therapist chose to confront him in front of us about a problem concerning a disabled girl with missing fingers on one of her hands and an unsteady gait with one leg shorter than the other. She reportedly came to the speech therapist crying, saying Matheus had told her he did not like her. Along with the speech therapist, I had my doubts that the girl's accusations were completely true. I shared with Matheus later how proud I was to be able to tell his speech therapist that I did not believe this was true. His teacher further added before he came in that she felt the girl was overly aggressive in her demeanor and tended to play on the heartstrings of others by exploiting her disability to gain attention.

Matheus was forthright about the incident, even smiling in a jovial manner. He was at ease with himself and clearly explained that he told the girl he did not like what she was doing; he described being uncomfortable with her overly assertive ways of verbally engaging and constantly touching him. He was able to account for himself rather easily, making it easy for the adults to believe him, and see that he was unfortunately targeted by the girl in her attempt to gain attention.

In comparison to a year ago, despite the hostility he had been holding toward me at the time from the fall-out the night before, the dramatic change in Matheus's confidence was a sight to behold. Matheus made it to the art competition the following year, in which he competed with poise and confidence. By mail we learned that had landed one of the top scholarship prizes to attend the art academy's summer program.

Chapter 30

See You Tomorrow . . .

Older children separated from their families of origin typically do not have ready access to information about their personal histories, other than what they may remember, however distorted the truth might be. It can become more difficult for them to develop a strong sense of self while struggling to reconcile with the bits and pieces of their past. With Matheus and Davi's adoption, a divisive tear forever separated them from their convoluted past; physically, their slates were wiped clean. I sought to construct a life book as a metaphor to bridge the gap between the cavernous hole in their physical sense of themselves and the tendrils of a greater sense of permanency in the world. I hoped it would be a unique testament to how their life began . . . anew, instilled with hopes for their future.

Even before leaving for Brazil I planned the creation of the life book, prepared for the lack of any physical remnants of their history with their family of origin. Instead, I began with where *we* started out . . . as strangers in anticipation of the forging of our union as a family. For the first page, I pasted my two favored pictures of the boys together, taken by Lino when he first met and spoke with them about their feelings and interest in being adopted. On that page I reproduced the wording of the e-mail I sent to family and friends to announce my adoption of the boys after the Brazilian court's initial approval of their being adopted: *Dear family and friends, "It is not flesh and blood, but heart which makes us fathers and sons"—Friedrich von Schiller. So begins my long anticipated journey to finally realize my dreams to adopt as I soon depart to Brazil to bring home my two sons, Matheus and Davi. By choice, we [will] become a family, first in our hearts, and finally in breath and being. "Great expectations are good; great experiences [will be even] better"—Richard Fischer, adoptive parent. Please share in my joy as I get ready for the journey of a lifetime.*

On the second page, I pasted the three key pictures I'd selected of myself to be shown to the boys when they were first told of their impending adoption. I carefully selected these pictures, attempting to foster a whimsical first impression of me that I hoped would help allay initial anxieties of who this strange man was . . . this man they were now to identify as their father. At first sight, they saw me on top of an elephant at a conservation center in Chiang Mai, Thailand, posing alongside a bronze statue of the Cat in the Hat in the Dr. Seuss National Memorial Sculpture Garden in Springfield, Massachusetts, and standing alongside a red K2 telephone box in London, England. I also reproduced the wording of the letter I had sent to accompany the photographs: *Dear Matheus e Davi, Well, you both say that "all you need is love, love is all you need"* [as they sang on the video e-mailed along with their photos from Lino]. *I can't wait to share with you both all the love I have waiting to give to you. I am so excited to soon start our lives together as a family. So many family and friends here in Florida are excited to be meeting you both soon. My dear sons, so many wonderful changes are ahead for the three of us; together, life is going to be an amazing adventure! Until we finally meet, Your loving father.*

On the adjoining third page, along with the Portuguese translation of my letter, I pasted the three photographs taken of the boys after they first were told about their new father and impending adoption; they were wearing the Florida State University Seminole shirts and hats I sent ahead to them for that day. Although they were smiling, I could only imagine the shock, disbelief, and uncertainty behind their seemingly hesitant grins. The next few pages were dedicated to photographs of our first meeting at the orphanage, followed by photographed details of our days together in and travels throughout Brazil, the finalization of the adoption, and our arrival home in America.

Since completing the life book shortly after our return from Brazil, I often caught them at odd times in the first few months thumbing through it, sometimes together and other times separately. Maybe it offered some type of adoption security blanket, becoming a testament to the reality of life as they were coming to know it. A year or so later, I came across a forgotten collection of photos of the boys during their stay at the orphanage, given to me by the home's social worker. The majority of the photos on the CD were candid shots of them not much younger than when we started out together. I was disappointed when first looking through those photos in Brazil, desperately hoping to see a shot of their mother and/or older brother, or a glimpse of younger versions of themselves. A more careful look this time around revealed a trio of photos with them a bit younger in comparison to the other photos, perhaps as much as two or three years younger. I also came across the first set of those grainy photos from the initial referral. The few remaining photos were random shots of them at outings and with other kids from the orphanage.

In seeking to maintain whatever physical connections they had with their own past, I incorporated these photos into four additional pages in the life book, following the series of photos from our visit to the orphanage after finalizing the adoption. When I showed them these pages, the boys were pensive at first glance. Matheus brushed away any potential significance with claims that he did not remember anything about the photos. After fumbling through the clouds of his memory banks, Davi determined that the earlier photos of the two of them together were from when they'd first arrived at the orphanage. They were about five- and eight-years old at the time.

Although I could not see it in the photos, Davi pointed out, "See how our eyes were red?" I asked him what was going on. He simply replied, "Because we were sad," about having come to the orphanage. He avoided further attempts to reflect on any thoughts and feelings about that moment, preferring to focus on the other photos, recalling names and who others were to them. Matheus then joined in, also identifying children and staff of the orphanage, and sharing some of his own innocent memories about those pictured alongside them. Even if just for a little bit before they softly slid shut, these small cracked openings of the windows into their past were allowing more and more brief interchanges with their present.

* * *

For our second-year anniversary dinner we returned to our favorite, unpretentious Brazilian restaurant. Other than the treat of going out to eat on a Monday, simplicity was the main order of our celebratory outing. It was about being together and quietly acknowledging the deepening maturation of our family relations. At home we took out the life book and looked back on our earlier days together and watched the ten-minute video of them at the orphanage. The video was now two and a half years old; we were all surprised by how much the boys had matured in their presentation of themselves. Matheus's shy, awkward posture and Davi's overly assertive ways now seemed less ubiquitous in comparison to their younger selves. We mostly watched in silence, save for a passing titter between us, with each of us perhaps feeling a sense of self-satisfaction with the affirmative turn life had taken over the past two years.

Those unexpected, simpler moments best defining our family relations for the three of us tends to happen at times when we least expect them, and are mostly subtle in how they unfold. Each morning we awaken, get ourselves going, and meet up in the kitchen for breakfast. Although we may not exactly sit down together to eat every morning, we still congregate around one another, bouncing off one another our rambling thoughts and wants for the day. Most mornings tend to be simple affairs with some transcending the unassuming in ways most unexpected.

One morning, as Matheus gradually returned to a state of calm with the diffusion of the storm clouds from the latest upheaval, Davi sprang up at my side as I was eating breakfast and perusing the morning's newspaper. He read over the latest essay he wrote, which I readily praised for his wonderful expression of his thoughts and ideas and its organization and flow. I then encouraged him to take another look for the inevitable mistakes in grammar and spelling, which would be heavily scrutinized in his writing for the upcoming FCAT exam. As I turned back to eat my breakfast, Davi crowded in on my placemat, pointedly taking me through his thoughts and ideas sentence by sentence with his brother looking on.

On a few occasions, Matheus daringly pointed out a particular grammar correction—this from someone who often liked one to believe he could not string two words together to form a complete verbal thought. Sometimes he was right for which I praised him mightily. Other times he was wrong, for which I gently corrected him and nodded agreeably when he would reply, "Well, at least I tried." Again, I commended him for taking a risk, wanting to be helpful, and learning something along the way. As much as I might have liked to have eaten my breakfast and read the paper in peace, it was one of the more ordinary moments in our time thus far together that leave me with a sense of profound satisfaction, one of those treasured moments I live for. There was no pretentious sense of oneself, no friction between egos—just mutual acceptance and affable relations.

As simply as we began our days, the way we end them seemed even less complicated. From the beginning, taking advantage of the structured lifestyle they were used to at the orphanage, I made sure to consistently maintain the boys' scheduled bedtime routines. Unlike my nephew, Michael, who made it his mission to fight even the suggestion of a bed time, the boys usually took to their beds with rarely a protest, typically falling fast asleep once the lights went out. Gradually, bed-times became later, yet still within the context of a predictable routine.

Our good-night routine also kept to a customary routine, with specific declarations in bidding each other good night. In the midst of hugs and kisses, along with random utterances about events, experiences, and sentiments of the day, typical affirmations nearly always included, "I love you . . . I love you more," "Sleep good," and, "Have good dreams." I do not recall just how or when it was first uttered, now casually by Davi, yet unfailingly by Matheus, but "See you tomorrow" never ceases to surprise me in the simplicity of its assertion, yet complexity of its significance. Perhaps to counter a prolonged earlier history of familial instability, "See you tomorrow" became the all-important declaration that stability shall reign. The boys will not awaken the following morning only to find the lives they were getting to know and realize as their own have faded away with the whispering shadows of a dream, with life's promises just a ruse.

Regardless of whether the day ends on a positive or sour note, there is still always tomorrow to behold. Despite any ugliness that transpired over the course of the day, even if left unsettled by the time a head or two should be laid down on their pillows, there still may be the thought, the expectation that scattered pieces will be there tomorrow to contend with. With the deepened anchoring of the boys' roots, the still fragile budding of themselves in the context of their new lives continues to strengthen, and impresses upon them greater predictability in the rising of tomorrow's sun. No longer alone, unattached, or without a future to call their own, Matheus and Davi indeed can expect a brighter tomorrow as they continue to reassemble the pieces of their personal puzzles toward a more secure, happier, and more productive sense of themselves. Their personal pieces also are fitting within the family's puzzle. The family portrait increasingly is becoming more comfortably familiar to them as it takes shape and its details align.

As I lay my own head down every night, I often let my thoughts ramble about as I regard the day. I, too, tend to look toward tomorrow as a mark of stability I have come to rely on. However I may pull off my fatherly role for the day, I look to tomorrow as yet another day to look forward to. Whether it is to ride further the wave of affirmation and congenial relations or put into practice a new spin on the day's trouble spots, tomorrow is filled with the hope of what is yet to come for all of us. As Albert Einstein so fittingly remarked, "Learn from yesterday, live for today, hope for tomorrow," yet "The important thing is not to stop questioning."

Epilogue

The boys and I made another pilgrimage to LIMIAR's weekend-long reunion picnic toward the end of the summer, held at the same place. It had been two years since we had last attended the picnic. Sean traveled with us this time, and we made pit stops along the way at Chimney Rock Park in North Carolina, tackled the whitewater rapids on the New River Gorge in West Virginia, and ambled around Lancaster's Pennsylvania Dutch country. Even though we had been only once before, Bradford already held a familiar feel; we stayed at the same hotel, ate at the same pizza place with a jaunt to the Dari Hut afterward, and took in the same bucolic surroundings of the university campus where the reunion was held.

Several of the same families that were there before had made it to the reunion again. I was surprised to see how much their children had grown over the course of just two years; I wondered how Matheus and Davi might have appeared to them, as well. Yet the shine I had noted before on some of these children's faces seemed to have faded somewhat, especially for some of the older teenagers; many of their parents told in our groups together that they conveyed rather grandiose, unrealistic ideas, were behaving recklessly, and were lacking in motivation. One preteen from a family of four was noticeably absent, having recently started residential treatment for severe behavioral and emotional problems. I wondered how it was that these teens had lost their way; my heart skipped several beats that echoed my still lingering fears with how Matheus and Davi might fare in the all too near future. Even so, I felt relief hearing some of the other parents describe the same trials and tribulations that I had been managing: stubborn resolves, over-reactive tempers, and shifty behaviors. Yet headway was being made with many of these children, similar to what I felt that I had been making with Matheus and Davi.

Lino had unexpectedly flown in from Brazil for the reunion. I was excited to see what he'd think about any changes he might notice in Matheus and Davi. They warmly interacted with one another; the boys left a favorable impression on Lino, and appeared to him to be more comfortable with themselves. The boys also interacted well with the other Brazilian children. This time there was no language barrier, and they made some new friends.

I was recruited to lead two of the parenting groups, which I kept loosely structured, hoping to facilitate discussion around a few key topics we all likely had in common: disrupted attachment, school adaptability, behavior management, and maintaining optimism in the face of pessimism. Even if just for those two hours, I felt awkward putting on my professional hat, possibly having to be regarded as an expert, and expected to dispense expert counsel. Even when I should happen upon my own success in redirecting my sons' challenging behavior and attitudes, self-satisfaction would too often be short-lived. Just when I thought I'd find the right key, the locksmith would change the locks on me . . . and I was expected to offer the other parents foolproof ways to rear their adopted children? I was really no different from any of the other parents in the room; I was just as keen on swapping my own personal anecdotes in exchange for different keys that might better unlock my parenting potential.

Over the weekend, I had met up with one of the single fathers who was the first I had spoken to when I had started to consider adopting from Brazil, and who had openly shared with me his struggles raising his two sons. When we spoke at the reunion, he remained upbeat in his loving regard for his two sons, brothers who were now essentially beginning to make their own way as young adults. He had more of a difficult go-around with his sons than what I had been experiencing with mine, yet I felt a shared camaraderie. We both had started out with the same intentions to love a troubled child, and see him through to adulthood and beyond. As cautious as I was in my decision making that led me to adopt Matheus and Davi, what might have happened beyond that was anyone's guess . . . and still is.

Together, we have become a family . . . exactly what I had hoped for. Matheus's black-or-white attitudes and Davi's passive-aggressive ways still cause conflicts and frustration, yet continue to subside in frequency as well as intensity, in favor of more harmonious familial relations. As I continue to work on my parenting with greater patience and humility, I have become better able to defuse the tension that they still hold inside and struggle to come to terms with. We left the reunion as we came: a family bonded together by the promise of what tomorrow will bring.

Davi might have expressed it best when a promising job I had interviewed for several months later, which would have had us moving to New England, did not pan out: "Father, let's not move . . . because we're in the middle of our lives right now." When I queried him about his thoughts, he spoke of how he liked his friends and "most of my family is here." He also told me how he liked our house, and that he was looking forward to transitioning to the neighborhood middle school the following year. Indeed, we had reached somewhat of a midpoint in our lives together, where there was a sense of self-satisfaction for each of us with the stability and strengthening of our roots underneath. Trying to pinpoint exactly when and how we had actually reached this point and where we might be headed did not matter; it was all a part of our enduring life's journey together.

www.ingramcontent.com/pod-product-compliance
Lightning Source LLC
Chambersburg PA
CBHW051936290426
44110CB00015B/1993